THE SANDS OF DUNKIRK

RICHARD COLLIER

PENGUIN BOOKS

TRANSWORLD PUBLISHERS

Penguin Random House, One Embassy Gardens,
8 Viaduct Gardens, London SW11 7BW
www.penguin.co.uk

Transworld is part of the Penguin Random House group of companies
whose addresses can be found at global.penguinrandomhouse.com

First published in 1961
Reissued in 2022 by Penguin Books
an imprint of Transworld Publishers

A CIP catalogue record for this book
is available from the British Library.

ISBN 9781529176827

Typeset in 11/13.75 pt Van Dijck MT Pro by Jouve (UK), Milton Keynes
Printed and bound in Great Britain by Clays Ltd, Elcograf S.p.A.

The authorized representative in the EEA is Penguin Random House Ireland,
Morrison Chambers, 32 Nassau Street, Dublin D02 YH68.

Penguin Random House is committed to a sustainable
future for our business, our readers and our planet. This book
is made from Forest Stewardship Council® certified paper.

To all the men and women of Dunkirk

'So long as the English tongue survives
the word Dunkirk will be spoken with reverence . . .'

New York Times, 1st June 1940

CONTENTS

Introduction by James Holland   xi

 1 Next Time I'll Come For You   1
 2 What, Dunkirk in Scotland?   21
 3 Make for the Black Smoke   42
 4 Any Road, Jerry Shan't Have 'em   56
 5 Into Hell and Out Again   102
 6 Like Southend with the Old Woman   158
 7 Just the Odds and Sods, Sir   188
 8 It May Seem Strange, But We Are . . .   209
 9 Most Chaps Have Gone, You Know   234
10 Have You Seen My Johnny?   261

    Facts About Dunkirk   287

INTRODUCTION

One of the very first books I ever read about the Second World War was *Eagle Day* by Richard Collier, his account of the Battle of Britain, and almost the very next one I devoured was *The Sands of Dunkirk*. I've still got the old battered hardback I picked up in a second-hand bookstall at an air show at Duxford back in 2002; its dust jacket is a bit dog-eared, and the pages are yellowed with age, but the words remain as fresh and vivid as when I first read the book, and indeed when it was first published more than sixty years ago back in 1961.

When people ask me what I think is the best book ever written about the Battle of Britain or the British evacuation from Dunkirk, I always cite these two books. For me, they're what popular history should be: rich in human drama, as compelling and readable as the best adventure story or thriller, and full of the kind of detail and atmosphere that transports the reader into the cockpit of a Spitfire or to the beaches during the evacuation. These books have exercised a huge influence on my own writing, not least in how to drive along a narrative that follows the fortunes of real people who were there, and by using a novelistic style.

Nor does this somehow make it 'lightweight' history. It is perfectly possible to write a history book that is full of scholarship and wonderful primary research, but which is still highly readable, and also, crucially, extremely entertaining. Richard Collier showed me that. Reading *Eagle Day* for the first time, all those years ago, was really quite a Damascene moment. *Ah-ha*, I thought. *So, this is how a history book should be written!*

Richard Collier was born in Croydon, south of London, in 1924 and on turning eighteen joined the RAF. Much of his active service was spent as a forces war correspondent in the Far East, however, where he became associate editor of the South-East Asia Command magazine, *Phoenix*. After the war, he continued working as a journalist and tried his hand as a novelist before his first big success with *Ten Thousand Eyes: The Amazing Story of the Spy Network That Cracked Hitler's Atlantic Wall Before D-Day*, which was published in 1958. The title might have been a bit of a mouthful, but Collier had cleverly picked a little-known story and corresponded with or interviewed a raft of people who had been involved, from spooks and senior intelligence officers in London during the war, through to secret agents who had served in the field and members of the French Resistance. The book was a huge success and led him to pursue a long and successful career as one of Britain's foremost popular historians.

Collier certainly had an ear for a good story and his journalistic background also gave him the ideal grounding for writing with a novelist's sense of style and flourish. A new kind of writing had emerged from the war – one that had been spearheaded by the American war correspondent Ernie Pyle. Until Pyle had arrived on the scene, first writing about life as he saw it across the United States as a roving reporter for the Scripps-Howard newspaper conglomerate, and then from the front line of the war, no one had thought to write from the bottom up – that is, from the perspective of the ordinary young men – and women – at the coalface of the conflict. Pyle also met generals and war leaders, but his prime interest was always everyday folk, ordinary young men who suddenly found themselves uprooted from their lives in the US and packed off to the anomalous and extraordinary situation of the front line thousands of miles away.

Taking the position of the interested observer, Pyle would watch what was going on around him, talk to some of the people he met, and record what they said and what he saw and observed. It proved a winning formula and by the time the North African campaign was over in May 1943, he was the most famous war correspondent in the free world. Tragically, Pyle was killed on Okinawa by a Japanese machine-gunner in April 1945, so he never had the opportunity to continue his career once peace had returned.

His influence outlived him, however, and it was hardly surprising that others followed his lead, first in newspaper and magazine print during the war, but then later, in the books that followed. Cornelius Ryan, a former wartime correspondent for the *Daily Telegraph*, was one, publishing bestsellers such as *The Longest Day*, while the duo of Larry Collins and Dominique Lapierre were two others, who wrote internationally successful books such as *Is Paris Burning?* Both Ryan and the pairing of Collins and Lapierre based their books around the personal testimonies of those who were there.

And, of course, so too did Richard Collier. In the late 1950s and into the 1960s there were still huge numbers of veterans with memories going back fifteen to twenty years and still fresh. On the other hand, a large number of primary documents had yet to be either organised or released; Collier had none of the access to source material available to today's historians. Nor was he writing in an age of photocopiers or digital cameras, which enable the modern researcher to scour and record a huge amount of original paperwork.

Not that it matters. What Collier may have lacked in terms of archival sources, he more than made up for with the vast number of people he was able to interview or with whom he could correspond. In writing *The Sands of Dunkirk*, Collier uses information collected from over a thousand eyewitnesses. They include sappers, civilians, privates, sergeants, sailors, airmen, gunners, brigadiers, majors, generals, drivers, bombardiers, lifeboatmen, guardsmen, WRENs, stationmasters, signalmen, marine superintendents, coxswains, deck-hands, British, French, and German. Although Collier follows the fortunes of a good number of individual participants, this wider group of eyewitnesses helps inform every page he writes and allows him to paint an incredibly rich picture of what was happening over the course of that extraordinary week of the evacuation.

And what a week it was – arguably the most dramatic seven days in Britain's long history; one in which Britain began looking down the barrel of total defeat but which ended with the country in a far better position than anyone back home or the Allies had possibly dared hope, a potentially catastrophic crisis averted. By the end of that week, Britain was not only still very much in the war, but also in a position from which it could grind back the initiative and, ultimately, play a major part in the eventual victory.

Collier begins the book on the evening of 26 May 1940, sixteen days after the Germans began their assault on the West, and at the moment Operation DYNAMO, the planned evacuation of the British Expeditionary Force (BEF), was given the green light to begin.

It's perhaps worth explaining, though, how and why it was that by Sunday 26 May the BEF was falling back on Dunkirk and, along with France and Belgium, facing defeat – and in such a breathtakingly short amount of time, something touched on only lightly in *The Sands of Dunkirk*.

When the Germans marched into France and the Low Countries on 10 May 1940, very few would have thought that just ten days later Hitler's forces would have reached the Atlantic coast, or just six days after that, the whole northern front would have completely collapsed and that millions of men were about to be enveloped in a massive encirclement.

After all, France alone had begun the battle with more tanks, more guns, more trucks and vehicles, and much the same number of aircraft as Germany. Add the Belgians, the Dutch and the British, and the Allies had a comfortable numerical advantage. Yet France had thought this new war would be fought much like the last one and had not reckoned on the speed with which the German forces advanced. Nor did French commanders have the communications they needed to respond quickly. While the Germans relied mainly on radios, the French were dependent on telephone lines and dispatch riders. With the German air force, the Luftwaffe, cutting many of these lines, and with fleeing civilians clogging the roads, the French army was swiftly bogged down.

The British had the world's largest navy and a decent-sized air force, but their army was tiny – and, to be fair, traditionally so. Britain and France were formal allies and it had been agreed that the French would provide most of the land forces while Britain's contribution would lie mainly at sea, blockading Germany, and in the air. As a result, the BEF comprised just eleven divisions compared with over a hundred French and twenty Belgian divisions.

Nevertheless, before the BEF could really contribute their forces, the Belgians to the north, and the French to the south, had collapsed. This was because while one group of German armies, Army Group B, had blasted their way into the Low Countries, a second group, Army Group A, had moved through the dense forests and hills of the Ardennes, which with its rivers and narrow road network was considered by the Allies to be impassable to massed armoured formations. Not only had the Germans disproved this, they had managed it in just three days, crossing the

River Meuse, the main French line of defence north of the well-defended Maginot Line, on the fourth day and at three different places.

No one in the French high command had expected this, despite numerous intelligence warnings and aerial reconnaissance to the contrary. Although only sixteen of the 135 divisions used in the German attack on the West were motorised – the rest used horse, wagons and foot soldiers – the mechanised tip of this spearhead consisted of highly trained, motivated and brilliantly led all-arms formations of motorised infantry, artillery, anti-tank and anti-aircraft, reconnaissance units, and of course tanks. Because of the wide dispersal of French forces and because of their woeful lack of modern communications, these German spearheads were able to blow away the weak French defences on the Meuse and then charge on, cutting a swathe westwards towards the coast while the bulk of the Allied forces were still plodding north into Belgium. And because the French forces were not expecting to move with the same kind of speed, the Germans were able to surround and annihilate Allied units in penny packets, rather than as a far more formidable massed whole.

Even by 14 May, it was clear that the Allies had fallen for the German plan hook, line and sinker, and were in danger of being completely encircled. Either side of the BEF contingent, the Belgians on their left flank and French on their right, began falling back. This forced the BEF to do the same in order to keep the line roughly straight. Before they knew it, they were in full-on retreat but also facing an enemy that was now bearing down on them from the north, south and east.

British and French troops now found themselves caught in a long finger-shaped wedge stretching back to the channel coast around the port of Dunkirk, with German forces pressing from the north, east and south. Both in Paris and London, political and military leaders were stunned by the speed with which this strategic assault was happening. In England, a plan to evacuate the BEF and what French forces they could also take was hastily put into action by the Royal Navy under the command of Admiral Ramsay in Dover. This was to be called Operation DYNAMO.

Any servicemen not fighting were picked up beforehand – the so-called 'useless mouths' – and while the flanks of the pocket were held, so the bulk of the BEF began to fall back to Dunkirk.

With each passing day the pocket shortened, so that on 27 May the evacuation of troops was able to begin. To start with, it was painfully slow and the chances of getting many men back across the Channel seemed slight. To make matters worse, the following day Belgium surrendered to the Germans, making the defence of the pocket even more precarious.

In Britain, King George VI called for a 'National Day of Prayer', so bleak was the situation. Winston Churchill, still so new to his premiership, now faced what was probably the greatest crisis of his entire political career. Major decisions were being made by the five-man War Cabinet in consultation with the Chiefs of Staff, that is, the three service chiefs of the Army, Royal Navy and RAF. Two of the War Cabinet were Clement Atlee and Arthur Greenwood, both Labour politicians and new to government and the War Cabinet. The other two were Neville Chamberlain, the previous Conservative Prime Minister, who had been forced to resign on 10 May, and Lord Halifax, a former Viceroy of India and without doubt the most respected politician in the country, known for his calm, steady hand and good judgement.

It is hard to over-emphasise just how shocked Britain's war leaders were at the totally unexpected events taking place just across the English Channel. A lot of people were imagining that if the Germans were rolling over France so easily, Britain would be next and that German paratroopers would soon be landing over southern England and the Luftwaffe pulverising British cities, followed by an inevitable invasion. In the shock and panic, not enough wise heads were considering the logistical unlikelihood of this or reflecting on Britain's very strong naval defences and burgeoning air-defence system.

With this in mind, Halifax had begun a dialogue with Giuseppe Bastianini, the Italian ambassador to Britain, about the possibility of using the Italians to send out peace feelers to Germany. During the three War Cabinet meetings held that day, Sunday 26 May, Halifax repeatedly raised the possibility of exploring peace talks and Churchill repeatedly refused to countenance such a course of action.

By the time Operation DYNAMO was given the green light at 6.57 p.m. that Sunday evening, expectations for its success were extremely low. The Chiefs of Staff reckoned that if they were able to get 40,000 troops off the beaches, they would be doing well. The Germans were pressing hard on Dunkirk and after what had happened so far in the campaign, few would bet against the British and French troops now in the hastily prepared perimeter lasting more than a day or two. Furthermore, with Dunkirk's port facilities already wrecked, the only feasible way of lifting men onto ships was via little boats ferrying troops from the beaches to larger vessels waiting offshore. Clearly, that was a hopelessly inefficient means of getting men away safely.

Britain's army might have been small, but the psychological effect of losing almost all of the 300,000-plus troops would have been enormous. Whether the government would then have survived was also a very moot point. And if it collapsed, the consequence of hastily conducted peace talks would be highly likely.

The next day, Monday 27 May, it was reported the evacuation was still not going particularly well, and in all just 7,669 men had been evacuated. News also arrived that the Belgians were about to surrender, which meant part of the northern flank would need to be hastily filled by British troops heading into the gap left by their vacating ally. At the morning's cabinet meeting the subject of peace talks was skirted over, but it resurfaced at the second meeting, which began at 4.30 p.m. in the Cabinet Room at 10 Downing Street. And this time, Halifax completely lost his temper. Churchill was insisting they could not even begin to go down the route of peace talks – open the door ajar, that door would then blow wide open, and it would be impossible to shut it again. Halifax simply could not understand why and then threatened to resign.

Had this happened, it would almost certainly have triggered the collapse of the government, but instead, the War Cabinet broke up and Churchill took Halifax out into the garden where they had a man-to-man chat. No one knows what Churchill said to Halifax but by the next cabinet meeting, at 10 p.m., there was no more talk of resignations and the following day, Tuesday 28 May, Chamberlain supported Churchill in not pursuing even the most tentative of talks with the Italians. Chamberlain is still the object of much scorn and criticism, but for this stance alone he deserves our enduring gratitude. He and Halifax were long-standing colleagues and friends, yet Chamberlain stayed true to his convictions.

By this time, Captain Bill Tennant, the Senior Naval Officer, who had been hurriedly sent to Dunkirk the previous day, had discovered the East Mole at Dunkirk: a largely wooden structure that extended out from the Dunkirk harbour as a limited break-water. It was not designed as a mooring for ships, but he recognised its potential in this role and after ordering up a cross-Channel steamer to test it – which it did, successfully – he realised that so long as it held, it could offer salvation for the BEF. That second day, 17,804 men were evacuated, and the perimeter around Dunkirk was still holding.

Tennant is rightly one of the heroes of Collier's book and his transition from staff officer at the Admiralty in London to man on the spot at Dunkirk is brilliantly and vividly told, right down to him cutting out 'SNO' from a cigarette pack wrapper and sticking it onto his tin helmet using fish oil. Small human details such as this vividly emphasise the makeshift nature in which DYNAMO was put into action and carried out.

Back in London, Churchill called a wider cabinet meeting at 6 p.m. that Tuesday, 28 May, and gave a stirring speech in which he stressed the importance of fighting on no matter what. 'We shall never surrender!' he told them. Everyone cheered, and after that Halifax never mentioned peace talks again. Churchill had won a vital political battle, one that enabled Britain to continue a fighting battle in the war. I reckon that the afternoon of Monday 27 May, when Halifax had threatened to resign, was in fact the closest Britain ever came to losing the war. No one was to know that then, however, and across the Channel at Dunkirk the most extraordinary drama was continuing to play out.

The next day, Wednesday 29 May, a staggering 47,310 men were evacuated from the beaches of Dunkirk, with 28,225 from the East Mole, as ships lined up along it, double packed, and hurriedly sailed back across the Channel. Fortunately, hitting a comparatively small target like a cross-Channel ferry or a Royal Navy destroyer was incredibly difficult without guided missiles, and hitting moving targets even harder. This is why the Luftwaffe, despite their best efforts, never hit the East Mole and destroyed surprisingly few larger ships during the evacuation. Ten-tenths cloud cover and a mill-pond sea for much of that week also helped enormously, as did the thick pall of smoke from burning oil stores that had been bombed. In fact, of the 231 ships sunk during the entire evacuation, only eleven were from the Royal Navy, and 202 of the total were little vessels – coastal craft, pleasure boats, skiffs and whalers hurriedly sent to aid the evacuation of troops from the beaches. An Admiralty report into Operation DYNAMO concluded that 70 per cent of the losses were due not to enemy bombs or artillery but to 'collisions and misadventure' – that is, vessels mostly sunk because they were overwhelmed by too many troops scrambling to get aboard.

As the week continued and the Germans were unable to break through over the flat, deliberately flooded and waterlogged land around Dunkirk, still tenaciously held by British and French troops, so the numbers of men who were lifted to safety increased. An astonishing 58,823 troops were evacuated on Thursday 30 May, 68,014 on Friday 31 May, 64,429 on Saturday 1 June, and 24,309 on Sunday 2 June. By 11.30 that night, every single fit and able soldier had been transported back to England from Dunkirk. More French troops were evacuated the following day, at which point Operation DYNAMO ended. A total of 338,226 soldiers had escaped and the British Army could live to fight another day.

This epic, astonishing drama is played out with compelling, nerve-jangling tension in *The Sands of Dunkirk*, so that even though we know what happened, reading it still makes me shift anxiously in my seat. How good it is to be writing an introduction to this fabulous book and to know that it will be reaching new audiences. Trust me, you're in for a treat.

James Holland

CHAPTER ONE

NEXT TIME I'LL COME FOR YOU

Sunday, 26th May
6–12 p.m.

Afterwards, looking back to that evening, it was the silence that Augusta Hersey remembered most. Already, as on any other day in the café, she had helped Maman array fresh coffee filters behind the worn zinc bar, polished oil-cloth table-tops – yet still the Café L'Epi d'Or (The Golden Ear of Corn) stood silent and empty. It was as if the shadowed rooms, like the city itself, were listening for something.

It was 6 p.m. on Sunday, 26th May, 1940. The city of Tourcoing, in northern France, lay bathed in golden sunlight; after that day's rain the pavements glistened like wet fresh slate. In the fields girdling the city the young corn pricked the furrows and the cuckoo was calling, but other more ominous sounds came faintly on the still air: the barking of hungry tethered dogs, the lowing of unmilked cattle. For farmers no less than factory workers had fled.

It was just sixteen days since Augusta, after eight long months of waiting, had seen the Second World War erupt in deadly earnest. Sixteen days since 117 German infantry divisions and ten armoured divisions had smashed from Aachen in Germany into Maastricht in Holland, and then with a wide left-handed sweep into neutral Belgium. Twelve days since the bulk of Lord Gort's British Expeditionary Force had crossed the frontier like conquering heroes, with lilac in their hats – among them Augusta's husband of six weeks, Private Bill Hersey of the East Surreys.

Only ten days since Bill, a storeman in his Brigade's anti-tank company, had arrived triumphantly in Brussels – yet now, on this Sunday night, Bill was less than two miles away, quartered with his unit in the suburbs of Roncq, after a headlong sixty-mile retreat.

To Augusta, a dark vital 21-year-old, it had all happened with terrifying suddenness, as breathlessly improbable as the whirlwind six-week courtship Bill had carried out with the aid of a pocket dictionary, as disturbing as her father's sudden departure to Bordeaux to find quarters for his family outside the battle zone. Even the news in the papers was vague and contradictory: it was hard to grasp that seven German armoured divisions had speared through the disorganised French Ninth Army at Sedan, their tanks moving easily through the hilly Ardennes forests the experts had said were impenetrable.

Yet the British too had abandoned riverline after riverline – the Dyle, the Dendre, the Escaut – seemingly without a fight.

As with most women on this golden May evening, the grand strategy of the nightmare campaign was beyond Augusta Hersey. As a woman she knew only that despite her father's forebodings she loved the fair-haired young soldier with the profile of a Greek god whose language she barely understood, and knew that she was loved in return.

No matter that Papa had exploded with violence when Bill, opening his pocket dictionary one night, had pointed to the word *mariage* and said simply, 'Your daughter.' No matter that he had roared, 'He is no good, that fellow. He spends too much on cognac.' Augusta had answered, 'But he will change', in the sure knowledge that she was right. The first pay-day following their engagement Bill had laid his whole week's pay, 175 francs, on the zinc and announced the drinks for his mates were on him. But he himself had settled for a cup of coffee.

But tonight, moving distractedly about the café, sometimes chatting with Denise, Madeleine and Raymonde Marquette, the three girlfriends who had sought refuge with her family, Augusta chafed. It was three days since she had seen Bill, and she knew that he was desperately worried for her. Only three days back a German fighter had swept down on Augusta's bicycle as she ped-alled briskly towards Roncq, scything the white dust with a hail of bullets.

Incredulous, she had shouted at the pilot, 'What do you think you are playing at?' Only with realisation had the tears flowed freely, and as she wept on Bill's shoulder he had told her firmly, 'It's too dangerous for you to make the journey any more. Next time I'll come for you.'

But Augusta Hersey was not the only one to know disquiet. On this May Sunday night an old dream was dying, and with its death France was a puzzled land.

For eight long months most of the 390,000 men of Lord Gort's British Expeditionary Force had had the time of their lives. Each day, secure in the illusion of the 40-mile-long Maginot Line far to the south, they had built more than 400 concrete pill-boxes, spaded slit trenches six feet deep, four feet six wide, the rigid First World War pattern, and waited for the German might to dash itself against impenetrable concrete and steel. At night, in thousands of estaminets like the Café L'Epi d'Or, they had made friends with the local girls, celebrated each pay-day with the Brit-ish soldiers' favourite diet of fried egg and chipped potatoes.

Merry on ten francs worth of white wine, they sang the songs their fathers sang – 'Tipperary', 'A Long, Long Trail A-Winding' – with a new one that had pride of place, 'We're Going To Hang Out The Washing On The Siegfried Line'.

On hoarding after hoarding blazed a slogan as staunch as the Maginot Line itself: *Nous vainquerons – parce que nous sommes les plus forts!* (We shall win because we are stronger!)

Not for years had an army gone to war so confidently – or so light-heartedly. The signs in the cafés read 'On Active Service – Keep your bowels open and your mouth shut', but somehow the caveat had a hollow ring. The newspapers had dismissed it as 'The Phoney War' or 'The Bore War', and most men had eagerly awaited a leave trip home on the *Maid of Orleans*, or else the coming of summer. All winter Private Robert Sellers, of the East Yorks, had kept shining up his dancing pumps, mindful of the fleshpots of Paris. Graham Jones, a young signalman from Birmingham, had sent home for a Li-lo, intent on a spot of sunbathing. It was the same with Captain Geoffrey Sutcliffe, of the 139th Infantry Brigade; if no one had equipped him with a pistol he had still remembered to bring his tennis racquet.

It was the same at all levels. The favourite place to take champagne cocktails was the American Bar of the Café Jeanne in Lille; for choicer eating, gourmets plumped for the faded charm of the Huitrière hard by – chicken stuffed with truffles, rice pudding and Napoleon brandy. Others moved on to the Miami or to Madame Ko-Ko's establishment in the Rue de Seclin, ornate with red plush drapes, its foyer a forest of red-tabbed greatcoats. The three major sicknesses ailing this army were gastric ulcers, scabies and venereal disease: the result of strange food, strange beds and stranger women.

There had been signs, too, that the Germans felt the same way: in the twentieth century war needed the light touch. When a French newspaper charged that hard-pressed housewives could no longer obtain cosmetics, the Germans hit back with a two-bomber raid, bombarding the citizens of Lille with face powder and phials of perfume.

As recently as October, 1939, the then Secretary of State for War, Leslie Hore-Belisha, had told the House of Commons that the Army sent to France was 'as well if not better equipped than any similar army'. It was 'equipped in the finest possible manner that could not be excelled'. Even General Edmund Osborne, whose 44th Division had gone equipped with six mobile cinemas, had hoped that he would be up to strength on anti-tank weapons when it came to a showdown.

From 10th May on this dream was slowly dying, so that by the evening of 26th May no man, general or private, could know, any more than Augusta Hersey, what this night would bring.

Two hundred miles away across the English Channel, at the Nine Elms, South London, depot of the Southern Railway, John Pelham Maitland was waiting for the phone to ring. As Running Shed Superintendent, Maitland's responsibility was traffic control on the fifty-mile stretch of the London, Brighton and South Coast railway which linked London with the Channel ports.

Hence Maitland's unease, for four days earlier he had been alerted that he must stand by to move an unknown quantity of troops inland from the coast – any number from 20,000 to 240,000. In that event he must move fast to new headquarters at Redhill in Surrey, twenty miles south, the nodal point of the London-Brighton line. The Admiralty's code word for this mammoth exodus, 'Dynamo', derived from the lofty naval ops room, which had once housed an electrical plant, at Dover Castle, Kent.

But as the long day dragged on the phone stayed silent and just after 6 p.m. Maitland gave up; a devout churchgoer, he left word that he was bound for Evensong at Southwark Cathedral. That very morning the Cathedral, like every other English church, had held a service of intercession for the British Expeditionary Force in danger – but it seemed too late for much to happen tonight.

Twenty minutes later in the crowded nave he was on his knees in prayer when a tap on the shoulder brought him upright. The black-gowned head verger stood hovering: Maitland was wanted on the vestry phone.

Breasting through heavy dust-smelling curtains, Maitland lifted the receiver. It was District Traffic Superintendent Percy Nunn, barely audible above the soaring notes of the organ: 'Operation Dynamo has commenced. You will proceed now to Redhill.'

Night came to northern France, a chequer-board of flat green fields laced by dykes, and with it a strange unease. A halo of mist hung above the dark canal waters and more prosaic smells mingled with the fragrance of hawthorn blossom: the smells of corned beef stew and freshly brewed tea.

In a hundred vehicle parks and market towns and châteaux the sentries had been posted and the orderly officers prepared to make their rounds for the night. Along the canals from Nieuport to Seclin, from Carvin to Gravelines, a 130-mile front curving inland from the Channel in the shape of a bent hairpin, the 200,000 fighting men of Lord Gort's force, the Belgians and the French First Army gripped tight on their rifles and waited.

The question looming largest in most minds remained unspoken: 'When do we stand and fight?'

Most, lacking up-to-date knowledge, took comfort in their faith; the top brass had a plan which would make it come all right. Lance-Corporal Thomas Nicholls, a young anti-tank gunner defending the market town of Wormhoudt, took comfort from an old sweat's dictum: 'This is Mons all over again – we're forming a thin red line to throw them out.' A few streets away Chaplain David Wild chose an apt text from Job I for that evening's visit to the billets: 'In all this Job sinned not, nor charged God foolishly.'

Occasionally a note of cynicism crept in. At Ypres, where the 4th East Yorks prepared to blow the famed Menin Gate, Major Cyril Huddlestone opened the War Office telegram routed to all units: 'We are holding a National Day of Prayer for you.' Angrily he crumpled it into his pocket: 'Why the hell don't they send us some 25-pounders?'

Many were mortally afraid but would have died rather than admit it. South of Houthem, on a railway track bordering the Ypres-Comines Canal, Lance-Corporal John 'Warrior' Linton wasn't uttering a word: waiting for action, the fear sounded in your voice, making it pitches higher. The forward man who lay ahead might hear that fear and double back, abandoning his position.

Linton had reason to be fearful. Aged twenty-eight, a wiry, soft-spoken West Countryman with strongly marked eyebrows and a granite jaw, he had seen his unit, the 43rd Light Infantry, in headlong retreat from Brussels across three vital riverlines – the Dyle, the Dendre, the Escaut. With every river had come the same do-or-die order: 'Last man – last round.' Then, within days, the order that sent morale dipping: 'Prepare to abandon positions – we're pulling out.'

Dead-beat, filthy, unshaven, Linton was well aware he couldn't go on much longer. In the last week he had marched almost sixty miles, so that now each extra mile had become a personal battle waged by his will against his exhausted body, carrying not only his own rifle, but another man's besides, harrying the two men who carried the anti-tank gun parts to make them keep up. And at each resting point the officers had issued the same grim warning: stragglers and wounded must be left behind. The Germans are on our heels.

Few men were aware that the words sent a chill through Linton. Though he would raise his fist to scrimshankers and curse a blue streak, there was always a scramble to make his six-strong section up to strength when burly Major Rupert Conant, the Company Commander, reorganised after a battle. They knew that Linton, a regular soldier of eleven years' standing, would look after them, just as he had looked after Private Curtis, doubled up with appendicitis on the march from Hollain. When the dead weight of carrying Curtis became too much, the men who'd agreed to aid him had grumbled that he must be left behind.

Linton had agreed with suspicious readiness, bright brown eyes surveying them, head cocked on one side, his voice dropped to the soft lilt they knew well. 'All right, my dears, we'll leave him.' Then his voice hardening, he had looked every man straight in the eyes. 'But who's going to do it? *Who'll* be the one to leave him behind, eh?' As they shouldered Curtis anew, bound for the baggage truck that carried him to England and safety, Linton knew that a precious fraternity had been forged.

The son of a Bristol craftsman, one of a solid working-class family of eight, Linton had always fought not to be left behind. Every landmark in his life was marked by privations or sudden unexpected treats: Armistice Day, at the close of the First World War, stood out as the day six-year-old Linton had tasted his first doughnut. Even before he was twelve, realising the grim need to help out the family budget, he'd run all the way from school to Mr Skene, the newsagent, to apply for the newsboy's vacant job at 3s. 6d. a week. Then on to the Youth Employment Officer at the Labour Exchange; the law decreed only twelve-year-olds could work, but when his birthday came in three months' time Linton knew the job would be filled – and other newsagents paid only 2s. 6d. The small freckle-faced red-head had looked so earnest, pleading for the right to help support the family, that he got his permit – and the job.

Now, in the darkness, Linton lay on the railway track, a man spaced neatly five yards on either side of him, steel helmeted, haversack and water-bottle slung. His belly throbbed gently with pain; the only food he had foraged that day was a handful of dried prunes and apricots. Sometimes a German plane droned steadily in the distance and the white splash of a parachute flare split the darkness, but the night stayed quiet. Facing the German might with six rounds in his rifle and an empty bandolier, Linton thought again: I won't be left behind – but no one else must be. Somehow, someone must have a plan to get us out of this.

At G.H.Q., Premesques, a small stone château six miles southeast of where Linton lay, one man had set the seal on the only plan that offered a shred of hope. Brooding alone at the scrubbed trestle table which served him for a desk, General Lord Gort, commander-in-chief, had ordered two entire divisions – General Harold Franklyn's 5th and General Giffard Martel's 50th – to abandon all plans for a dawn attack south with the French First Army.

Instead 3,500 men must hold the eight-mile line of the Ypres-Comines Canal while the bulk of the British Army drew back to the coast, as the Secretary of State for War, Anthony Eden, had authorised that very morning. Already 27,000 non-combatant troops – 'useless mouths', as Gort styled them – had gone, but with the Germans pressing in on all sides time was of the essence. Three days earlier Boulogne had fallen; in Calais the garrison could hold out only for a matter of hours.

Only that morning Gort had cabled Eden: 'I must not conceal from you that a great part of the B.E.F. and its equipment will inevitably be lost even in best circumstances.' Then turning on an aide in a rare moment of self-revelation: 'You know, the day I joined up I never thought I'd lead the British Army to its biggest defeat in history.'

A Guards officer and a First World War V.C., Gort, a burly blue-eyed monosyllabic man nicknamed 'The Tiger', had always held that, come the day of reckoning, his Army would accomplish great things. All winter he had urged his officers, 'We must keep fit for the struggle to come'; for three days, ever since his sorely pressed troops went on half-rations, Gort's own breakfast had been two hard biscuits smeared thinly with marmalade. A non-smoker who cared little for food, his keenest pleasure was the punishing two-hour tramp he took each evening with his military assistant, Captain the Viscount Munster. There followed a brisk sherry . . . dinner . . . then a marathon conference at which Gort, whose whole life was the Army, chewed over such points as: on which shoulder must a soldier carry his steel helmet.

At these times the port, by Gort's order, circulated once only – a rule from which even his Chief Liaison Officer, the Duke of Gloucester, wasn't exempt.

Yet tonight, though strong in courage and loyalty, Gort faced a bitter decision. Not only was he forced to fight a losing battle but to deny the French High Command, who were his masters. Already, reports made plain, the whole Belgian Army was cracking under pressure; the retreat plan which Lieut.-Colonel the Viscount Bridgeman, of Gort's staff, had finalised a day back, working against the clock on a diet of whisky and chocolate, must be adopted without delay. The one hope now was to fight back down a corridor fifty miles long, fifteen miles wide, to the thousand-year-old port of Dunkirk – in the grim likelihood that more than 300,000 men would be prisoners by the week's end.

A few men faced problems as crucial: had their troops the stamina to fight at all? As Brigadier Miles Dempsey, commanding the 13th Infantry Brigade on the eastern front, made his night rounds in the meadows perched above the Ypres-Comines Canal, he had cause to wonder. From one group of forward posts, a 500-yard stretch held by the Royal Inniskilling Fusiliers, there had come no challenge, no sound. Approaching noiselessly across the spongy ground, Dempsey found the bulk of the sixty-strong company fast asleep in their slit trenches.

Since Dempsey knew the Canal – really a dry overgrown channel seventeen yards across – formed the vital eastern flank of the whole British front, his first reaction, as a regular soldier, was typical. The men should be court-martialled, if not shot.

As things turned out, compassion — and the memory of two weeks' gruelling retreat — blocked the impulse: Dempsey didn't wake them. Instead, tiptoeing to Battalion Headquarters as noiselessly as a physician from a bedside, he told the C.O., Lieut.-Colonel Frederick Lefroy, 'Those chaps out there are sleeping — but let them. They're dead beat and they may not get any more sleep once this attack starts.'

Accepting that for one night five hundred yards of the eastern front should lie naked to the enemy, Dempsey couldn't know that a massive thrust by two infantry corps of Generaloberst Fedor von Bock's Army Group 'B' was planned for dawn on the Monday — or that the five armoured divisions which had mysteriously halted three days back were racing east to entrap the Allies from the rear in a mesh of steel.

Three days had now passed since Generaloberst Gerd von Rundstedt, commanding Army Group 'A', had issued the order that was to set the entire German High Command by the ears. At 6.10 p.m. on Thursday, 23rd May, to all Panzer commanders on the western front twelve miles from Dunkirk, had gone the order: halt at the line of the Aa Canal and close up.

At the general's own headquarters, though, the old creeper-covered town house at Charleville, in the Ardennes, no man so much as raised an eyebrow. It was, thought Oberst Günther Blumentritt, von Rundstedt's operations officer, affectionately all of a piece with the general's outlook: walk warily, consolidate, never court risks.

A reserved 65-year-old patrician with a lined handsome face, von Rundstedt no longer worried too much about keeping pace with modern methods — or men. Shunning strangers, his off-duty routine never varied now . . . a few chosen staff officers to share his favourite dinner, meat-and-vegetable stew, then a long silent evening solving crossword puzzles or wading through piles of paperback whodunnits.

Much the same in working hours: to von Rundstedt the whole new concept of tank warfare – mobile Panzer divisions advancing under their own steam as the Army's spearhead – was fraught with peril. Time and again in the Ardennes campaign he had clamped down brief 'Halt' orders – the tanks were advancing too far and too fast for the infantry to catch up, leaving a long danger-ously exposed flank. And though dashing Panzer leaders like Generalmajor Erwin Rommel and General Heinz Guderian never ceased to chafe at the bit – 'When my panzers start on a journey,' Guderian snorted, 'they have a ticket to the terminus' – von Rundstedt, cautious and canny, had stuck to his guns.

To other top brass, too, the order made sense – at first. At Munstereifel, south of Bonn, Germany, Generaloberst Franz Hal-der, Chief of Staff to the Army High Command, shrugged when he read the flimsy: to him von Rundstedt was always a com-mander lacking drive but the man on the spot knew best. West of Montreuil, Oberst Kurt Zeitzler, chief of staff to General von Kleist's tank group, thought grudgingly the order had a kind of logic. Of von Kleist's 1,250 tanks, some 50 per cent did need emer-gency repairs and it would be foolish to risk a breakdown in the dyke-seamed terrain beyond the canal. Even so, in the daily report they always rendered to Hitler they'd stressed some 360 would be serviceable within two days.

Now the Army's Supreme Commander, Generaloberst Walther von Brauchitsch, stepped in. The tanks, he felt, were wasted in the west; the British there were a broken reed, no longer a force to be reckoned with. Instead, von Brauchitsch ordered, the entire Panzer contingent plus the German 4th Army must transfer from von Rundstedt to General Fedor von Bock, whose Army Group 'B', attacking the Allies from the east, lacked any armour at all.

Then, at 11 a.m. on 24th May, Hitler paid a surprise visit to von Rundstedt's Charleville headquarters. It began, as Oberst Günther Blumentritt recalls it, pretty much as usual . . . the black open Mercedes purring easily through the cobbled streets . . . the Führer as always in snuff-brown jacket and breeches, the Iron Cross at his breast, sitting stiffly in the back with Generalmajor Jodl, his operations officer . . . his aide, Oberst Rudolf Schmundt, keeping the chauffeur company.

And as always, knowing Hitler's prejudices, the staff had to scuffle like guilty schoolboys to put a good face on things. General von Sodenster, Rundstedt's chief of staff, a man who took his liquor strong and often, piling cointreau bottles into a filing cabinet . . . an orderly flinging wide von Rundstedt's window, wafting out the heavy tobacco fumes of a chain-smoker.

Only von Rundstedt, as ever, remained calm and impassive; without too high an opinion of the Führer, he knew the value Hitler placed on his judgements. And today, as always in von Rundstedt's presence, the Führer was quiet, almost docile . . . standing beside the general as he flicked a pointer over the big operations map . . . nodding quietly at intervals . . . asking finally what did von Rundstedt intend to do with the armour now he had it halted?

Von Rundstedt was puzzled. Surely the Führer realised the armour was no longer his to command? Von Brauchitsch had transferred it to Army Group 'B' twenty-four hours back.

In the chill silence that followed, every man divined now that something was wrong. Plainly, though Hitler's only comment was a quiet 'That order will be cancelled', he'd known nothing of the switch.

And he went on: von Rundstedt had done right to halt the tanks. Not only had they outrun themselves, but the marshy Flanders plain just wasn't tank country. There was 'Plan Red' to consider too, the already blue-printed armoured thrust across the Somme River against the heart of France. Supposing the French attacked from the south in force while the Panzers, bogged down in the marshes round Dunkirk, merely snarled up things for the Luftwaffe?

Von Rundstedt nodded sagely; a born diplomat who spoke four languages, he had had long discussions at the funeral of King George V with General Georges Gamelin, Supreme Commander of the Allied Forces until General Weygand took over three days back. Tapping the map of southern France, von Rundstedt, who expected great things of the French, would say time and again: 'My little friend Gamelin will certainly come up here with a counter-offensive.'

And there seemed other reasons for not getting too excited about the British. A week back, in this very room, Hitler had launched into a half-hour eulogy of the British and their Empire: 'I hope and believe we will come to an agreement with Great Britain . . . *she* should rule the globe and the seas . . . I should rule Europe.' And he wove other flights of fancy: supposing England made peace, then got embroiled in a war with another power? Such was his admiration he'd even lend them the Luftwaffe and the German Navy to help them out of it.

The session over, Blumentritt recalls how von Rundstedt commented dryly: 'Well, if he doesn't want anything else from England, we'll have peace in about six weeks.'

Neither man was much surprised: they'd heard Hitler talk this way too often. In 1937, as Chief Operations Officer of the 7th German Army, Blumentritt remembered many discussions as to whether Germany should ally herself with Italy or Britain – and how Hitler sneered: 'I'd rather have a British thoroughbred than an Italian donkey.'

Convinced they'd read the Führer's mind aright, neither von Rundstedt nor Blumentritt took much further interest in the proceedings. But by now the stage was set for a high-level wrangle. By 3 p.m. on the 24th, Hitler was back at his hunting-lodge headquarters in the forests at Munstereifel. At once, sending for Supreme Commander von Brauchitsch, he threw a mammoth tantrum. By what right did von Brauchitsch transfer the Panzers without consulting him? The tanks had no business in the Flanders marshes — the order was to be cancelled right away.

A sensitive dignified aristocrat of the old school, von Brauchitsch couldn't even bring himself to talk back — often the effect of a brawl with Hitler made him physically sick. As his chief of staff, Generaloberst Franz Halder recalls, he came back 'shaken and distressed . . . convinced the Führer's decision might alter the whole course of the war.' Halder, a dapper, precise Prussian with a terse manner, upbraided him: 'The way you let him push you around, it serves you right.' And he added: 'Why don't you hand in your resignation? He can have mine at the same time.' But Halder knew he was wasting breath; the tortured conscientious von Brauchitsch would surely do no such thing. He urged Halder, 'Whatever happens, there is our loyalty to the Army . . . and you mustn't dream of resigning either. You're the only man with everything at his fingertips.'

These were command decisions. At lower levels, for twenty-four hours things stayed quiet. Then, from every side, as the top brass grasped the full implications, came one mighty yell of protest.

In Brussels, headquarters of Army Group 'B', General Fedor von Bock knew as little as his own privates. Why had the tanks halted in the first place? Why hadn't they transferred to him as promised? His chief of staff, Oberst Hans von Salmuth, rang General von Kluge, whose 4th Army controlled the Panzers, and the mystery deepened. Von Kluge had had the order right enough but no reasons had been given.

Now von Bock took over. Snatching up the phone, he called

von Brauchitsch, but the Supreme Commander, perhaps unwilling to admit that he had yielded to Hitler, was cagey. 'Unfortunately,' he explained, 'the tanks have been halted for the day.'

Von Bock replied angrily: 'But it's essential they attack at once! If Dunkirk isn't taken, the British can transport their army wherever they want.' As Chief of Staff von Salmuth remembers it, von Bock was one of the few men who already grasped the vital import of Dunkirk.

Others were early into the fray – and none more eagerly than Reichsmarschall Hermann Goering, Commander-in-Chief of the Luftwaffe. Generalleutnant Josef Schmid, Chief of Staff to the Air High Command, never forgot how Goering, on 23rd May, heard that the Panzers had almost reached Dunkirk. At once, pounding the table with his fist, he cried: 'I must talk to the Führer immediately. This is a special job for the Luftwaffe. Get through on the phone.'

Within minutes, Schmid recalled in wonder, Hitler had agreed without demur – a day before he'd even consulted with von Rundstedt. Dunkirk should be left to the Luftwaffe after all. The Panzers should stay where they were.

Others were beside themselves. At Munstereifel, General Greiffenberg, of Hitler's operations staff, burst out: 'What is the meaning of this insane order? Are we building golden bridges for the British?' When one of his colleagues, General von Lossberg, sought out Generalmajor Jodl himself, Jodl soothed him: 'The war is already won. Why waste tanks doing what the Luftwaffe can do economically?' Distraught, von Lossberg hastened into the sunshine to find Generaloberst Wilhelm Keitel peacefully puffing a cigar. Again, though, he drew a blank. Keitel assured him: 'Flanders is too marshy for tanks – but don't worry, Goering will finish the job.'

In fact, only Goering had such faith. Feldmarschall Albert

Kesselring, ebullient chief of Air Fleet Two, whom the British called 'Smiling Al', was appalled when he heard the news. From his Brussels headquarters he at once rang Goering to protest. Surely Goering realised that three weeks' air war had reduced some of his units by 50 per cent? Worse, the Panzers had ripped ahead so fast that the Luftwaffe's supply-chain couldn't keep up. Most available bombers were still based at airfields south of the Rhine River, more than 300 miles from Dunkirk.

But at last convinced that Goering's desire for vainglory overrode all other factors, Kesselring, with a curt 'Nicht lösbar' (It won't work), slammed down the phone.

Thus for three long days, while British and French regrouped, the arguments raged like a forest fire and not until lunch-time on Sunday, 26th May, did a gleam of light emerge. Then from Brussels, von Bock's intelligence officer, Oberst Hasse, made his daily routine call to General Greiffenberg at Hitler's headquarters. He wheedled: wasn't there the smallest chance of the tanks advancing? But Greiffenberg had cheering news. Lord Gort's 'useless mouths' plan hadn't gone unobserved – and on hearing that six transport ships had left Dunkirk that morning crammed with troops, Hitler had again changed his mind.

The Panzers, five divisions of them, had permission to advance – though only to within thirteen miles of Dunkirk, the artillery range of 15-centimetre guns. As for Dunkirk, the Panzers were to bypass it altogether – again, Hitler stressed, that was the Luftwaffe's job.

One man at least was determined that they would do it with all their might. In his farmhouse headquarters near St Pol, fifty miles south of Dunkirk, General the Baron von Richtofen had chafed for days now. A tense trigger-tempered go-getter of 44, the Baron was the cousin of Manfred 'Red Devil' von Richtofen, the famed First World War air-ace with 80 planes to his credit – and he rarely forgot it. As the ruthless dynamic head of the 8th Flying

Corps, a picked body of crack pilots based within striking distance of Dunkirk, the Baron had flown with the famed Condor Legion in the Spanish Civil War and since then had specialised in close infantry support.

He, too, had been rocked on his heels by the halting of the tanks; but as usual, in an attempt to pull strings, he'd put in a personal call to his good friend, General Hans Jeschonnek, Chief of Staff to the Luftwaffe. It was a pipeline other Luftwaffe officers knew and dreaded. Von Richtofen's appeals to the all-highest for aircraft and personnel seldom went unanswered – though supply and training chiefs computed his missions in terms of cracked-up planes and crippled aviators.

This time, though, von Richtofen, who contemptuously referred to Hitler as 'Adolfchen' (Little Adolf), wasn't within an ace of success. No sooner was the call over than his chief of staff, Oberstleutnant Hans Seidemann, saw him burst from his office 'cursing like a colour sergeant'.

'What the devil is Adolfchen playing at?' he yelled. 'Jeschonnek says he's withdrawn the tanks from Dunkirk to save the British from a shameful defeat. What kind of crazy talk is that?'

And on this damp Sunday night von Richtofen had special reason to be pleased with the changed orders. At Castle Dyck, near Cologne, he had experimented long hours with the Junkers 87 or Stuka dive-bomber and had come up with a device to make the plane immediately more terrifying; the brain-child of air-ace Ernst Udet, inspired by the U.S. Navy's 'Flying Jenny', its engines turned over so smoothly that von Richtofen scoffed: 'It's like a man walking in wet socks.' Only recently a close friend had remarked, 'You ought to give up playing with toys.' For von Richtofen, after much thought, had equipped each of the Stuka's bombs with four small cardboard whistles, each keyed to a different pitch, with a tiny rotating propeller on the plane's wheels.

Von Richtofen ignored the jibe for now, when plane and bombs ripped through the stratosphere as one, they made a sound like all the devils of hell. He wondered how the British at Dunkirk were going to like that.

As yet few of Lord Gort's men knew that trouble was afoot – but the news was spreading. In a stable on the outskirts of Roncq, Private Bill Hersey of the East Surreys was knuckling sleep from his eyes; abruptly an uncivil hand had jerked him into wakefulness: 'Stand to! Company Commander's parade.' Ten minutes later, lined up on the cobbles outside, Hersey heard spine-chilling news from Company Commander Captain Harry Smith: 'We are making a general retreat to the coast. The idea is to get back to England with the whole object of returning to France later.'

There was no time to lose. As Battery Sergeant-Major Richard Whiley signalled 'Dismiss', Hersey cut in front of Smith, snapping to attention. 'Sir, is there anything you can do for my wife?' Hersey knew and trusted Smith, a kindly thick-set man, who had even arranged that Captain Joseph Gardner, the Brigade's Catholic priest, should intercede with the local clergy, who had disapproved of the mixed marriage. As ever, Smith was helpful if succinct: 'Go and get her.'

Grabbing a bicycle, Hersey pedalled hard for Tourcoing, the tyres slithering and bumping over rain-washed cobbles. The whole concept of retreat, even of returning to England, had paled before the thought of leaving Augusta behind.

Before the Germans invaded, Bill Hersey had known a unique distinction: from his wedding day, 17th April, he was the only man in the B.E.F. granted a permanent sleeping-out pass. From then on, each night at the Café L'Epi d'Or had seemed like England, with old friends dropping in: 'Nobby' Clarke, 'Dicky' Dumper, 'Gutty' Bedford. Right from the wedding breakfast of steak, chips and anisette, they had all shared warm moments: quiet games of pontoon, sing-songs, spirited evenings on the café's rifle-range, locals versus troops, with Augusta, whose father had taught her to shoot, handling her .22 as gamely as any man.

And strangely, for Bill was always thumbing through his pocket dictionary, and Augusta spoke no word of English, the marriage seemed right from the start. A lean, devil-may-care rolling stone, who had soldiered all over India and spent many nights in the guardhouse, Bill Hersey had secretly yearned for a wife and home; in his own home things had never been good since his father, a water-cress farmer, lost heart keeping pace with new methods. The longing had stayed with him until the December day when Bill, cooking steaks for lunch, had burned his hand badly on an open-air petrol stove and gone to the café for first-aid.

At once Papa Paul Six, Augusta's father, had insisted that his daughter must attend to it. Was she not learning first-aid and in need of practice? Augusta's method had seemed a shade primitive at first, for the douche of 90-degree alcohol she splashed on the burn sent Hersey leaping for the ceiling. Yet somehow Bill Hersey, who had never troubled with minor ills, found he needed his wound dressed at least once a day. There seemed no better excuse in the world for holding hands.

Still pedalling for dear life, Hersey swerved his machine into the familiar length of the Rue Clinquet – his home for three whole weeks – then glanced at his watch. It was just 11.30 p.m.

Within minutes, five women were stirring uneasily inside the Café L'Epi d'Or. Huddled on palliasses in the big downstairs bedroom, a precaution against air attack, Augusta, her mother and her three friends had retired early for the night, but no sleeper could have resisted that thunderous knocking.

Struggling through the darkened café in her dressing-gown, Augusta never forgot the sight of her husband's face as the blackout curtains parted: the relaxed nonchalant charm had gone, leaving a new Hersey, urgent and tense. His greeting was a command: 'Get your things – we're leaving.'

CHAPTER TWO

WHAT, DUNKIRK IN SCOTLAND?

Monday, 27th May
1 a.m.–8 p.m.

Augusta Hersey needed no time to make up her mind. It was her nature to accept what fortune offered. At 21 her life had followed no set pattern; the world had willed it otherwise. Her father's daughter, boyish, impetuous, she had taken readily to exchanging banter and half-understood jokes with the khaki-clad strangers who had invaded Tourcoing last winter, with their oddly nasal twang and their humorous stubborn leathery faces.

Now, as a British soldier's wife, it was her duty to go wherever her husband went. Slipping back to the bedroom, she contrived to waken her mother fully without even disturbing her girl-friends, explaining, 'It is Bill – he has come to take me to England.' For minutes the old lady was too distressed to speak. But as Bill Hersey urged, 'She is British now; only this way can she be safe', she seemed to understand.

Swiftly, methodically, Augusta packed a suitcase – linen from her trousseau taking pride of place. Inside ten minutes she was dressed: white linen blouse, pleated skirt, jaunty French beret, a new blue topcoat to ward off the night chills. A swift investigation of her handbag revealed 2,400 francs – about £14. Leaving 1,000 francs with her mother, she embraced her once again.

'*Dépêchez, dépêchez*' (Hurry, hurry), Bill kept imploring as she wheeled her bicycle from the back room. It seemed a night for speed. Machine-gun fire hammered faintly from the east as they pedalled through silent streets; the curfew was four hours old. By the roadside, as they went, sappers were laying mines.

Once at Roncq all was business: the stealthy grumble of transport moving off, the glow-worm rear-lights of trucks, the clatter of boots on *pavé*. As Bill presented Augusta to his company commander, Captain Smith made a swift decision. He explained to Hersey: 'She can go ahead in my P.U. (personal use) truck with my batman. But first you'd better get her kitted up.'

For Hersey and his wife, the strangeness of it all almost numbed the pang of parting. First the separation . . . then this bitter-sweet reunion . . . now within half an hour, Hersey, the skilled storeman, was fitting up his wife as a prototype British Tommy – khaki greatcoat, steel helmet, respirator, Lee-Enfield rifle. A swift conclave with Smith's batman, Driver Johnnie Johnson, then Smith signalled 'Off'.

At 12.30, the convoy, a dozen trucks strong, moved off into the damp pitch-black night. Transport was short and some, Bill Hersey among them, were marching. Rumour along the column was firm: destination Ostend.

Ironically, Ostend, on the Belgian coast, was one more port the British must soon yield – as none knew better than Admiral Sir Bertram Home Ramsay, Flag Officer Commanding Dover. This morning, after weeks of anticipation, the aloof silver-haired little admiral faced a nightmare task: the evacuation of an unknown quantity of troops from the one bolt-hole remaining – Dunkirk, twenty-four miles up the coast from Calais.

No man was better fitted for the job. Long known as a trouble-shooter – until eight months back he had been in retirement after consistently tangling with his superiors – 57-year-old Ramsay was as famous for his sharp, incisive brain as for his ruthless perfectionism, his cutting contempt for the second-rate. As immaculate as the black satin tie he always wore, the admiral was no easy man to get along with; most mortals found his standards in everything from port to polo ponies too high to make friendships feasible. But he could judge a situation, as he judged a man, with one X-ray glance – 'and if he found the man wanting,' an aide recalls, 'he would cut him short in mid-sentence, his mind irrevocably made up.'

This morning, in his small iron-balconied office carved from the sweating chalk of Dover's East Cliff, Ramsay's mind was again made up – and he saw the chances as slim. Aside from Dunkirk, the northern coast now offered no other egress. Yet the main harbour, with its seven fine dock basins that had made it France's third port, was out. As a point of routine, Feldmarschall Albert Kesselring's Air Fleet Two had begun pounding it to rubble eight days back on 18th May.

That left the twenty-five miles of shelving sandy beaches – and Ramsay, a First World War veteran of those waters, at points no more than two fathoms deep, remembered them too well. To use heavy craft was out of the question: the tortuous shoal-ridden Dunkirk coast, known as 'the graveyard of ships', made this a small-ship affair from the first. Yet out of the 202 destroyers the Navy could muster when war began, Ramsay could call on only forty by week's end. Norway, the Mediterranean theatre, the heavy toll of the Belgian and Dutch evacuations . . . all had combined to whittle down the total available.

Quietly, clinically, Ramsay chewed it over with Captain William Tennant, the lean eagle-faced officer who had been sent post-haste by Admiralty to help out. Already the pattern had been set – old Isle of Man steam packets like the *Mona's Isle* and the *King Orry*, converted to armed boarding vessels, had set out hours earlier, as the spearhead of the evacuation force. But the slim whippet-like destroyers, as Tennant knew, crammed with guns and depth-charge racks, had not been built to carry men. Thus, the bulk of the lifting would fall on lightly-armed merchant ships – coasters, cross-channel ferries, flat-bottomed Dutch barges known as *schuits*. Only 129 of the British Merchant Navy's 10,000 vessels were at Ramsay's disposal on this warm May morning – but from a score of ports and landing berths more were coming.

Now Ramsay told Tennant: 'The Boche has got as far as Gravelines. That's the worst blow yet.' Tennant had no need to ask why. When the Germans closing in on Gort's army seized Calais to the south they had gained the prize of the Gravelines guns hard by. That meant that Route Z, the 39-mile short sea route from Dunkirk to Dover, now lay in reach of the lethal coastal batteries.

Thus the two-hour crossing must be abandoned, at any rate by day, and already Ramsay's hydrographer, Commander Archibald Day, was working out new routes. Route Y, an 87-mile dog-leg, cut inland from the Kwinte Buoy, off Ostend, approaching Dunkirk from the east. Route X, a 55-mile run, crossed the Ruytingen Bank and hit the inshore channel midway between Dunkirk and Gravelines.

Route X crossed minefields and Route Y was an unknown quantity, yet still Ramsay had been forced to accept the risk. Already before the channel had been swept he had ordered transports and hospital carriers to proceed by Route Y.

Both men could see the implications. The 87-mile route meant more than double the time, five and a half hours as against two. That meant more ships – and more ships in turn could mean a bloody field-day for the Luftwaffe.

Meanwhile as newly-appointed Senior Naval Officer, Dunkirk, the taciturn Tennant, with twelve naval officers and 150 ratings, was to control the entire evacuation from the port – for as long as Gort's army could stem the German tide.

As yet the secret was well kept; not one of the twelve officers clustered outside Ramsay's office in the damp chalk tunnel 500 feet above the Channel knew the real import of the summons.

Commander Harold Conway, playing croquet on the lawn at home, had answered a telephone summons: 'We've a little job for you . . . but don't bring anything but a toothbrush.' Commander Renfrew Gotto, still on the 'active' list, had come straight from church parade at Portsmouth in 'Number Ones', full service dress. Commander Hector Richardson, knowing just as little, had packed some tennis shirts and a revolver.

Even the ships knew little more, but all round the coastline of Britain from the Tees to Plymouth Sound, there was a pleasant tingle of expectancy. If something strange was afoot, the Navy was ready.

Some learned the news in devious ways. At North Shields on the Tyne, Chief Petty Officer Wilfred Walters had been queuing outside a pub when a policeman approached: 'Return on board immediately, you're on an evacuation job.' Now en route for Harwich in the old coal-burning minesweeper *Ross*, Walters had the romantic notion they were speeding to the rescue of the Dutch Royal Family, who had been evacuated fourteen days previously.

On the bridge of the minesweeper *Kellett*, outward bound from Newcastle, Commander Reginald Haskett-Smith arched his eyebrows. The radio cabin had intercepted an urgent signal: 'From Captain, *Mona's Isle*, vice-admiral, Dover: I am being shelled off Gravelines.' Thumbing through a school atlas to locate Gravelines, Haskett-Smith blenched. Whatever they were going south for, it wasn't healthy if the Germans had reached the Channel coast.

Yet even those on the spot knew as little. Lieutenant Victor de Mauny, skipper of the contraband control vessel *Ocean Breeze*, was breakfasting in the shore naval base at Ramsgate, Kent, when a Scots Guards officer came hareing in: 'The Dynamo's working . . . the Dynamo's working.' Convinced the man's brain had gone, de Mauny tried to soothe him with coffee until the officer exploded: 'What are *you* supposed to be doing here anyway?'

As de Mauny explained that his last instructions concerned Belgian refugees, the officer was withering: 'Refugees? Good God, it isn't *refugees* – it's the B.E.F.!'

Few had it as straight from the shoulder as the officers of the minesweeper *Leda*. Finger stabbing at a map of the coast, Commander Harold Unwin told them: 'The situation is bad, almost as bad as it could be . . . we are going over tonight to bring off the B.E.F . . . and now we are for it, boys, good and hearty.'

The way things looked, 'night' was the operative word. As Tennant left Ramsay's office, the admiral almost casually had added one last word: at the most, Tennant and his staff could hope to bring off 45,000 men.

Across the Channel, the predicament was different. Few men as yet knew they were going home, but slowly, along 100 miles of front, the word was passing.

For some the intelligence had an almost holiday flavour. As the sergeant announced they were off to Dunkirk for a rest and a bathe, Gunner William Medlyn almost whooped with joy. Private Mervyn Doncom, of the Hampshires, a seasoned soldier of fortune who kept a sharp eye on the main chance, heard it from the adjutant, Captain Humphrey: 'Nice day for a walk – know where you're going? You're going to England.'

There were grimmer ways to hear. Along with his mates of the 2nd East Yorks, Corporal Jimmie Trodden was retreating north of Waterloo – 600 men moving silently through a milky dawn mist, for the sun hadn't yet burned the dew from the grass. Then slowly, from a pale sky, the surrender leaflets came floating. A brief scuffle, and the East Yorks were the first unit to realise that the B.E.F., with their backs to the sea, were clamped inside a monstrous horseshoe. The text was chilling:

British Soldiers!
Look at this map; it gives your true situation!
Your troops are entirely surrounded!
Stop fighting!
Put down your arms!

Major Eric Rippingille, taking a long look at the blank faces around, asked, 'Well, men, what are we going to do?' There was a muffled growl of unanimity; for too long had the unit been short of toilet paper. Trodden and all of them marched on, strangely heartened, not knowing why.

Some, still in the dark, interpreted small pointers. North of Ypres, Gunner Hugh McGowan felt uneasy to see the officers changing from battledress into service dress – winking buttons, polished Sam Browne belts. Corporal Thomas Dunkley, delivering a message to 5th Brigade H.Q. near Béthune, overheard a muttered conference mentioning 'Dunkirk' behind closed doors. Abruptly, as a subaltern sniggered, Brigadier Gerald Gartlan grated: 'Bloody young fool, nothing to laugh at.'

At Poperinghe, a sergeant-major, using the slang of an older war, told Regimental Artificer Jack Boxey: 'It's a blighty move, Tiffy. Make for Dunkirk.' Yet to the bulk of the 150,000 rear-line troops first affected, the place-name conveyed nothing. 'What,' Trooper Herbert Barnard sang out, 'Dunkirk in Scotland?'

A few took the news philosophically: if death and defeat were at hand there was still just one way to do things. Near Arras, Sapper Jimmy Ross's unit, printing maps in a sawmill, got the word to evacuate just before the morning's routine inspection by Lieutenant Birkmore. In silence the lieutenant licked his finger, bent down and ran it along the floor. It came up with dust on it; Germans or no Germans, Ross had to re-sweep that floor.

Even the men nearer the top knew little more. At Steenvorde, Brigadier John Gawthorpe, commanding 137 Infantry Brigade, was mulling over plans to secure the town of Cassel when a staff officer jumped from a halted car: 'Sir, your orders are to take no further aggressive action . . . report to 3rd Corps headquarters at Teteghem, near Dunkirk, with all you've got.'

When Gawthorpe protested that Dunkirk was on the English Channel, the officer was terse: 'We happen to be going that way.'

In truth they were lucky to hear it. On this fresh May morning many men were fighting not to return to England but to stay alive at all. Already, at 4 a.m., the Very lights burst with the white lustre of Roman candles over the fields beyond the Ypres-Comines canal: General von Bock's Army Group was closing in. On the railway embankment running parallel John 'Warrior' Linton squinted at them, rifle butt cuddled tight against his shoulder. He said to his bosom friend 'Raygo' King, 'No Christmas party lights those . . . they're calling up the artillery.'

Linton worried over 'Raygo', a blue-eyed lad, with a sandy moustache, who smiled a lot; for twenty years he had followed Linton's lead, in the Army and as far back as boyhood, in trips to the stream by the old snuff mill on Saturday afternoon, over the trees they climbed and the caves they explored. Linton felt responsible for all his men, but even more so for 'Raygo'.

Fifteen yards away lay Lance-Sergeant 'Ginger' Dawson, another of Linton's mates – if he was hit, fifteen yards was a long way to crawl. But supposing 'Raygo' was hit at the same time? Crawl first to Dawson and then to 'Raygo'? If he got back to Bristol and 'Raygo' didn't, Linton would never live it down. 'Raygo's' mother would say, 'But, Jack, you were right next to him, surely you could have given him a hand?'

It was just 6 a.m. Now as Major Rupert Conant passed along the line, he told them: 'Don't fire, you'll give your position away. You're here to stop them coming, not to engage them.'

Linton knew that Conant worried over him because he could no longer sleep at night, but he thought that Conant would never understand the responsibility he felt, any more than the secret pacts they had all made that the wounded would help each other. 'Raygo' could sleep, of course, but then 'Raygo' was a private.

It was no time for sleeping. All along the eight miles of front the battle was flaring. The sloping valley echoed to the deadly hammering of machine-gun fire, the tearing ripping whoosh of mortars. Saplings toppled and fell and shredded leaves drifted like green snow amongst the stink of cordite and the coughing, crouching men.

High above them, on the upper canal road, the last men of General Giffard Martel's 50th Division were piling from lorries, a khaki-clad emergency force waiting to take up positions. As they doubled, Lieut.-General Alan Brooke, the dark, poker-faced Commander of 2nd Corps, kept exhorting them: 'You've no time to lose – no time at all – the attack is coming.'

It was Brooke, alerted by captured German staff papers, who had prevailed with Lord Gort to give him virtually the strength of a corps to stem the flood from the east – though Gort, at first preoccupied with the menace to the south, had felt that on the whole Ypres-Comines Canal two machine-gun battalions could do the trick. Until only a few hours earlier, Linton's brigade had been the one unit in position: less than 2,000 men to defend the eight-mile front.

Few men apart from Brooke knew the real significance of this stand and the knowledge turned him cold. Already the Belgian Army was retreating northwards under enemy pressure – and as the gap widened there would be nothing to stop von Bock's infantry from pouring westwards to link up with von Rundstedt's armour beyond the canals. If the forces on the two canal lines did not stand fast there would be no Dunkirk bridgehead into which the rest of the Army could retreat.

Could the lines hold, even with ten divisions ranged against the Germans? On the eastern front Brooke knew only that the men were desperately tired – those sleeping Inniskillings that Brigadier Dempsey had unearthed were proof enough of that. Weapons, too, were pitifully inadequate, as they had been all through the campaign: the Cameronians, the famous Scottish rifle regiment, were holding a 4,000-yard front between Houthem and Hollebeke with ammunition for 3-inch mortars in plenty, but no mortars. Their mortars had been withdrawn for adjustment two weeks before and they had never been returned.

Instead, stores had issued them 2-inch mortars – but without ammo or sights. It was the same all along the canal.

At 6 a.m. Brooke was certain of just one thing: only the steadfastness of the men up front could win time for the thousands in retreat.

Near Houthem, Lieut.-Colonel George Gilmore, commanding the Cameronians, faced as grave a problem as any. Already the German barrage had been so deadly that Gilmore had sanctioned a hair-trigger withdrawal back to the ridge overlooking the canal; now, to his horror, he saw that the retreat had overspilled. Bleeding, demoralised, dragging their wounded as they came, the men had fallen back in their hundreds down the far side of the ridge to the dirt road on which he stood.

The Cameronians' front stood undefended, and back on the ridge almost 400 of his men had been cut down by shells and machine-gun fire. On that flat terrain it had been impossible for them to dig in.

But Gilmore, a cheerful ruddy-faced man known as 'Pop', saw

a way out. If the five armoured carriers worked as a screen, boxing the men in from front and sides, the ridge could be retaken – even with the 180 men and ten officers left to him. Mustering his force in the ditch by the roadside, Gilmore gave them the rifleman's age-old order: 'Fix sword.' Then, as the sun struck white fire from the serried bayonets, he pointed to the crest of the ridge: 'That is our objective – advance.'

It was a heart-rending moment. Slowly, the carriers with their caterpillar tracks lumbering ahead, Gilmore in the lead, the long thin line of the Cameronians, spread over 400 yards, flagging in the cruel heat, moved grimly back up the mile of hilly pasture. Towards the crest, a murderous cross-fire of incendiary bullets and machine-gun fire cut into them; all round men were doubling up in the turnip fields, but Gilmore's tactics were working. As the light machine-guns opened up from the scrubby grass, Gilmore's carriers turned nose-on to them, charging like tanks. Within seconds von Bock's gunners had fled.

But Gilmore, haunted by the faces of the dead who lay on all sides, was nagged by a strange thought: where and when had he seen those faces thus grouped before? Then, as the incendiary bullets cut a bright path towards him, he remembered. Twelve years ago, at Catterick Camp in Yorkshire, the year he was Father Christmas, these had been the young faces grouped candle-lit round the regimental Christmas tree.

As he, too, fell, shell splinters ripping into his thigh and stomach, he knew a strange peace. For him the long journey back to England by ambulance had begun, but at that moment his runner, Corporal Taylor, was doubling back down the ridge to tell Brigadier Miles Dempsey: 'We are back where we were ordered. We shall hold on at all costs.'

And the commanders on the western front were as determined; outmanned and outgunned, they must still contrive ways and means to hold von Rundstedt's armour back.

On the high ground above La Bassée Canal, the Queen's Own Cameron Highlanders were almost surrounded, but Lieut.-Colonel Peter Rose-Miller had a personal reason for not giving up; a battalion that defied Lord Gort must never yield to the Germans. Despite a War Office order that highland battalions must no longer wear the kilt on active service, the Highlanders had for months fought a delaying action on paper. Surely there was some mistake? What should be worn in lieu? Where would they hand the kilts in? On 10th May, when the Germans struck, Rose-Miller knew they had won: from now on G.H.Q. would have other things to brood on.

Yet the still-kilted Highlanders faced a near impossible task – to halt the entire 7th German Panzer Division, 400 tanks under the personal command of Generalmajor Erwin Rommel. In the farmhouse cellar that was his H.Q., Rose-Miller had pleaded by field telephone for close artillery support, but Brigadier Gerald Gartlan was uncompromising: 'You won't even have any anti-tank guns, they're all going back to Dunkirk – but the Germans must not cross the Canal.'

The tragedy was, Gort's Army had arrived in France in top gear to fight an old war. Against the Germans' 2,700 tanks, Gort could marshal only the 120-odd tanks of the 1st Army Tank Brigade – whose 25-ton 'Matildas' had been so heavily armoured to carry a frail 2-pounder gun that the crews, back in England within twenty-four hours of Ramsay's Dynamo signal, had left them to act as pill-boxes, bogged down for ever on Vimy Ridge, north of Arras. Major-General Roger Evans's 1st Armoured Division (328 tanks) only made it weeks later, with mock-up plywood vehicles – their training had just finished as the Germans invaded Belgium. Even the French tanks, 2,400 strong, moved cumbrously, geared to infantry support, often running short of fuel during the battle.

The result was disaster from the first. The only real armament against von Rundstedt's tanks were 25-pounder guns detached in an anti-tank role to fire solid shot against the advancing Panzers. Infantry used the .55-inch rifle, the Boys, whose bullets, far from puncturing the tanks solid hide, bounced back like peas off a window-pane. The artillery was as bad. Not one gun which Gort possessed had much more than half the range of the latest German models. Of these many had never been fired before 10th May – the firing locks hadn't arrived from England.

But on a sudden, watching the might of 400 tanks, Mark IVs and Mark IIIs massed in parade-ground order on the plain below, Ross-Miller had a brainwave. If infantrymen with rifles couldn't hold up tanks, at least they could stall their advance. Now he ordered his scratch force – twenty-one men commanded by Second-Lieutenant Donald Callender: 'If you see a block hole, fire at it!'

It was a daring ruse, yet it worked triumphantly. As the tanks droned on at a steady 30 m.p.h., Highlander after Highlander, nursing his rifle, aimed for the black slits. Meanwhile, bubbling with fun like an uncle organising nursery sports, Rose-Miller mustered a scratch force of company clerks and cooks, pressing grenades on them: 'Go out and see how many tanks you can bag.'

The results were better than he could have dreamed. As the anti-tank bullets whanged home, tank commander after tank commander shut down his periscope and clamped down his visor; a crack marksman's bullet, penetrating the tank, would zoom amongst the tank crew like a crazy bee. Now shorn of vision, the tanks lurched across the fields like drunken men, and even a gunner seeking a breath of air risked a hastily-lobbed grenade through the gun turret.

No wonder Rommel later wrote: 'Prospects did not look too good for an attack across La Basée canal . . . the situation was extremely critical.' For thirty-six hours, Rose-Miller had fought a delaying action – his orders not to withdraw without permission – until Brigadier Gartlan phoned again: 'Where are they?'

Rose-Miller, who had already converted his carriers into ambulances and seen his wounded out, answered, 'In the back yard.'

'What are they doing?'

'Burning the roof over the top of my head.'

Gartlan was final. 'Time you got.'

Rose-Miller wasn't slow to act. Within seconds he had ducked from the cellar into the smoke-filled street. As a German tank closed in on him he dived head-first into the canal, emerging 'like Neptune covered in weeds and blowing bubbles'. Joyous in the knowledge that he had cost Rommel twenty-one tanks – though the Panzers crossed the canal by early afternoon – Rose-Miller retreated across the fields. Scrambling through another ditch he found his adjutant, Captain Peter Hunt, had thoughtfully arrived from base with a truck: 'Your car, sir.'

In England it was hard to tell what was happening; if some ships had been briefed others stayed completely in the dark. Aboard H.M.S. *Wakeful* in Plymouth Harbour, Warrant-Engineer Tucker had had full steam on all boilers for hours – but no one knew why. To Able Seaman Geoffrey Kester, one of the guns' crew, it all seemed highly suspicious: never before had they hit Plymouth without leave being piped.

Leading Seaman James Ockenden thought it much of a piece with *Wakeful*'s war to date: only recently the ship's magazine had published a cartoon of an admiral with a spyglass exclaiming: 'What, *Wakeful* in port? Send her to sea again.' To the 150-strong crew it seemed that *Wakeful* had collected more than her fair share of patrols and most of them dull ones.

In some ways *Wakeful* was typical of the ships on which Admiral Ramsay must pin his faith in this perilous week. Twenty-three years old, one of the 'V' and 'W' class of destroyers, she had seen better days. Her grey paint was chipping and she reeked of oil; her oil-leak was so permanent that Sub-Lieutenant Bill Mayo always knew how long they'd been at sea. A week, and the oil-leak had peeped from the skirting of his cabin; a fortnight and it had crawled like a cockroach right across the deck.

She was a cramped fusty old war-horse, built for another age; some of the cabins lay under the after torpedo tubes, so that when they were trained no one could open the hatch to go below. The crush was as bad in the wardroom, with the edge of the dining-table jutting clean into the cupboard-sized ante-room; even with ten officers, meals had to be taken in two sittings. When her Captain, Commander Ralph Fisher, wanted a bath, he went aboard an oil tanker or checked in at a hotel; the *Wakeful* could rustle up round iron tubs for a sluice-down but no baths.

But now it seemed that *Wakeful*, too, had a part to play. By 2.30 p.m. on 27th May, the signal tower at Plymouth was flashing urgently: 'Get under way.' Once outside the harbour, the crew drew a deep breath; on the bridge Fisher, a stocky, capable man with grey humorous eyes, had ordered 'Hard-a-port.' That meant up-Channel – Portsmouth or maybe even Dover.

As they churned eastwards, white wake trailing, the tension kept pace with the bustle . . . navigating officer Wilfred Creak checking the Dover charts up to date . . . Sub-Lieutenant Bill Mayo 'bagging' all the confidential books that would not be needed . . . Fisher on the bridge, keeping the ship at her full 30 knots. Suddenly to the west driven fires pulsed like a blast furnace and Fisher cleared the lower deck: 'That is Calais. Eventually we are going to another port near there.' Amongst the ranks Able Seaman Geoffrey Kester heaved a contented sigh: there'd be some excitement at last.

En route for Dunkirk, Captain William Tennant and his party had all the excitement they wanted. Once aboard the old destroyer *Wolfhound*, their task had become a chill reality: scarcely had they cleared the Downs beyond Dover when the first German dive-bombers came snarling from the hazy sky. For the next two hours, while Captain John McCoy kept the ship swerving from port to starboard to dodge the rain of bombs, Tennant's party, crouched on deck below the 'X' gun, strained their ears to hear their captain's briefing. They heard little enough: as *Wolfhound*'s guns pounded until the barrels were almost red-hot, a spattering hail of empty gun-cases showered down on the after superstructure, drowning out Tennant's words.

But the salient points were clear. Dark, precise Commander Jack Clouston was to liaise with the ships as they came in . . . Commander Renfrew Gotto would handle troops from the harbour end . . . Commander Harold Conway was to reconnoitre the beaches from west of the harbour . . . each officer would have a party of a dozen ratings to act as go-betweens.

But as Dunkirk drew in sight, Tennant's heart sank. Never in his wildest dreams had he imagined a scene like this. From the burning oil refineries of St Pol to the west a dark slowly spreading stain of smoke drifted like a pall across the sun, enveloping the harbour in a cold eerie light. The miles of warehouses and quays seemed on fire from end to end. High in the sky, the dive-bombers wheeled and without cessation the bombs came screaming.

Even as Tennant's party watched a stick of bombs fell with hammer-blow precision beside the quay and concrete and white water were founting. Commander Renfrew Gotto muttered, 'A nice welcome to Dunkirk.'

Tennant, of course, couldn't know it, but already German planes and shells were taking their toll in the Channel. At 7 a.m. before Ramsay could even close down the short sea-route, shells and bombs had holed the motor vessel *Sequacity* off Gravelines, the ship sinking so fast that Second Mate Reg Field hadn't even time to salvage his bank book or false teeth. And as the *Mona's Isle* limped into Dover, Commander John Dowding tallied up grimmer losses . . . twenty-three killed . . . sixty wounded . . . the funnels colandered by machine-gun bullets . . . the decks slippery with congealing blood.

But nothing showed in Tennant's face as *Wolfhound* tied up and the Officer Commanding Dunkirk, Colonel Gerald Whitfeld, came to meet him; a strong disciplinarian with a quarter-deck manner, Tennant was no man to give his feelings away. Surveying him, Whitfeld's first reaction was human: 'That beautiful starched white collar won't stay like that for long.'

He was right. Even as the first greetings were exchanged the bombers seemed to darken the sky . . . Tennant, Whitfeld and all of them hit the quayside as one . . . again the bombs came raining and from the town came the smothered roar of toppling buildings. As the raid passed and they scrambled to their feet, Tennant's collar was now the fashionable shade of Dunkirk black. With quiet humour Whitfeld murmured, 'I can always lend you a khaki one.'

It was just 6 p.m. – twelve hours since von Bock's Army Group had struck at 'Warrior' Linton and the others all along the Ypres-Comines Canal. Now Tennant took swift stock of the situation and what he saw appalled him: the Luftwaffe had done their work well.

For four days there had been no water in the town. Although the undersea cable came ashore at La Panne, ten miles up the coast, only one telephone link remained between Dunkirk and London. On this bloodstained Monday alone the bombers of Feldmarschall Albert Kesselring's Air Fleet Two had hit the port with a non-stop rain of 30,000 incendiary bombs and more than 150,000 high-explosives, the bulk of them 500-pounders – smashing the railhead, buckling the overhead cranes, gouging great chunks from the quayside. The 115 acres of the docks, the five miles of quays – all were rubble. Farther on, in the ruins of the town, a thousand men, women and children lay dead.

Aside from the beaches, which lay open to the roaring northern winds, the sole embarkation facilities the port now offered were the East and West Moles — long wooden gangways, merging into a concrete substructure, that thrust 1,400 yards into the roadstead. But the moles had been set up on cement piles to protect the port from the swirl of the tide along the coast; they were not designed for berthing ships. At this season of the year, known to mariners as High Water Springs, a surging three-knot tide raced between the piles and it was hard if not impossible to bring craft alongside.

What of the Army? Here, too, the situation looked black, though a start had been made. Along the last perimeter of all, General Sir Ronald Adam's men already manned the bridgehead from Nieuport to Gravelines, dug in behind the gleaming loop of canals that girdled Dunkirk. As unit after unit fell back, Brigadier John Gawthorpe, who had only heard of Dunkirk that morning, was one of many officers who stood by the perimeter bridges sifting the troops. While some — tank crews and skilled specialists — were slated to return to England now, others, artillery-men and sappers, were to man the defences of the bridgehead, until the main force took over.

As they jogged through, Gawthorpe kept up a soothing flow of patter. 'Right, you join your division over there . . . yes, you're all going together but you can't go without tickets . . . Division's got the tickets.' Deliberately, Gawthorpe was playing it by ear: he thought that men who had scented the fresh air of home wouldn't relish the prospect of a last-ditch stand while others got away.

There is no doubting Gawthorpe was right. Already inside the perimeter groups of men deserted by their officers prowled like hoodlums in an ugly mood of violence: out of defeat and shame was born a savage anarchy.

Driver Ernest Holdsworth, like hundreds of others, had arrived in Dunkirk earlier that day: a teetotaller, his first reaction to the news of evacuation was to drink himself senseless on a lethal mixture of rum, whisky, benedictine and brandy. He awoke in a hotel cellar to a nightmare scene: British, Frenchmen and Senegalese slumped together against vast casks of cider, singing, weeping, screaming, vomiting. To Holdsworth the spectacle 'worse than Dante's Inferno' was like an ice-pack on the brain; the horror sobered him at a glance.

Others were less impressionable. As Tennant and his men marched doggedly through the blazing town to reconnoitre the beaches, they saw sights to turn them cold . . . soldiers smeared with lipstick howling and screeching, their arms discarded . . . a sergeant blind drunk sporting a woman's feather boa . . . the litter of pigskin brandy flasks and toilet-cases discarded by hastily departing officers.

Farther along the beach, rifle-fire cracked sharply and a bullet whined. To Commander Harold Henderson, Dunkirk's naval liaison officer since war began, it seemed high time to turn back: a snarling trigger-tense mob of soldiers, rifles at the ready, was advancing through the dusk. Then, as Henderson marvelled, Tennant, approaching the ringleader, gently but firmly disarmed him.

'Here, old chap,' he invited, producing a hip flask, 'have a drink of this . . . you'll feel better.'

For one electric moment, Henderson thought the troops might open fire but the ice was broken. Convinced the Navy was there to help them, the men were now pathetically docile, forming readily into queues.

Now Tennant gave crisp orders. Commander Harold Conway and his ratings to take over at Malo-les-Bains. Commander Hector Richardson and fifteen ratings to take over another sector of the beaches. Back in the dunes, the troops to be organised into groups of fifty, in charge of an army officer or a seaman, later to be led to the water's edge on the same principle. No man must embark without arms.

The last words of Rear-Admiral Tom Phillips, Vice-Chief of Naval Staff, as Tennant left the Admiralty had been, 'Mind you bring the guns back.' If Britain formed the last line of defence, even rifles might soon be at a premium.

But these were minor crises compared with what Tennant must still face. Through a freakish chain of mishaps, the port of Dunkirk now lay almost wide open to the worst that the Luftwaffe could do.

Already some units, like Brigadier John Slater's 4th Ack-Ack Brigade, had blown their massive 3.7 guns before even entering the perimeter; the bulky carriages and tractors, they felt, might only block the roads at crucial moments. Then, too, as Major-General Henry Martin, commanding all Dunkirk's anti-aircraft defences, had it from his liaison officer, Captain Sir Anthony Palmer, all ack-ack gunners were to pull out that night.

These orders hadn't come in writing – Palmer was talking from notes made in a briefing at General Sir Ronald Adam's headquarters – but Martin was used to that; rarely in the whole campaign had he been sent a written order, and in battle, out of touch with headquarters, he had acted mostly on his own initiative. And Martin, at Malo-les-Bains, had no immediate way of contacting General Adam, nine miles away along traffic-choked roads at La Panne.

But it was plain that if the gunners were going home, every gun, save a few light Bofors guns covering the docks and beaches, must be wrecked before they went. A little after 8 p.m. Martin sent this order out.

Not until 1 a.m. – five hours later – did Martin meet up with Adam in La Panne – to find to his horror that somehow through no fault of Palmer's, the order had been misinterpreted. The heavy ack-ack, numbering over a hundred guns, had been scheduled as a vital part of perimeter defence, but now it was all too late: the guns were no more than a cooling mass of riven metal.

Save for the old-type French ack-ack, the embattled port's only defence against the Baron von Richtofen's Stukas were Bofors guns, which rarely registered beyond a 1,500-yard range.

As yet Tennant knew nothing of this disaster. Back at Bastion 32, the vast underground concrete warren forming the headquarters of Admiral Jean Abrial, the French commander at Dunkirk, he went into swift conference with Brigadier Geoffrey Mansergh, Lieut.-General Alan Brooke's chief administrative officer, who had come on ahead to help the evacuation.

Almost dead with fatigue, racked by ulcer pains, Mansergh could paint only the blackest of pictures – though lacking hour-by-hour contact with G.H.Q., it was hard for any man to know how the battle was going. Already the 10th Panzer Division had taken Calais, and from there the coast road ran, straight as an arrow for twenty-four miles, to Dunkirk. Knowing nothing of Hitler's decision that the tanks must bypass the port itself, Mansergh told Tennant flatly: 'We expect German tanks on the beaches within twenty-four hours – thirty-six at the most.'

At 8 p.m., in a hot, airless office fifty feet below ground level in the Bastion, Tennant, his face expressionless, dictated an urgent signal for Admiral Ramsay in Dover to his signals officer, Commander Michael Ellwood: 'Please send every available craft to beaches east of Dunkirk immediately. Evacuation to-morrow night is problematical.'

CHAPTER THREE

MAKE FOR THE BLACK SMOKE

Monday, 27th May
8–12 p.m.

In some ways Captain Tennant was supremely lucky. At 8 p.m. on this cheerless May evening he could at least face the facts of the situation squarely, in so far as he knew them. Thousands, moving dazedly back along the white dusty roads of France, had no such comfort. They knew only that their own small world had splintered into fragments.

At Proven, an officer told Corporal William Mitchell and his mates of the Army Service Corps: 'Make for the black smoke.' Mitchell could see the smoke pall rising but he didn't know it was Dunkirk or that the port was eighteen miles away; he didn't even know that he and a third of a million men were joined in a general retreat. Jam-packed in a truck with sixty others, he jolted unhappily through the night, wondering how it would all end.

Still, defeat was not a reality; it was people's own problems that had pride of place. Bouncing towards the coast in Captain Harry Smith's canvas-covered 15-cwt. truck, Augusta Hersey was more vexed that she couldn't exchange one word with Driver Johnnie Johnson. Her problem was that Bill had so far taught her only two words of English – 'Good night' – and this, he had explained to Johnson, must be Augusta's signal if she desired privacy.

Now, despite the steel helmet clamped firmly on her dark sleek hair, the rifle nursed between her knees, the lively Augusta felt the stir of adventure – yet she must stay obstinately silent. Twice, moved by the beauty of the star-pricked sky, she had exclaimed, 'Oh . . . good night.' Each time, despite all her protests, Johnson had jammed on the brakes, solemnly vacating the truck until she dragged him back.

Miles behind, on the road to Dixmunde, Bill Hersey, too, had personal problems. Though he had managed to hitch a ride on an open Bedford 3-tonner with his mate, Nobby Clarke, Hersey himself could barely drive. Now it struck him urgently that this skill could prove vital. But Nobby, preoccupied in swerving fast round corners, had insisted that this was too tall an order. Later he could identify gears and ignition for Hersey – but he couldn't, all in a space of hours, teach him to drive.

As the Bedford groaned through the night, small worries nagged in Hersey's mind: could he learn to drive in time – in time to be of help to Augusta? And when and where would he see Augusta again? He had no idea as to how far ahead Smith's truck had gone, or even if the convoy had been bombed, so that now each dark mile became an agony of suspense.

All over northern France the reaction was the same: as if the mind, recoiling from disaster, sought personal distractions to keep hold on sanity.

Driver Sidney Morris, retreating through the Belgian lines to Dunkirk, clutched tightly on to a present for his small son Trevor – a magnificent chromed-steel and mahogany model of a French seaplane, a Loire Nieuport 40. Morris had never seen his son, who was only eight months old, but he had bought the gift with his savings months ago, using the long period of the phoney war to make a special wooden case for it. The one thing on his mind as he retreated was the vision of his small son's face when he first sighted the plane.

Others had problems as pressing: near Cassel his unit was almost surrounded by Germans, but Lance-Corporal John Norman, the officers' cook, was pondering tomorrow's menu. A dedicated man, still wearing a spotless white coat, Norman had served up tinned salmon fish-cakes for lunch, a chicken dinner with tinned fruit – but could he get enough coal to cook a bacon and egg breakfast with sauté potatoes? Private Mervyn Doncom, the soldier of fortune, had a special worry. Somehow he hadn't bargained for a retreat on foot and the kitbagful of watches he had acquired was slowing him up.

Captain Edward Bloom had solved one burning problem and was within an ace of resolving the other. A dapper, normally immaculate officer in charge of a petrol convoy, Bloom hadn't bathed in days, but today, based in a flat over a deserted lingerie shop in Port Avendin, the captain had celebrated his birthday with a scrub down – his batman, Private Clewys, had drummed up a galvanised tub and filled it with kettles of boiling water.

Now faced with a demand for clean underwear, Clewys, poker-faced, had retired to the shop below, returning shortly with their first loot: 'I have cut the lace off the bottom, sir, and at least they are clean.'

Few men nursed a greater grievance than Private Walter Osborn of the Suffolks. Officially Osborn was the only man of Lord Gort's fighting troops who was in close arrest: on 10th May a General Court Martial had sentenced Osborn to forty-two days' detention. The charge: writing an anonymous letter to Mr Winston Churchill, then First Lord of the Admiralty but already, through his visits to France, idolised by the troops.

Osborn had not signed his name to the missive but he'd enclosed it in an envelope addressed to his wife, Louvain, back in Ipswich, which the censor had opened.

'What about a drop of leave for the lads?' the letter led off – language which the Army had considered 'prejudicial to good order and discipline'.

What galled Osborn most, as he slogged back with his escort, Sergeant Frank Peacock, was that his status was not defined. As a Suffolk, one of Major-General Bernard Montgomery's crack 3rd Division, Osborn had stood to in seven rear-guard actions since the great retreat began. Then he was a soldier with a Lee-Enfield and a bandolier of ammunition – yet no sooner did the fighting cease than he was in close arrest again, bundled into a barn under police escort.

He told Sergeant Frank Peacock: 'I'm just like a perishing Jack rabbit, Serge – into clink when the fighting stops, out again when it starts. A man's got a right to know where he stands.'

Peacock, smuggling him a forbidden cigarette, wisely counselled patience. That night at 9 p.m. they were moving northwards again, from near Roubaix to the line of the Yser River – nobody knew why, let alone where all this would end.

One man knew why – but the outcome of the whole perilous move worried him sick. In the lyrically-named Ferme d'Alouette (Farm of the Lark) Lieut.-General Alan Brooke, dry-mouthed and fearful, lay awake in a ground-floor room – lulled almost to sleep by the steady grumble of transport, jerking instantly to wakefulness the second the rumbling stopped.

It was a mighty gamble. All that day Montgomery's Division had been poised before Roubaix, fifty miles from Dunkirk, in the heart of the German Sixth Army. Now, with the Belgians cracking to the north, it was imperative that the whole Division should be side-stepped north beyond Ypres, to fill the gap on the left of the Ypres-Comines Canal and prevent the Germans sweeping across the Yser River to cut the road to Dunkirk. Only thus could Brooke procure a solid flank to the east.

To Brooke it seemed a near impossibility even though Montgomery, faced with the problem that morning, had bubbled over with glee: 'Right, look here, I'm going to do it – do it like this.' As Brooke watched, Montgomery even seized a map and charted the route: across the River Lys just east of Armentières . . . past Ploegsteert wood . . . up by second-class roads northwards, within 4,000 yards of the front where Linton and the others fought.

That afternoon Montgomery had made his plans. All through the phoney war, mindful of such a moment, he had practised these streamlined tactical withdrawels: an 80-mile night trek to take over a riverline, a noiseless 80-mile retreat. And at 9 p.m. as the dusk deepened, the stage was set. Already every inch of the 36-mile route had been reconnoitred in daylight, first by Lieutenant Charles Sweeney, Montgomery's aide, later by Brigade liaison officers.

As he clinched his final orders, Montgomery summed up the whole adventure in a sentence: 'Well, chaps, if 3rd Division can get away with this it can get away with anything.'

Hour after hour, as Brooke lay fitfully courting sleep, the vast convoy snaked its way through the night, Charles Sweeney tut-tutting ahead on a motorcycle. Bolt upright in his staff car, Montgomery watched the fury of the Ypres-Comines battle raging only 4,000 yards away – the white, green and magenta flashes of the Very lights, the night sky turned to day by the pounding of the giant guns, often, as was his wont, impaling a message for intelligence officer Kit Dawnay on his swagger cane and thrusting it through the car window: 'Quite sure you've got the way right?'

But Montgomery's plans were foolproof. Men like John 'Warrior' Linton, manning the Canal, never even knew the convoy was passing behind them: the differential of each truck, daubed with white luminous paint, was lit up by a tail-lamp beneath the vehicle. The hawk-eyed drivers had no other problems but to watch the rear of the truck in front.

At each tricky bend and junction, small colza oil-lamps twinkled by the roadside; red-armleted regimental police did traffic duty. In the inky darkness, along jam-packed roads, 600 vehicles – 13,600 men – were slipping to safety, forming a solid defensive flank with General Bougrain's Second Motorised Division to the north.

Montgomery had made military history – though the only temporary casualty of the move was Montgomery himself, whose staff car 'with a great deal of fearful language' got bogged down in a cul-de-sac for twenty fretful minutes.

Still Brooke lay awake wondering – hastening from the farmhouse every now and again to watch the transport sliding past along the road. Unless the convoy had quit the roads when daylight came, von Richtofen's Stukas, Brooke knew, could wreak a deadly havoc.

The same fears, the same aching sense of responsibility, were common to all men this night. In a Dutch barn near Steenvorde, Sergeant Leslie Teare, of the Sherwood Foresters, couldn't sleep with the worry of it; the bulk of his battalion, the 9th, were nineteen-year-olds, Territorials from Nottingham's Bestwood Colliery, and Teare, a pithead official, had known them all since their first days down the shaft. For days he had walked double distances down the column, coaxing them on, feeling for them like a father.

Tomorrow they would move in as one more unit to strengthen the Dunkirk perimeter but none of them knew that, and in the darkness Teare felt their perplexity and unease.

Suddenly, espying a furtive movement in the straw, Teare peered closer; he saw that one of his men, Private Crossland, was trembling in every limb. 'What's the matter, lad?' he asked, but as Crossland answered, 'Nothing, Sergeant', Teare sensed the boy's voice was trembling too.

'Are you all right?'

'All right, Sergeant.'

The voice was still trembling, battling with fear, and on an impulse Teare felt the need to pay tribute to 'the bravest man I ever saw in France'. He edged sideways in the straw and unobtrusively, like any father, cradled the boy's head in his lap. He was asleep within minutes, Teare recalls – 'just like a poor little kid, he wasn't no more than that'.

In England, the sense of pity was dormant as yet: it would take time for the truth to sink in. It wasn't that the people had no heart for the tribulations of others. But for eight months they had lived each day in the belief that Lord Gort's B.E.F. was the invincible force that would deliver them from evil; and it would take time to readjust. Only twenty-four hours back, Dover's Clerk of Committees, Bill Ransom, had sat with scores of others on a beach innocent of barbed wire, drinking in the evening sun. But early that morning the air-raid siren had shrilled over the town, and all day there had been the small signs adding up to disaster.

At Dover's Air-Raid Precaution Centre, Joan Bruce Lane, a comely switchboard operator, noted two of them. For days the little grey port had shaken to the sound of the guns, besieging Calais. Now there was only aching silence, the silence before the storm. Her fiancé, Alex, who ran the engine-sheds at Dover Marine Station, was quiet, too, even cagey: 'I may say I'll be around one day, then not turn up. Don't ask me why.'

Like all the others in Dover, Joan Lane felt that something big was going to break: that morning Chief Constable Marshall Bolt had visited the centre more agitated than she had ever seen him.

Going up for a breather later, Joan Lane saw why: the doorman had a rifle and bayonet now.

Then, too, the town swarmed with harlots; some rumour had drawn them like a magnet from all over the country and the police were clearing them out as fast as they came. If nobody knew what would happen next, everyone guessed what was in their neighbour's mind. Up in St James's Cemetery, on the hillside, labourers were already digging the vast communal graves – enough, they said, for several hundred people.

All that day, in the Kentish ports, the rumours mounted, unchecked . . . a sailor had brought a revolver and two rounds of ammunition home for his wife . . . some women were carrying knives and poison capsules . . . one old soldier, they said, had already committed suicide.

To some it was stark truth: the police came to the Castle Avenue flat of Billy George, the bicycle merchant, with an ultimatum – his wife, a cripple, must be out of Dover by week's end. George asked why and the reply held a note of doom: 'Only those who can run stay in Dover now.'

The security blackout was total. Only a few journalists – the *Daily Express*'s Hilde Marchant and H. L. McNally, the *Daily Herald*'s Reg Foster – had checked in to Dover's Grand Hotel, the massive Edwardian pile overlooking the sea. But already there was the palpitating feel that a story would break. As head-waiter, George Garland, served the fish in the lofty green-carpeted dining-room, Foster and McNally glanced only briefly at the entry of two naval officers. Then, glancing again, they held their breath. A trail of blood and oil marked the visitors' progress across the pile carpet.

Whoever they were, they were early in the fray: the bulk of the mighty evacuation fleet had not yet been blooded. In the main harbour, around this time, H.M.S. *Wakeful* was just making fast alongside the oil-tanker *War Sepoy* when an Aldis lamp flickered urgently from Dover's Port Wall Signal Station. Seconds later Commander Ralph Fisher and Yeoman of Signals Leonard Gutherless scanned a priority message: 'From Vice-Admiral, Dover. The last chance of saving the B.E.F. is tonight. You are to proceed with all despatch two to three miles east of Dunkirk and embark troops in your own boats. Return at your discretion not later than 0330.'

It was enough. At once Sub-Lieutenant Bill Mayo got the curt command: 'Land all confidential books on the oiler – we're leaving now.' As Mayo swiftly finished the job of sorting them into mailbags, he knew something was up: the ship was now left with only the skeleton set of active service codes known as 'Dangerous Water Books'.

Dashing on deck, Mayo just managed to sling the mailbags aboard the oiler as *Wakeful* slid past her stern. They had been alongside exactly three minutes.

It was a night of surprises. In Ramsgate, seventeen miles up the coast, Mrs Rosa Bishop had gone early to bed; her husband, Sergeant Tom Bishop, whom she loved deeply, was away in France with the Catering Corps, and there was little reason to keep late hours. Drifting into sleep she had been comforted by one thought: if Tom arrived home on sudden leave, she would know in an especially tender way. He would, he had promised, serenade her with *their* song – the old hillbilly classic 'Home on the Range' – before entering the house.

Suddenly, in the darkness, Rosa Bishop was wide awake: outside in the street, not one but three-score voices had launched into 'Home on the Range'. Though her hair was in curlers, Mrs Bishop didn't even bother to remove them; hastily donning a dressing-gown, she bolted for the front doorstep. From end to end the blacked-out street was choked with lorries. The singing came from scores of grimy but cheerful troops who were piling into them from the railway station hard by.

It was ludicrous but somehow pathetic: though Rosa Bishop hadn't realised *their* song was shared by half the Army, she went back to bed deeply disturbed. Why should soldiers, singing or silent, be arriving at this hour? She resolved that first thing in the morning she would go to the railway station; if a crisis was brewing, there might be a way in which she could help.

All those who could say that to themselves felt better this night. As the Liverpool-London express racketed through the night, Sub-Lieutenant William Tower, R.N., relaxed in a first-class compartment, knew that he, too, was on the way to something big. That morning an Admiralty signal to his base ship, H.M.S. *Somali,* had ordered Tower south with all despatch.

A vital fair-haired twenty-one-year-old, Tower's first appearance was deceptive. His gentle manners, the pink-and-white skin that maiden aunts envied, suggested a man content to take life as it came. Amongst friends and family his lightheartedness was a legend . . . his resourcefulness after missing a late-night liberty boat, using his taxi's headlights to signal transport from his ship . . . his gift of mimicking pompous admirals . . . the dashing little blue Renault, christened 'The Top', that he drove everywhere.

This was typical of Tower, whose mellow voice and champagne sense of fun masked a core of steel. As a hot-tempered five-year-old he had suffered the displacement of a ligament in his femur; for nine months he had lain on his bed in agonising pain, a weight dragging at his leg to straighten it. In those months Bill Tower learned a hard lesson for a five-year-old. He learned not to cry out and to keep his temper in check; equally he learned to channel his will.

Out of this had emerged a new Tower, the ten-year-old who had taught himself to swim, battling on until every stroke was mastered, the eleven-year-old who had built himself a wireless set from scratch, the fourteen-year-old who spent every hour of one holiday teaching himself to skate. Now, seven years later, he had already seen more war than men twice his age; three weeks back, as gunnery officer of H.M.S. *Bittern* off Norway, he had been strapped in the gun-turret for twenty-four hours. His gun-crew was halved by the end but Tower's guns only ceased firing when the ship was sunk.

Now he, too, was bound for Ramsgate, only half guessing what lay ahead, but well content if it meant more active service. In one recent letter home he had written to his parents: 'I must admit it – I *do* enjoy the adventure of war.'

Back at Dunkirk Captain William Tennant was in no such buoy-ant mood. Another quick sortie to the shallow shelving beaches had only confirmed his worst suspicions: probably no stretch of sea coast in the world offered worse conditions for the task that lay ahead. Now at low tide, the grey Channel waters had receded a full half mile – and some Medical Corps men, stretchers lifted head high, were struggling towards two solitary whalers that had rowed within a hundred yards of the sand.

Yet their parent destroyers, *Wolfhound* and *Wolsey*, were dark grey specks a mile off-shore. Every whaler that pulled painfully inshore to pick up troops would face this backbreaking twenty-minute pull and the boats could load, at most, twenty-five at a time.

Clearly the answer was more small boats – but there was the question of wind, too. Tonight, the wind, blowing off the land from the east, was ideal – but the beaches and the port itself faced north. The slightest hint of a north-easterly wind would cause small craft to broach to – swing broadside on to the shore and swiftly capsize.

True, a destroyer could pack in 1,000 men, but the loading might take six weary hours and Tennant knew that time was of the essence.

Only an hour earlier, after a scratch meal in the Bastion, Signals Officer Michael Ellwood, lightheartedly suggesting that his chief needed more identification, had trimmed the letters 'S.N.O.' from a cigarette packet's silver paper, gumming them to Tennant's steel helmet with gravy. To Tennant, it seemed a gloomy symbol. He was indeed Senior Naval Officer, and every decision, right or wrong, must be his.

It was 10 p.m. In the flickering darkness, along with Lieut.-Commander Bruce Junor and Commander Jack Clouston, Tennant tramped back to the East Mole. Surveying it yet again he broke silence. 'Here's something quicker – if *only* we could get a ship alongside.'

It was a grim decision. Despite its length, the Mole was still no more than a narrow plank-way stemming from the old fortifications and merging into a concrete breakwater. Just wide enough for three men to walk abreast, it was flanked for most of the way only by railings of stout timbers. At intervals along the railings larger piles projected – Samson posts by which a ship could be warped in an emergency.

But it seemed there was no other way. Taking a long look at the leaping fires that glowed like crimson lacquer on the dark water, Tennant growled, 'Well, we'll try it – tell that nearest one to come alongside.' At once the Aldis lamp blinked out: 'Enter the harbour – tie up alongside the jetty.'

As the ship, *Queen of the Channel*, cut a path towards them the minutes seemed to crawl. First Captain W. J. Odell had to ease her bow in, at a gingerly seven knots decreasing . . . swiftly a head rope was made fast . . . then, as Tennant and the others watched tensely, the ship's stem eased gently to nudge against the East Mole. Ten minutes later the *Queen of the Channel* was secured fore and aft.

At 10.30 p.m. Tennant breathed a sigh of relief. Only 7,669 men had left Dunkirk this day, but it looked as if a solution had been found. If only the Army held its line steadily from the sea inwards they might at a pinch clear the 45,000 that was Ramsay's target. Even as Tennant stood, the heavy clump of Army boots sounded on the planking, rumbling above the crackle of the fires like distant thunder. The first contingents were under way.

Tennant didn't know it yet but there were other problems. Around this time Lord Gort was arriving at Bastion 32 for an urgent conference. Already Gort had spent precious hours of that day searching for General Georges Blanchard, commanding the First Group of French Armies. The mission was vital: at that moment Blanchard still believed in the chances of defending Dunkirk to the last – but with a perimeter that stretched forty miles south to the River Lys.

Now Gort must make it plain there was no such chance. A British commander subordinate to the French High Command, Gort's terms of reference from the British Government had always been that in the last resort he must preserve what he could of his own Army. Now that time had come. Only that afternoon Anthony Eden had cabled again: 'Sole task now is to evacuate to England maximum of your forces possible.'

As he strode into Bastion 32, service cap, as always, tilted back on his forehead, Colonel Gerald Whitfeld, Dunkirk area commander, could only marvel at the man. From the night sky the Luftwaffe were launching the twelfth air-raid of that day. Black oily smoke wreathed and curled about the Bastion entrance and livid flares lit up the skeletons of the dockside cranes – yet Gort's bright blue eyes were shining.

Though Gort had often found the political tangles of his command beyond him, he reacted to danger and the prospect of battle like a cavalry charger responding to the bugle.

In the fusty underground dug-out, banked with telephones, Gort went into brief conference with Admiral Jean Abrial, the precise, handsome naval officer who was French commander of the port. Among the others grouped round the long table were Whitfeld; Admiral Le Clerq, Abrial's chief of staff; Commander Harold Henderson, British Naval Liaison Officer; and the French General Koeltz, who was Chief of Staff to the Supreme Commander, General Weygand.

Though there was no sign of General Blanchard it seemed vital to Gort to settle the details of the Dunkirk bridgehead. But as yet, although Abrial was technically Supreme Commander of Dunkirk, political reasons decreed that no mention should be made to him of total evacuation – for conference purposes this was a limited withdrawal of non-essential troops.

The meeting droned on, chewing over essentials: the British to hold from Nieuport along the canals through Furnes to the town of Bergues; the French westward from Bergues to Gravelines; on the British front, General Alan Brooke's 2nd Corps ultimately to hold the Nieuport sector; General Michael Barker's 1st Corps placed at dead centre; General Sir Ronald Adam's 3rd Corps to hold the area round Dunkirk itself.

As yet barely 20,000 men had filtered back into the perimeter, but Gort, eyes still shining with exultation at the distant rumble of bombs, assured Abrial that there was hope yet.

It was now 11 p.m. In the sudden silence General Koeltz asked nonchalantly: 'Is Lord Gort perhaps aware that the King of the Belgians has asked for an armistice from midnight?'

Now for twenty miles the whole left flank of the British Army lay open to the sea. Gort sat quite still, palms outspread on the table, staring into space. Watching him, Whitfeld thought his expression might have meant anything.

CHAPTER FOUR

ANY ROAD, JERRY SHAN'T HAVE 'EM

Tuesday, 28th May
1 a.m.—12 p.m.

The news of the Belgian surrender had not yet reached Augusta Hersey, yet, somehow, with a woman's instinct, she had known. Tonight, in a farmhouse east of Dixmude, all a French liaison officer's pleadings had not softened the Belgian farmer's heart: he had no beds for the British and their kind.

At last, worn out by the wrangle, Augusta had settled for a heap of dry straw in the farmyard. Later, when she and Driver Johnson sought to quench their thirst, they found that the farmer had locked the well.

A Frenchwoman, Augusta Hersey understood better than most the anguish that had befallen the land: she sensed that the farm-folk, like millions of others, were groping in the dark. Eighteen days back, when the British crossed the border, they had pressed wine and flowers upon them: priests in black vestments had stood all day outside the churches as the Army streamed past, asking a blessing on the cavalcade.

Now the liberators were pulling out and for the second time in their lives the people sensed that the Germans were not far behind. As fear crept like a shadow across the landscape, family after family lost heart and took to the roads.

As they flooded northwards, the troops were aghast; nothing in all their peacetime training had prepared them for this. From Lille onwards, 800,000 refugees jammed the roads in a honking, shouting, ear-splitting cavalcade . . . old women on foot, their shoulders draped with the ever-present red blankets, clutching vast bundles like laundry . . . the rich in glossy chauffeur-driven coupés . . . peasants in milk-carts drawn by dogs . . . a fat man pedalling an ice-cream tricycle with his wife and two daughters jammed in the refrigerator compartment . . . whole families in old rattle-traps piled high with mattresses, their sole pathetic armour against the swooping fighters.

In some areas the road-blocks stretched for fifteen long miles — abetted now by the creaking gun-limbers, ammunition carriers and old wood-burning field kitchens of the Belgian Army. Mingling with the grimy khaki-clad troops as they wrestled back to the coast, they blocked the vital ammunition and supplies that were moving inland up the line.

On such roads the provost could do nothing: every man, general or private, was his own traffic controller. On the bridge at Poperinghe the immaculate Lieut.-Colonel Bootle-Wilbraham of the Coldstream leapt from his staff car and himself did traffic cop duty for two fuming hours. Farther north, towards Bergues, Trooper Dennis Cartwright of the Royal Dragoon Guards left his tank time and again to brandish his revolver; it was the only way for the Mark VI (B) tank to move coastwards an inch at a time.

Even in the midst of chaos, few men could believe their eyes. Private Edgar Smith, recalling old movies of the Spanish Civil War, thought: But *I'm* part of it now — it can't be true. At Strazeele, Private Jack Evans, a young territorial of the Queen's Royal

Regiment, summed up the puzzlement of many: 'Perhaps this is what war is *supposed* to be like.'

In fact it wasn't, but despite the storm-clouds of the nineteen-thirties, right until the morning of 10th May, the Belgians had always pinned their faith in armed neutrality. Thus, when King Leopold assumed command of his troops, he took over a cumbersome 700,000-strong force armed only with rusty rifles and horse-drawn cannons. Committed to static defence, it was from the first an army innocent of tanks, planes or sea-power.

All this Gort, briefed by the reports of shrewd advisers like Lieut.-General Alan Brooke, had long known. Having seen the Belgian Army in the field, Brooke had opined they were in no shape to fight. Within ten days Belgium had lost three-quarters of its territory – and the few square miles of Belgian soil that remained held only fourteen days' food supply.

None of this truly surprised Gort. The poker-face which so impressed Colonel Whitfeld was born of foreknowledge. At one painful interview he himself had seen the King in tears over the tragedy that had befallen his country; and eight hours before the final collapse was announced at Dunkirk's Bastion, Leopold had sent Gort warning that he would be obliged to surrender before a debacle.

Incensed, Gort had burst out to Captain George Gordon-Lennox, one of his staff officers, 'My God, Geordie, they're swine.' Blundering from the room he had seized a rifle, relieving his feelings by potting from the standing position at a low-flying German plane.

From a soldier who saw dying for his country as the greatest honour a man could covet it was a human reaction – yet logically it held no water. At Ypres, on 21st May, in more sober mood, Gort had asked Admiral Sir Roger Keyes, Britain's representative in Belgium, 'Do the Belgians think us awful dirty dogs?' Twenty-four hours before the Belgian surrender, Gort had already begun the slow withdrawal of *his* Army – without informing Leopold. The King, too, had a duty to his people.

None of these high-level political manœuvres were known to Gort's men; there was only blank incomprehension that an ally could give up. Lieut.-Colonel Geoffrey Anstee, commander of the 5th Northamptonshires, passing through Furnes, could not understand why Tuesday should be washday in every household. It was hours before he identified the unending clothes-line of snowy sheets and pillow-slips for what they were: the tokens of surrender.

On every side the troops slogging northwards among the refugees saw the same despairing sights as Augusta Hersey: white flags flapping from the bayonets of Belgian soldiers; a Belgian General, his staff car halted by the roadside, calmly stripping off his uniform and changing into sports coat and flannel trousers; a farmer's wife, mindful that the oncoming Germans might be thirsty, setting the tea-kettle to boil. In every Belgian village their reception was the same: the bitter glances, the handles wrenched from pumps to deny water, the hail of flints from angry villagers.

To Sergeant Sidney Tindle, a puckish, irrepressible little Irishman of the King's Own Royal Regiment, it seemed the world had turned upside down. A day back his battalion had fought a bitter battle against German tank gunners disguised in French uniform – and had only escaped at night by crawling on their bellies through a flock of sheep. Now they were marching he knew not where, and Tindle, like a puzzled child, asked Sergeant-Major Bonnier, 'Why have they turned against us?'

'Search me,' the sergeant-major replied, 'but you never know who'll win this flaming war.'

It wasn't surprising that fear was abroad. By the morning of Tuesday, 28th May, at all levels, suspicion and distrust were rampant – and every man nursed the belief that you could no longer tell friend from foe.

The innocent no less than the guilty stood in jeopardy; near Ploegsteert, in the nick of time, Father Geoffrey Lynch, attached to a Yorkshire artillery regiment, established the bona fides of two Jesuit priests by a hasty quiz in Latin. Convinced they were German spies, the gunners had them earmarked for the firing squad. It was worse for Fräulein Gerda Kermisch, a nineteen-year-old Austrian Jewess in flight from Hitler's Germany; every hour in the refugee column moving north seemed fraught with peril – if the British didn't shoot her as a spy, the Germans would surely send her to the gas-chamber. At Malo-les-Bains she tore her passport into tiny shreds, flushing it down a toilet – condemning herself to five more years of flight and fear.

As the rumours multiplied they found eager ears. English-speaking Germans dressed as officers were infiltrating the lines to misdirect convoys, spread panic. Civilian snipers were picking off the unwary. A new phrase denoting treachery trembled on every lip: 'The Fifth Column.'

Near Dixmude, Second-Lieutenant Alexander Lyell scanned an embarrassing order from Divisional H.Q. Just as in Holland, para-chutists were plummeting from the sky dressed as nuns. But the ruse, the order stressed, would be easily spotted by interlocutors: the marks of parachute straps would be plainly visible on the saboteurs' behinds.

It was stark fact to some. At dawn that day, Gunner William Brewer and four mates, retreating to Dunkirk, were drinking tea near a farmhouse when Bombardier 'Geordie' Allen came dou-bling white-faced. 'Did you ever see a bloody nun shaving?' Stealing across the pasture, all five men saw what they'd always taken to be the tallest of tales: two German paratroopers, white coifs discarded, crucifixes dangling, shaving behind a haystack.

Seconds later, the 'nuns' fell dying, riddled with .303 fire, the blood a dark spreading stain on the black habits.

And it seemed that treachery was everywhere. From a barn

near Mount Carmel, Signalman Alan Hall and his mates watched a farmer scything a perfect fig-leaf – the identity mark of General Sir Ronald Adam's 3rd Corps – in the wet lush grass; they pulled out minutes before low-flying Messerschmitts zoomed from heavy clouds to shoot up their transport. Sapper Alf Bate, looking skywards to cheer a flight of eight British Spitfires, suddenly piled for cover with all his unit; with the sun behind them, the decoy planes had dived, machine-guns chattering. Hot cartridge cases rained upon the sappers' naked hands, scoring deep wounds.

Near Armentières, Signalman Victor Glenister, with two others, warned to keep an eye open for suspicious characters, saw a movement behind a hedge, challenged, then shot. None of them ever knew what the civilian they killed had been doing there. Sometimes the fear hardly justified the cause. Near Bachy, the Hampshires were sand-bagging a house when the sweet sickly smell of peardrops tinged the warm air: at once the company sergeant, suspecting Fifth Columnists were spraying the area with phosgene gas, bawled 'Respirators on!'

It was some time before the unit latched on that Private Mervyn Doncom, the soldier of fortune, had put aside his kitbagful of watches to acquire – and open – a bottle of nail varnish.

On a morning when it seemed the world had gone mad, it would have been easy for any man to put his own needs first – yet thousands torn by pity for the refugees set aside their own troubles to help.

Nursing orderly Kenneth Roberts and his mates gave the refugees almost all the supplies their field ambulance possessed – bandages, ointment, tinned milk – then realised they had nothing left to treat their own casualties. The Rev. Hugh Laurence, carrying bread supplies to the 6th Lincolns, just couldn't resist the hunger in people's eyes, the children's haunting cries of '*J'ai peur, j'ai peur*' (I am frightened). Without hesitation – though the unit hadn't seen bread in days – he doled out all fifty loaves. Hour after hour Staff Sergeant Frank Chadwick stood by the roadside with freshly-brewed buckets of tea; the refugees couldn't fancy the unfamiliar brew but equally Chadwick couldn't give up.

Private Walter Allington, a big gentle man like a boxer, felt the same pang. Already, on the way to Dunkirk, Allington, who always tried to help his neighbour, had given most of his rations to the refugees; what puzzled him as he toiled through an afternoon shower was a Belgian on crutches trying to catch the rain in his cupped hands.

Suddenly, Allington realised the man couldn't use the village water fountains — no man could stand upright on crutches and operate the button that regulated the flow of water. Compassionately, with his mate, Private Heap, Allington led the Belgian to a fountain, cupping his hands while Heap pressed the button. As the man lapped greedily, Allington saw his lips were cracked with thirst, his hands red-raw from the chafing of the crutches.

Solemnly Allington took out his field dressing — though to use it without sanction was an indictable offence in the Army — and bandaged the stranger's hands. As the Belgian cried and kissed Allington, the big man felt a sudden stabbing pain in his right side. Gasping, he doubled up, then, after a moment, shrugged it off — it was all too long, he knew, since he had eaten.

To every man on this warm overcast Tuesday, pity took on a different guise. To Lieut.-General Alan Brooke, driving non-stop in his staff car to keep tabs on the Ypres-Comines line, it was the vacant smiles of lunatics freed from the asylums, thronging the roadside in drab brown corduroy. To Corporal Thomas Dunkley, it was the twin refugee girls aged about six, dressed in trim white blouses and Scottish plaid skirts. When Dunkley. a family man with a twin-brother, pushed through the throng to speak to them, the shamefulness of war hit him like a blow in the stomach. Terrified, in abject surrender, the little girls put up their hands, recoiling.

Some men saw sights which filled them with deadly anger. Moving north from Steenvorde, into the Dunkirk perimeter, Sergeant Leslie Teare espied two refugees on an empty village street – a boy of eight holding his little sister's hand, trundling their baggage in an orange box on wheels. Suddenly a German fighter fell from the sun, bullets rattling on the *pavé.*

When Teare uncovered his eyes again, the fighters – and the children – had gone. Then, as he watched, both children scrambled from the ditch, and slowly and with dignity went on their lonely way. Twenty years later Teare recalls: 'I never thought it possible to hate anyone like I hated that bastard then.'

There was pity for animals too. In Lance-Corporal William Cole-Winkin's provost company orders were specific: release canaries and budgerigars in any derelict house you find. Others did what seemed best: Private Jack Hampson, of the Border Regiment, milked the entire dairy herd on one deserted farm, then shot them one by one. With poignant memories of Top o' th' Brow, his own Lancashire farm, Hampson thought it might be days before another samaritan chanced along.

Then there were the dogs – hungry, shivering with fear, they swarmed everywhere, tagging on to any Tommy too merciful to shoo them away. Lance-Corporal Eric Stocks of the Manchesters felt his heart wrung by the sight of them – but for more than three weeks his hands had been full with 'Tippy', a tawny dachshund pup, her paws and tail tipped with white. Today, passing through Poperinghe, Stocks was cut off from all his unit – but already he felt that 'Tippy' symbolised good luck. Early that morning he had halted at a farm to boil her some cocoa; now, as he slogged the twenty miles towards Dunkirk, there were no malevolent glances, only smiles and waving hands. Seeing 'Tippy' peeping from his pack, the French farmfolk cheered loudly: '*Voilà la petite chienne!*'

Captain Edward Bloom, the dapper immaculate convoy officer,

faced a larger problem altogether; shortly after celebrating his birthday with that hot bath he'd dined with the local doctor. On the point of flight, the doctor and his wife explained their midget car just wouldn't accommodate Hugo, their mammoth Belgian sledge-dog who had lain alongside Bloom all evening, licking his hand. Pity had prompted the captain to take Hugo along – but even now as the Humber staff car bore him and the massive hound north, he didn't realise their destination was Dunkirk.

In the line it was different: men had no time for pity, not even for themselves. Already in the dawn light John 'Warrior' Linton, lying on the railway embankment, had watched the first German patrol move cautiously through wet waist-high grass: two men dressed in field-grey with heavy coal-scuttle helmets, the 'get-away' man moving a little behind. Linton knew the point of that: if anyone fired on the forward men the 'getaway' man would double back and report.

Still Linton held his fire – orders apart, there were still only six rounds of ammunition between him and annihilation. He had asked Sergeant Adams, five yards up the line, for more but Adams had none either. The odds seemed so hopeless, Linton couldn't resist gibing: 'What are we going to *do* when the Germans come? Bite them?'

Linton thought that every man along the line must feel much the same as himself and 'Raygo' King. Squatting down cleaning their rifles the previous night, 'Raygo' had been frank: 'This is a tidy pickle. If you get home and I don't, you go and see my mother . . . and I'll go and see your folks if you stop one.'

Linton had tried to sound more reassuring than he felt: 'Minutest bit of chance and we'll stick together.' But that was before Major David Colvill, the second-in-command, had told them this was a last stand: 'You are to fight to the last man and the last bullet.'

Now another patrol of three Germans had succeeded the first, even standing on a wall, but still the front stayed quiet – ominously quiet, Linton thought, but not for long. Now, as noon approached, explosions shattered the quiet of the valley, the swift crushing noise of shells passing too close overhead and slow, lazy puffs of smoke rose from the ridge behind them. More puffs of smoke, closer now, then the pounding breath-blasting shock of the barrage.

Linton felt no pain, didn't even feel the shrapnel strike him, but something tore at his body like a shock-wave and he fell forward, trying to push his head into the railway track. He knew how bad things were now; he had seen 'Raygo' slump over as the shell landed.

Next instant Linton went down the bank in a diving roll, tumbling over and over. Briefly he glimpsed the needles of shrapnel poking from both knees, impaled in the white gristle; still he felt no pain. Two soldiers whose names he never knew came tumbling after him, then Linton, gasping, cannoned to a halt: 'Go and have a look at "Raygo."'

But the men had never known the childhood name. 'Who's he, Corp?'

'King, for God's sake. Go and look at him.'

It was only seconds before they doubled back again. 'He's had it.' In a kind of frenzy Linton urged them: 'How do you *know*? Go back and make sure.' But when they returned again he knew it was useless. 'Raygo' could have known nothing. The dagger of shrapnel had driven clean through the back of his head.

For a second then thought blurred in Linton's brain, and there was only the timeless mindless agony of remembering and not remembering. He saw now the futility of the pacts and promises; nothing, least of all grief, could help 'Raygo' now. Time would make the pain less but he could not all at once blot out the memory of those Saturday afternoons by the snuff mill; the white line of stepping stones across the clear water, the stout trees they had climbed, the fires they lit to bake potatoes. Sometimes Daisy, the pedigree bulldog, had been with them; her Sunday name had been Polite Duchess, but it even hurt to think of that now . . .

But the two men with Linton saw one thing: the corporal must be got to the regimental aid-post and fast. Bending down, they stripped off his empty bandolier, haversack and water bottle, loosening his battledress at the neck.

Now, half stumbling, half shuffling, the little party set out . . . across a cottage garden backing on the embankment . . . through a cottage, brushing aside an old Frenchwoman's offer of clean rags . . . out into the front garden . . . into the deep roadside culvert that carried floodwater.

Now, across the road and up a dirt drive, Linton could see the farm buildings where the first-aid post was sited – but suddenly, to his astonishment, an officer bobbed up from the ditch on the other side of the road. His command was final: 'You know the orders about wounded. Leave that man and get back into the line.'

Whoever he was, the officer had good reason; in Linton's sector the whole Brigade front was crumbling. In his own regiment every company was cut off from the other. His own company commander, Major Rupert Conant, was dead; the commanding officer, Colonel Ernest Whitfeld, had been carried wounded from the field. On the left the 8th Royal Warwicks had already pulled out; the Gordon Highlanders' machine-gun battalion had gone too.

Hours earlier General Harold Franklyn, co-ordinating the battle, had told Lieut.-General Brooke: 'I'm uneasy about the 143rd Brigade . . . they have given and are being pushed back.' Already at Comines the Germans had crossed the Canal, and were a thousand yards inland, working steadily round Linton's unit to the rear.

Linton, of course, knew nothing of this, but as the men who had helped him doubled back he thought fast. The horror that he and 'Raygo' had tried to guard against had happened now; free from pain, not even bleeding, he was wounded none the less, to be discarded on the scrapheap of war. Now the thought struck him: 'But if I can reach the doctor, *he* won't leave me. Doctors swear oaths. Two men have risked court-martial to help me. I must be meant to get back.'

Inch by inch, dragging his legs behind him, he slithered along the ditch. After a long time he was lying level with the track across the road that ran up to the farm buildings. He eased his hands to the lip of the ditch, striving to pull his exhausted body after him, then abruptly fell back. From somewhere close at hand a machine-gun had beat an excited tattoo and the dust was spurting.

Minutes passed. Again Linton scrambled painfully up; again, like a reflex, the gunner fired. He lay exhausted and panting, legs spreadeagled behind him, but suddenly a warm glow spread through him. From across the road had come the welcome voice of Lance-Corporal Norton, who had served with him back in India.

'Don't get coming over this road, they'll get you sweet as a nut,' Norton warned. But Linton, near to tears, thought only: 'At last – a friend who'll help.'

Succour was indeed at hand, not only for 'Warrior' Linton but for all the men along the Ypres-Comines line. Disturbed by General Franklyn's report of withdrawals, Lieut.-General Brooke had lost no time in driving post-haste to Major-General Harold Alexander at Lille. Urging Alexander to lend him three battalions to stiffen Linton's sector, Brooke stressed: 'We're for it if they break through.'

Without demur Alexander agreed. The three crack battalions of his 1st Division were Brooke's for the asking – the North Staffordshires, the famous Highland regiment, the Black Watch, and the 3rd Grenadier Guards, Lord Gort's old battalion.

There had been no time to lose. Major Allan Adair, the courtly, dashing commander of the 3rd Grenadiers, had been with his battalion near Ploegsteert Wood when the news came through; tired and hungry, the whole battalion were just lining up for their first square meal in days, a rich lip-smacking chicken stew prepared by Quartermaster Fred Turner. But a brief roadside conference with General Franklyn had changed Adair's mind. The Ypres-Comines Canal was the first testing-point of the strength of the Dunkirk perimeter, thirty-odd miles north.

If the Germans broke through and reached Ypres before the bulk of the B.E.F. they might also be first into Dunkirk.

Now Adair told Lieutenant Turner: 'Fred, you'll have to take the food back . . . we haven't got time.' Turner urged a change of heart: it would take less than ten minutes to dole out the meal. But Adair was adamant: 'We must move immediately – and you must take the transport back towards Dunkirk. I think we're going into a sticky action and it'll only be another target.'

If the Guards' tradition was to snap to an order without protest, the Grenadiers lived up to it now. Detached from their own Division and Brigade, Adair's men now had nine miles to march across tussocky twilit fields – to drive an unknown strength from an unknown terrain. But not a murmur came from the ranks as they moved off, marching as blithely into the sunset as if it was a field exercise on Pirbright Heath, in Surrey, the rich savoury smell of chicken a fading torment in their nostrils.

Sadly Lieutenant Turner and his troop of sixty retired to a nearby wood to eat the chicken themselves. Every mouthful seemed to lodge in their gullets.

Adair had been right. The wedge that the Germans had driven through Linton's sector was a vital one, and even though Lieut.-General Brooke had now secured another infantry brigade and the entire heavy artillery of 1st Corps, to regain lost ground would be a bitter no-holds-barred action. Yet as Adair's Grenadiers reached the Ypres-Comines Canal they saw a heart-stirring sight – the blazing fires of Comines to the east and the men of the Black Watch, lunging forward with fixed bayonets, silhouetted against the flames.

And to Gefreiter Karl-Heinz Neumann, a twenty-year-old machine-gunner covering the German assault wave, it seemed that within minutes things had gone terribly awry. That morning, as the infantry doubled forward carrying light wooden boards to help them ford the canal, it had all been such a walkover. Neumann's heavy water-cooled machine-gun had kept blasting away, a steady 400 rounds per minute; word had come through that the British had fallen back fully three-quarters of a mile; no one could doubt that the Germans had swept the board.

Yet now, in the night, there was fear and howling confusion on all sides . . . men he knew well were scrambling back in desperate flight up the dry shelving banks . . . the rumour came that forty men, including two officers, were already dead. In a moment the truth was plain; there were steel-helmeted Tommies within yards of them. Hastily grabbing their machine-gun, Neumann lurching under the weight of the 60-pound tripod, the gunners fled.

Little by little the Grenadiers were thrusting the Germans back, but it was uphill work: in their first catastrophic bayonet charge nearly 100 men were wiped out. Worse, not one of the three forward companies had proper entrenching tools; Captain Stanton Starkey's company, lining a field ditch, had to scoop it deeper still with their bayonets. All that day the Germans pressed home the same dogged attack – a whistling red-hot mortar barrage that had the Grenadiers ducking, then a steady thrust of German infantry, doubling in clutches of twenty, spaced out in wide arrow-head formation.

And Adair's men, too, stuck to their own routine: wait tensely until the Germans closed in, near enough to see every detail of their equipment, then let the forward bren-gunners bowl them over like rabbits. Then, as a glowing curtain of German artillery fire descended, the bren-gunners swiftly withdrew.

Once . . . twice . . . three times . . . the Germans kept coming; in the sticky heat, Captain Stanton Starkey couldn't understand why they were all wearing greatcoats like an engraving of the Crimean War. Each time the deadly muted stutter of the brens, the bark of the mortars, drove them back.

From the German lines, Karl-Heinz Neumann watched in numb despair. All along he'd felt that his regiment, the 176th Infantry, were treating this war like a field exercise; even now the officers strolled confidently amongst the troops, their highly polished leather belts and shining silver buttons almost inviting British fire. Beside Neumann, Oberleutnant Georg, his own company commander, was standing bolt upright, scanning the battle with binoculars. Like all the other German officers he felt it unworthy to take cover.

For this false confidence they paid dearly. A few minutes later Georg slumped forward, a Grenadier bullet ploughing into his chest. But, a soldier to the last, he still felt duty-bound to make a final report to the company: in sick silence the men watched as he struggled bloodily to his feet, announcing '*Oberleutnant Georg meldet sich ab, tot!*' (Oberleutnant Georg reports his death in action!). Then, saluting, he fell back dead.

But Adair's Grenadiers faced a desperate situation. Ammunition was pitifully short; the rout of the last sixteen days, severing lines of communication, had cut off vital supplies. Now, at noon on Tuesday, 28th May, the steady surge of the refugees northwards had completed the confusion.

The scant ammunition that had been unloaded at Dunkirk before the Germans put the harbour out of use for good and all couldn't even reach the men who needed it most. Armed with 100 rounds per man at the outset of the battle, the Grenadiers, after sixteen bloodstained hours, were down to one round apiece, a pittance of grenades.

As they waited for the Germans to come yet again, Captain Starkey and his company, faint with hunger, broached an abandoned drum of raw suet, cramming it into their mouths by the handful.

Only one solution remained: at Allan Adair's Battalion Headquarters, a farmhouse a quarter of a mile away, there was still some ammunition on which to draw. Now Lieutenant Edward Ford, the carrier officer, made a desperate attempt. Bumping perilously across the rutted ground, his armoured carrier loaded with wounded, Ford ran the gauntlet of fire. His carrier burst into flames, the wounded were jolted off within minutes – but Ford made it finally on foot.

At Battalion Headquarters, Ford found Adair, who embodied the Guards' officer's traditional devotion to his men, calmly dressing a corporal's wounds. Courtly, even in crisis, he greeted Ford like a diplomat at a soirée: 'My dear chap, how *nice* to see you . . . have you time for some tea?'

But Ford hadn't. It took only minutes for Ordnance Stores to load ammunition on to two more carriers, then a breathless bumping ride back to the beleaguered Grenadiers – fifteen minutes in all.

Gratefully, with a whoop of joy, Starkey and the others began prising open the coveted boxes – then an eerie chill settled upon them.

The hard-pressed ordnance officer had moved too fast. Their ammunition for the most part was made up of Very light cartridges.

But Starkey had noted one salient fact. The Germans, true to type, were conforming to a rigid pattern. To keep the Grenadiers pinned to their trenches they first called down a withering barrage, signalling their mortars with a fixed Very cartridge pattern:

red-white-red. Then, while the Grenadiers hugged the earth, ears singing, the Germans would signal the 'stop' by the opposite pattern – white-red-white – and charge.

As the afternoon wore on, Starkey resolved on a last fling of the dice. As the Germans again surged forward after the barrage, he raised his pistol and sent an urgent red-white-red pattern trailing to the heavens. On all sides the Germans doubled in confusion as the molten mortar fragments showered amongst them like a brazier upended from the sky. With incredulous fascination, Starkey saw man after man toppling.

From the German forward posts an imploring white-red-white went soaring: within seconds the barrage died. Recovering themselves, their rifles at the trail, the Germans moved forward once more. Again as Starkey fired, the barrage came showering.

Now, as the Germans strove to countermand the order, red and white tracer spangled the evening sky like a millionaire's firework display. But as Starkey grimly kept firing, the Germans gave up. Abruptly the mortaring ceased.

For all those on the route to Dunkirk, the Grenadiers had won precious time – but how much time they could not know. From Adair had come firm orders: their sector must be held until 10 p.m. Only then could they fall back.

Huddled in their trenches, the evening shadows lengthening, men had strange, almost ethereal thoughts. Deliberately Lieutenant Edward Ford emptied his pockets, laying on the lip of the trench before him a few grenades, a few bullets, his naked bayonet. He thought: 'If it's got to come, then let it . . . but by God I'll show them something first.' And Starkey, a hundred yards up the ditch, recalls thinking: 'Now the gap between life and death had narrowed, I felt I knew and understood all of them here so well . . . the mind went back over strange things . . . there was no need to put on the shell of formality . . . one was never more sincere.'

But in this sector the battlefield stayed quiet; at 10 p.m. the companies pulled out to Messines. Later, when a roll was called, Adair was down to nine officers, 270 men. The Ypres-Comines Canal had been held. The casualties along the eight-mile front: upwards of 1,000 lives.

Southwards on La Bassée Canal, the line had held too, but with appalling losses . . . the whole of General Noel Irwin's 2nd Division, 13,000 strong, reduced to brigade strength, 2,500 men . . . 90 men of the 2nd Royal Norfolk Regiment machine-gunned by an execution party led by Oberstleutnant Fritz Knoechlein . . . the 2nd Durham Light Infantry fighting to a finish in a burning barn . . . Lieut.-Colonel Rose-Miller's kilted Cameron Highlanders pulling back with 350 men dead, wounded or captured . . .

But the might of von Rundstedt's armour, that had flung four Panzer divisions forward against them, attacking the Ypres-Comines Canal from the rear to link up like the closing claws of a crab with von Bock's infantry, had been held.

Even those who were pulling out had to do so piecemeal. At Festubert, where the 2nd Dorset Regiment held out under tough flint-eyed Lieut.-Colonel Eric Stephenson, German planes delivered a walk-into-my-parlour invitation: leaflets that read: 'Do you really believe the nonsenses that German kill their prisoners? Come and see yourselves the contrary.' Stephenson, though, had no such intention; at the head of his 300 men he set out on a resolute seventy-two-hour hike across dykes and canals, once hiding his entire force up in a ditch within yards of a snail-crawling German armoured column. The colonel was still at their head, his boots in ribbons, when they marched in formation down the Mole at Dunkirk.

And these were professional soldiers, toughened by years of training. On the long canal line running south and west from Gravelines, the amateurs' sole armour was grim determination.

One battalion should never have been there at all. Days earlier, heading southwards to man the western canal line, Brigadier Nigel Somerset had had an urgent 3 a.m. message from G.H.Q. delivered to his staff car by despatch-rider: 'Detach one battalion for the defence of Hazebrouck. They will be commanded by Colonel Brown of Advanced G.H.Q.'

In the small hours, crawling fitfully along blacked-out roads, Somerset was in no position to contact the one regular battalion in his Brigade, the 2nd Gloucestershires. Instead he sent orders to the rear battalion of his column, who could most readily be detached as a body, the 1st Bucks Battalion of the Oxford and Buckinghamshire Light Infantry.

As the message went back along the column Somerset comforted himself that his grass-green territorials would be safe enough. The man from G.H.Q. would show them the ropes.

In some ways Somerset's choice was justified — within days a special German broadcast was to announce: 'The troops chosen to defend Hazebrouck are obviously amongst the best and most formidable of the British Army.' Yet the irony was tragic. It took the Bucks Battalion only two hours in Hazebrouck to realise the true position. There was no sign of Colonel Brown. Advanced G.H.Q. was already pulling out from its convent headquarters, leaving the railway station a paper-chase of confidential files — among them Lord Gort's complete Order of Battle.

Bequeathing to the defenders the one map of the area they were ever to hold, hastily departing G.H.Q. officers explained to the O.C., Major Brian Heyworth, that it was now his job to defend the whole south-western corner of the semi-circle ringing Dunkirk. They announced proudly that a few days earlier they themselves had actually been shelled by tanks.

A brisk tour of the town and the position to Heyworth was plain. He must defend the mile-long circumference of the old walled town with 500 men — the bulk of them orderlies and runners, non-combatants left behind by G.H.Q. Many were without ammunition or even rifles. For them it would be a fight to the death with hand-grenades and axes.

As things turned out, all Heyworth's fears were justified. At that afternoon's conference his officers were so tired that one man after another dropped quietly off to sleep. Within three days of the take-over Heyworth himself was dead – picked off by a sniper as he crossed the street. Already Brigadier Somerset, realising that G.H.Q. had slipped up, had sent word to the battalion to pull out and make for Dunkirk, but when Major Elliott Viney, who had taken over, tried to send word to his companies he realised it was hopeless.

Cut off from central command, Hazebrouck had become a battle of platoons. Using tanks, heavy artillery and probing groups of infantry, General von Kleist's armoured corps had effectively severed company from company.

But group after group did its utmost: twenty years later Oberst Kurt Zeitzler, Kleist's chief of staff, was to recall: 'They were tough all right – men of steel.' In a railwayman's cottage beside the embankment, Second-Lieutenant Amyas Lee and his men, staving off hunger with ginger cake from a grocery store, contented themselves for nine solid hours picking off every motor-cyclist and troop-carrier passing on the road below.

The tanks, Lee was noting calmly, got through unscathed, but it wasn't until they had actually gained the railway track, blasting round after round down the sleepers, that Lee and his men withdrew. Only then did Lee realise how tough things were – in the old town's main streets the only roadblocks were ten-foot high improvisations of trucks, furniture and packing-cases.

Now at 3 p.m. on this Tuesday Viney made a final decision: it was time to move out. Ammunition was low, the rifle companies on the outskirts of the town had been overrun, the troops left by G.H.Q. had been banished to the convent's cellars – few even knew how to fire a rifle. To the last Viney, a dedicated commander, stayed close to his men. A pre-war printer, he spent a long time in the cellars chatting about printing to Private Sydney Grimmer, a twenty-four-year-old Aylesbury lad, who had once worked with his firm. Grimmer could never have guessed why; mortally wounded, lying on a stretcher, he was to die within hours.

Then, discovering two boxes of fine cigars that he had put by in April, the major in the eerie silence quietly made the rounds of every strong-point.

As the rich aroma of Coronas mingled with the sickly smells of blood and cordite on the warm air, Viney was content: those were two boxes of cigars von Kleist's tank crews would never smoke. At 4 p.m. he determined they'd pull out.

But the resolution was short-lived. At 3.30 p.m. the barrage began again; now, as the Germans had the exact range, men were running from building after building. Trapped in a house with 100 men and only two bren-guns, Viney was spotted at the window by a sharp-eyed gunner as a tank rumbled past along the street.

As a grenade came flying through the window Viney acted fast. Promptly he leapt from the window and surrendered his party.

At the cost of 300 dead, wounded or captured, the siege of Hazebrouck was over – but whether any man got away was in the lap of the gods. Second-Lieutenant William Marshall, defending the station hotel and blissfully scrubbing his teeth in their best champagne, had word early; he and a party of eight slipped eastwards through the German lines. Platoon Sergeant Frederick Larkin got a later message: 'Head northeast, the password is "Beer and skittles."' Second-Lieutenant Clive Le Neve Foster bumped into some gunners on the railway embankment; he and a party of three headed with them for Dunkirk, not even knowing where that might be.

Few of the ships had known either – but more and more were realising now what the voyage entailed. Following swiftly on that hasty departure from the oiler at Dover, Commander Ralph Fisher had once again cleared lower deck in H.M.S. *Wakeful*. 'We are bound for Dunkirk to pick up as many as we can of 6,000 troops cut off in that region.'

Within minutes the ratings under First-Lieutenant Walter Scott were turning to . . . clearing the mess-decks of all tables and stools . . . brewing up vast urns of cocoa and tea . . . manhandling kegs of rum and loaves of bread up from stores. Yet still Fisher worried. His cramped old oil-ridden ship had all too much topweight – upper-deck cargo, increasing the roll of a ship. Yet the only solution at first seemed too hazardous to contemplate.

Like every destroyer in her class, *Wakeful* had two sets of torpedo tubes, sited on each side of the searchlight platform. As Fisher saw it, the one way to reduce topweight was to jettison the six tons of torpedoes and the 100-plus depth-charges stored in the chutes and throwers. That way *Wakeful* could pack in 100 more men – besides manoeuvring at high speed if the Luftwaffe showed up.

Though Fisher had to decide fast, the chances seemed good. Other ships must be bound on the same mission. If each destroyer could find room for 600 apiece, the lifting must be accomplished that very day. It would be a big risk to take, a risk not only involving his 150-strong crew but 600 unknown men, yet a risk that would hold good only for the space of hours. Soon enough they'd be back in Dover, their job done.

At 1.30 a.m. on 28th May, Fisher had made his lonely decision. He ordered Acting Gunnery Officer Townsend: 'Set the torpedoes and charges to safe and fire them . . . report when it's done.' The dark water scarcely bubbled with the impact of the missiles: few of the crew knew what had happened as the ship barrelled on towards Dunkirk.

Not all the destroyers had made this decision – and with good reason. H.M.S. *Codrington* was already off the beaches at Bray

Dunes, four miles east of Dunkirk; but Captain George Stevens-Guille didn't even know the score: orders had come to get there fast but not what to do. Following the example of other ships around, he sent in a whaler to pick up troops from the beach, then steamed into Dunkirk's Eastern Mole. At the Mole's end he sighted an old friend, Commander Jack Clouston, Captain Tennant's piermaster. He hailed him: 'Hallo, old boy, what the hell is all this about?' Clouston seemed strangely cheerful: 'Oh, well, you know, we've been defeated.' Only then did Stevens-Guille latch on.

Already Captain Tennant's brainwave was paying dividends. Clouston, piermaster at the seaward end of the Mole, was signalling the ships to come in while Commander Renfrew Gotto filtered the troops from the harbour area. Now word had come from Ramsay at Dover that the personnel ships – converted cross-Channel ferries packing in over a thousand troops – would also be routed to the Mole. There was still a chance of bringing off those 45,000 men.

Aboard H.M.S. *Wakeful* Commander Fisher fairly beamed: his decision about the torpedoes had been right after all. The Eastern Mole could berth only sixteen ships at top of high water and the approach had been a shade tricky, but the procedure was streamlined: bows in . . . head rope fast . . . swing the stern round . . . make fast fore and aft.

Then it became a routine all ships were to know . . . the muffled tramp of boots and sharp clatter of rifles . . . the oily smoke writhing to reveal the licking orange flames . . . dark winding columns of men etched against the fire-glow . . . little by little the silhouettes taking shape . . . dazed grimy soldiers stumbling aboard, scarcely capable of speech, slumping into a coma on the cold iron deck. In less than half an hour, with 600 men aboard, *Wakeful* was steaming stern first out of Dunkirk Harbour at a steady 25 knots.

But Fisher knew swift disillusionment. Back at Dover, as they tied up against the oil-tanker *War Sepoy*, came a sudden message from Admiral Ramsay: there was still no time to re-fuel. Within the hour *Wakeful* must return to Dunkirk – overall target, 30,000 men. For the second time, Fisher wondered about those torpedoes.

Back at Dunkirk, aboard the *Sabre*, Commander Brian Dean could have wished all his torpedoes at the bottom of the Channel. At that moment the handsome, red-bearded captain was holding his breath: with no opportunity to lighten ship, his deck cargo totalled a massive 70 tons – 800 bone-tired jam-packed Tommies. But Dean's route home, with a propeller draft increased from fifteen to nineteen feet, lay through Ramsay's Route Y, the 87-mile trip via the Kwinte Buoy.

Already the tide was falling – and to ground *Sabre* with 800 men, a sitting target for the bombers, was a grisly prospect. The echo-sounding machine, installed only a month before, still had teething troubles.

Dean did the only thing possible. As *Sabre* approached the Pass, dead slow, he hastened two able seamen to the 'chains' – small square platforms hinging outboard from the ship's side. From the bridge Dean listened tensely as each man, heaving the lead, laconically reported the depths like old-time Mississippi leadsmen: 'M-a-a-ark 5' . . . 'Dee-eep 4' . . . 'And a ha-aa-alf 3' . . . 'And a quarter 3.'

It seemed to Dean that he aged a little each minute: only six spare inches lay between *Sabre*'s propeller and the bottom now. But as he listened the leadsmen were chanting anew: 'And a ha-aa-alf 3' . . . 'Qua-aa-rter less 4' . . . 'Dee-ee-ep 4.' A sigh of relief went up from the whole ship. *Sabre* was out.

Astern of *Sabre*, along the beaches, there was only black despair: the whole assignment seemed too enormous, too disorganised, to stand any chance of success. Aboard H.M.S. *Harvester*, Lieut.-Commander Mark Thornton was at his wit's end; without charts, his only orders had been to follow the destroyer *Mackay* towards Dunkirk. Now *Mackay* was grounded on a sandbank – and Thornton, with no clues as to anchorage, cannily let his ship drift. Sweating anxious moments of tension until the tide, as Thornton knew it would, carried the 1,300-ton destroyer into the deepest channel. Now and only now could he lower his boats.

For most the problems only began there: already *Sabre*'s First-Lieutenant, Norman Parker, had had an unwelcome taste of them. As the destroyer's whaler, towing a sailing dinghy, had hauled in to the beach earlier, the troops, snatching at any straw, stampeded like maddened animals towards them. To Parker, as the little pulling boat bucked and heaved under their onslaught, it was the most terrifying moment he had ever known: only by flailing at the Tommies with oars could he restore order.

Even with docile troops it was no picnic. From the minesweeper *Halcyon*, Stoker Arthur Parry kept it up for three gruelling hours . . . first the ten-minute pull to the shore in the ship's whaler . . . anxious moments for the crew of four as the soldiers thrust wildly forward, threatening to capsize the boat . . . the bowmen steadily pushing the boat out, adjusting the growing weight of water-logged Tommies with an extra depth of water. Then, ferrying nineteen more soldiers to safety, the whaler began its grinding pull back to *Halcyon*.

On the bridge of the *Halcyon*, Commander Eric Hinton did some swift mental arithmetic and groaned. At this rate, it would take twelve hours to fill the ship and get under way.

The crying need, as Captain William Tennant knew, was for small boats – motor-boats, whalers, ship's lifeboats, any craft drawing not more than two feet six inches of water that was capable of inshore ferrying work. That very morning he had impressed the crucial facts on Captain Eric Bush, who was making a swift reconnaissance on Ramsay's behalf: small boats were needed and fast.

Already, a start had been made. Two weeks back the Admiralty's Small Vessels Pool had begun a register of privately-owned craft – though to date only forty had been unofficially commandeered. Apart from that Ramsay had barely another fifty available – drifters, passenger launches, the small craft of the Dover base.

In Dover, sitting impassively back above the grey lake-calm Channel, Ramsay heard Bush's report in silence. Then uncradling the phone, he called Rear-Admiral Tom Phillips, Vice-Chief of Naval Staff, in London. Always a troubleshooter, the Admiralty held no terrors for Ramsay; already his chief of staff, Vaughan Morgan, had urged Operations Officer Philip Martineau, who knew Ramsay well: 'For heaven's sake stop him talking to Phillips like that – he'll lose his job.'

Now, pushing over the phone, Ramsay invited Bush curtly: 'Here – you'd better tell him.'

Phillips listened for a time, then asked: 'Well, how many small boats *do* you want? A hundred?'

To Bush it didn't seem then that any man as yet appreciated the full gravity of the situation. His voice tight with emotion, he answered: 'Look, sir, not a *hundred* boats – every boat that can be found in the country should be sent if we're to even stand a chance . . .'

To the men on the spot, Captain Bush's urgency made simonpure sense. As *Halcyon*'s whaler tugged back for the beaches yet again, Stoker Arthur Parry, glimpsing the troops flanked like dark breakwaters against the pearly-grey sand, paused for a second on his oars.

'Any road,' he still recalls growling, 'Jerry shan't have 'em.'

The resolve was universal, though on the late afternoon of 28th May, less than forty-eight hours after evacuation began, it sounded perilously close to whistling in the dark. As things stood, no man, even Gort himself, could have predicted the outcome now.

Roaming disconsolately round the King of the Belgians' abandoned seaside villa to which he had shifted headquarters at La Panne, nine miles from Dunkirk, the commander-in-chief was as much in the dark as any of his Army. The villa had been chosen because the undersea cable from Dover came ashore here, giving direct contact with London – yet Gort's contact with the forces in the field was now virtually nil.

It was two days since he'd been in personal touch with Lieut.-General Brooke, commanding 2nd Corps, much the same time with General Michael Barker of 1st Corps. Eleven days since he had had any telephone link with French First Army H.Q. or H.Q. North-East Front. His staff was so tired that every reference on the vast mapboard was hours out of date.

But the situation was hideously simple. If 50,000 troops, the bulk of the British Expeditionary Force's 'tail', were within sighting distance of the perimeter, there were as yet nearly a quarter of a million men, the cream of any future British front line, who weren't. Worse still, of the men who formed the rearguard, thousands were, even by First World War training standards, ill-equipped to do more than die with dignity.

Of Gort's 390,000 men, more than 150,000 formed a vast unwieldy tail like a pantomime dragon's – untrained, for the most part unarmed. Only two divisions – General Alexander's 1st and General Irwin's 2nd – had been fully trained when war began. Thus few men had had a greater shock than Major-Generals Harry Curtis and William Herbert, commanding the 46th and 23rd Divisions – both untrained labour forces from the North and Midlands. On arrival in France Gort had greeted them warmly: 'Gentlemen, you're going to be a valuable reinforcement to me.'

Small wonder that Curtis and Herbert had gaped. Their War Office instructions had been cut-and-dried: a straightforward coolie job until August, building airfields and pill-boxes, back to England for stiff training, a gradual return to France as front-line soldiers. As things were, Curtis and Herbert now saw their divisions co-opted without plea of redress into the main fighting force. The equipment for 12,000-plus men: eight two-inch mortars, thirty-six bren-guns, twenty anti-tank rifles, two motorcycles and two four-seater cars. From the first they were without artillery, signals sections or anti-tank guns.

It was the same all down the scale. Sapper Thomas Marley, a civilian four months back, still couldn't load his rifle when he hit Dunkirk beaches. Sergeant Sidney Tindle's battalion, the 6th King's Own Royal Regiment, had gone to France like fourteenth-century mercenaries — one rifle per 100 men: a month later they were tackling German Mark IV tanks armed only with grenades. In Brigadier Philip Kirkup's 70th Infantry Brigade, which took in three battalions of Durham Light Infantry, three-quarters had never fired a bren-gun, a fifth hadn't even passed out on the rifle range. About this time their first rifles arrived — still packed in grease, minus ammunition.

North of Ypres, Second-Lieutenant Walter James would have settled for one of those: an officer of the pioneer-trained South Staffordshires, James didn't even have a pistol as his punch-drunk unit reeled back towards the coast. Suddenly a squadron of riderless Belgian cavalry horses clattered past while James, jog-trotting in pursuit for a humiliating one and a half miles, tried desperately to grab a revolver from a saddle. Finally the horses outpaced him; he gave up in disgust.

James, in any case, knew little enough about firing a revolver: like most Territorial officers, he had done his training in anti-quated First World War 'Fire Bays', squinting from his trench at the waving coloured flags which stood in for artillery fire.

Now, as the Army fell back, many men moved as blindly as in a fog — company cut off from battalion, battalion from brigade,

brigade from division. Captain Geoff Gee, of the Leicesters, severed from his company near Armentières, bumped into a staff colonel who couldn't locate Brigade let alone Corps Headquarters. Slapping Gee gaily on the back, he consoled him: 'My dear boy, we don't even know where our own divisions are!'

It was the same with Lieut.-General Alan Brooke, still shuttling from point to point along the Ypres-Comines front. He knew where his divisions were but, lacking communications, he had to pass almost every order to them by word of mouth.

No man on this day moved more dazedly than Sergeant Sidney Tindle. In the past twenty-four hours, the perky little Irishman had found keeping pace with events beyond all his powers . . . first that terrifying battle with the German tank-gunners dressed as Frenchmen . . . the eerie night withdrawal under cover of a flock of sheep . . . then a long march in wind and darkness, during which he'd completely lost his company. At dawn Tindle was stranded with just four others in a silent gutted town whose name he never knew.

Overwrought – for in nineteen years' service he'd known nothing like this – Tindle still wrestled to keep hold on a strength that was fast ebbing. He told his men firmly: 'I'm the sergeant here, my authority stands. If I see any man looting I'll do what's necessary – and you can guess what that is.'

But the men were tractable, willing to accept any lead – quietly following Tindle to a blitzed bake-house for a quick snack of stale bread, then on through the silent town. On the far side the little sergeant stopped, scratching his head in amazement.

For mile after mile the roads were jammed with the longest supply column he'd ever seen – brand new guns, tall packing-cases of ammunition, shining new trucks. A sudden wave of despair seized him: there'd be no chance to use any of this now.

To a sergeant in the Duke of Wellington's Regiment, Tindle confessed: 'We're bogged down – they've shifted all the road signs and we haven't a map.' The sergeant seemed friendly. 'How about stringing along with us? How many are you?'

Tindle was about to answer 'Four', when sudden instinct made him whirl round. Stupefied, he counted twenty-four men trailing behind him now – Borderers, Yorks and Lancasters, the King's Own Yorkshire Light Infantry.

Past patience, Tindle screamed: 'Where the devil did you lot spring from? Get the hell out of here – *I* don't want you.' But as the men didn't answer, only stood dumbly with the mute appeal of stray dogs, Tindle felt his resolution weaken. After a long pause he grumbled: 'All right – you can stop, I suppose. But I've no food to give you, mind.'

With the professional's bitter pride, he thought: *I'll* have to see them through this – and a bunch of Saturday night soldiers at that. Slowly the little party trudged off, each man knowing as little as the next.

The signals liaison which might have saved the day for many men broke down completely now – retreating before a non-stop rain of steel, the Army's linesmen had only the old First World War cable-drums, holding a meagre mile of cable which had to be wound by hand. Signals Officer Anthony Noble of the 2nd Lincolns had had eight miles of wire when the Germans invaded Belgium; this day, following withdrawal after withdrawal, he had lost it all.

It wasn't surprising that the Lincolns' 'B' Echelon – the supply arm – took the wrong turning when cut off from the main body and drove clean into the enemy lines.

Near Flêtre, within twenty-one miles of Dunkirk, Colonel 'Mollie' Sharpin and 200 men of the Royal West Kents made the same tragically false move.

And scores escaped only by the skin of their teeth. North of Arras, Gunner Alfred Futter of the Norfolk Yeomanry and three other wounded men swooshed clean through the enemy lines in a truck – only to run smack up against a German staff car. Methodically an officer searched them, then ordered: 'Get back in the truck and follow me.' Futter obeyed until the third cross-roads; then, as the Germans turned right, he forked hard left. After a nerve-racking ten-hour drive north he struck a first-aid post – and a coast-bound ambulance.

It was the same with Driver Leslie Jenkinson, playing follow-my-leader all night with the rear light of a convoy; it took the reddish dawn light to reveal the swastika emblazoned on the tank ahead. Guardsman Jack Boulton of the Coldstream, taken prisoner at Bachy, even did three days' kitchen fatigue, then slipped away to link up with the British. All through to the coast he puzzled: would this entitle him to prisoner-of-war leave?

Some met only the top brass. Sergeant 'Snowy' Mullins of the Dorsets, captured at Festubert, was led to the divisional commander's headquarters, a stone-flagged farm kitchen. When a staff officer led off, 'You're 5th Brigade, 2nd Division – and you've had a pretty good beating,' Mullins was truculent. 'Name and rank are all you'll get from me.'

As the officer agreed blandly, 'That's all we expect,' Mullins, glancing up, caught a fleeting smile of sympathy from the divisional commander, conning intelligence reports across the room. He knew the face later when it jumped into the world's headlines: the strong jaw and finely-etched features of Feldmarschall – then Generalmajor – Erwin Rommel.

Despatch-riders might have unsnarled the chaos but this, too, fell down. Men like Guardsman Alfred Brooks, of the 3rd Grenadiers, rode like zombies now, stuttering along choked dusty roads in an agony of fatigue. Today, as he hit Dunkirk beach, Brooks was almost blind with pain; clocking 12,000 miles in three weeks, he had rubbed coffee grounds into his eyes to keep himself awake.

By the end of the week despatch-rider casualties totalled 200 men – not all of them through accidents. Near Bergues, Trooper

Dennis Cartwright saw a sight to turn him sick: a German piano wire rigged fiddle-taut across a country lane had sheared one rider's head clean off.

Most men could have made Dunkirk by map, but maps were now as rare as corn in Egypt. Lieut.-Colonel Peter Jeffreys, commanding the 6th Durhams near Arras, had to refuse a tank commander who offered him armoured support – he just couldn't part with the battalion's only map. In the 139th Infantry Brigade, now inside the Dunkirk perimeter, Intelligence Officer Wilfrid Miron held the one map among 2,500 men.

Shorn of all directions, men did their desperate best. Driver Rowland Cole, taking the palm for know-how, used a compass – and the map on a crumpled German surrender leaflet. Lieut.-Colonel Alfred Lawe's 2nd Lincolns made the canals ringing Dunkirk by steering for the setting sun. Major Cyril Barclay brought what was left of the Cameronians back to Dunkirk with eighty Michelin road-maps, providentially bought for £4 10s.; eighteen months later he was still trying to collect from a War Office who claimed 'regulations offer no provisions for an officer to buy maps on active service'.

The Army had provided maps in plenty for an advance beyond the Belgian frontier; the need of maps for a full-scale retreat had not at first occurred to them. The maps they could have used were by this time in France, landed on Dunkirk's dockside, by the Channel steamer *Maid of Orleans* on Sunday night, but now it would always be too late.

There was no time for such inquests at 4 p.m. on Tuesday, 28th May, 1940. For five hours a graver problem had faced Lord Gort: that it would be too late for 25,000 men. At 11 a.m. that day, Gort had at last made contact with General Georges Blanchard, commanding the French First Group of Armies. In silence Blanchard had listened while Gort's chief of staff, Lieut.-General Henry Pownall, read out to him the contents of Anthony Eden's telegram – then recoiled in horror. To withdraw to Dunkirk was unthinkable. He had had no such instructions.

Now it was Gort's turn to be surprised. The British decision to pull back to the coast and embark had been communicated by the Government to the French Premier, Paul Reynaud, and to General Maxime Weygand, the supreme commander, two days earlier.

It was clear, though, that Blanchard knew nothing of this. He still stuck stubbornly to his guns – a bridgehead, yes, but a bridgehead over the River Lys, forty miles south. There wasn't a chance of embarking his men: the French First Army, under General Edmond Prioux, must stand fast south-west of Lille.

Now Gort grew desperate. The Belgians were out of the fight now. The enemy were pressing on the north-east – and on the south-west, by Cassel and Wormhoudt, they were thrusting steadily too. If the French didn't withdraw at the same time as the British, the entire Allied cause might founder.

The British were withdrawing to the Lys that very night, then northward to Dunkirk. Through Pownall, whose French was more fluent, Gort implored Blanchard: 'I beg you for the sake of France, the French Army and the Allied cause to order General Prioux back.' And he entreated further: the French Government would surely lay on ships for some of the troops? Wasn't it better to save some trained soldiers than to lose them all?

Now tempers flared – so hotly that Brigadier Oliver Leese and Lord Bridgeman, who'd been sitting in until now, felt like intruders on a family quarrel. They slipped quietly from the room.

But Blanchard, as Pownall still recalls, was adamant: a loyal soldier of France, he'd had no such orders. His head erect, he asked Gort formally: 'The question remains, are you going to walk out without us?' Gort understood French well enough; before Pownall could translate, he jumped in, 'Yes, that is so.'

When Blanchard left, after an hour's fruitless debate, things looked as bad as they'd ever been. Gort as yet couldn't know that while General Prioux and six of his divisions would be prisoners by that day's end, the 3rd Corps' General de la Laurencie viewed the whole gallant stand as foolhardy. On his own initiative, slogging at the head of his men, he brought his Corps north to Dunkirk to fight with the British.

But for the moment Gort faced an even bigger problem. Until he knew what the French would do, no final orders could go out to the two hard-pressed divisions manning the south-western canal lines – General Andrew Thorne's 48th and General Edmund Osborne's 44th. Gort didn't know that Hazebrouck had already fallen but he knew that every town on the western canal line – Wormhoudt, Cassel, Ledringhem – was under bitter pressure.

Only a few hours remained before Gort withdrew his rear-guard to a new line of defence running from Cassel to Ypres through Poperinghe – eight miles nearer to Dunkirk and freedom. Whether these two divisions would ever glimpse that freedom was still, at 4 p.m., a vexed point.

Past hoping for anything better, the men of the western front did the best they could – behind primitive barricades of farm carts and children's tricycles, behind tea containers packed with wet mud. In the Forest of Nieppe, Private Jack Evans and his mates of the Queen's Own Royal Regiment hopefully awaited the firing-pin which would make the two-inch mortar work; an officer had said it would be coming and an officer should know. Gunner Frederick Pendar and his unit, their heavy guns long abandoned, crouched behind a road-block of farm carts with a twelve-bore shotgun and two cartridges.

Things were as tough all along the line. Corporal Bill Chick and his mates of the West Kents had, apart from their rifles, just one farm cart and a roll of barbed wire to stop the German advance. To some it seemed the end was very near: Private John Feaveryear, of the West Kents, carved his name in the clay of his slit trench in between bursts of fire, his own primitive 'In Memoriam.'

For a few men in these last hours the war became intensely personal. At Wormhoudt, twelve miles south of Dunkirk, Lance-Corporal Thomas Nicholls, a young anti-tank gunner of the Worcestershire Yeomanry, entrenched behind a barricade of pianos, had been on pins all day. As yet there had only been small signs that things were going wrong but they were enough . . . French troops, bloody and unshaven, filtering back through their lines . . . orders to cover every slit trench with rhubarb leaves from cottage gardens to shield the naked earth from quizzing German spotter planes.

Worse, Nicholls and his mates couldn't even get a glass of beer. Crouched behind his two-pounder gun, Nicholls had to stay guarding the cross-roads near the gendarmerie, and the local estaminet proprietor would now only serve beer to drink on the spot. Things didn't look good and he wanted to be sure he got his bottles back.

Nicholls didn't even know that Wormhoudt was completely surrounded – he was too troubled by the memory of a conversation a few days back when his unit pulled out from Béthune. Then a French farmer's wife had reviled him: 'You English, when you came into our country ten days ago we garlanded you with flowers . . . we thought we would be able to stay by our firesides . . . and within ten days you are running.'

And Nicholls, colouring with shame, could only answer with a twenty-five-year-old's pathetic dignity: '*Nous reviendrons*' (We shall return). He believed it implicitly, too – hadn't the unit's old sweat explained that this was all a ruse to form a thin red line?

Suddenly, across the flat sunlit land, Nicholls and all of them saw a column of French troops, marching four abreast, pass behind the farmhouse to their right, 400 yards away. Then, as

Battery Sergeant-Major 'Danny' Ireland raised his field-glasses: 'Look lively, lads! They're Jerries!'

Next instant his whistle had shrilled but the Germans squatting momentarily on a log to rest their feet were quicker. As the Lewis-gun beat a relentless tattoo, a few lay where they had fallen, but more ran for the cover of the woods or to the farmhouse. The farmhouse was the target now, Nicholls thought, slowly traversing the muzzle of the two-pounder round.

Suddenly Nicholls gulped. Out of the wood ahead, at the fullest extent of his field of fire, had lumbered two mammoth German tanks – Panzer Mark IVs. His target, though the young territorial couldn't know it, was the cream of the German Army: General Heinz Guderian's 19th Armoured Corps.

Still Nicholls didn't hesitate, crisping the gunner's jargon: 'Target front . . . 1,000 yards . . . left a half . . . fire!' As the two-pounder shuddered, the leading tank, with fearful impact, blew up in an eye-searing sheet of flame. At once the other tank ground cumbrously away, moving fast out of range. Nicholls's first thought: My God, I got him. His second: If only that French-woman could see us now.

Then a strange thing happened – strange because that day's forecast had promised only fair weather. In the old château at Wormhoudt, Brigadier James Hamilton, commanding 144th Infantry Brigade, accepted the worst now. On every side his troops were surrounded . . . at Wormhoudt itself his own Brigade H.Q. and Major Peter Hicks's 2nd Warwicks . . . Tom Nicholls and his mates of the Worcestershire Yeomanry . . . the 8th Worcesters . . . all were boxed in tightly by Guderian's 19th Corps . . . with Colonel Buxton's 5th Gloucesters farther south at Ledringhem facing the same plight.

These units had formed a vital sector of the western rear-guard, blocking the German drive for the roads to Dunkirk, giving time for all those moving back to the coast. Now it seemed as if annihilation was their reward.

By this time all confidential papers were grey feathery ashes in the stone fireplace. Armed with rifles, Hamilton and his staff made ready for a last stand.

All at once Hamilton, a deeply religious man, felt the urgent need to ask for God's intervention. From the château's living-room, its silence broken only by the ticking of an ormolu clock, he passed to an inner room, away from his staff officers. His prayer was quiet, simple, like a man addressing an old and cherished friend: 'Look here . . . hold on a minute . . . we need help.'

Within minutes it was as if God Himself was answering – with a clap of thunder that split the sky apart. Massed inky clouds swelled on the horizon. At 4 p.m. a white hissing curtain of rain drenched the battlefield that was northern France.

Half an hour later Tom Nicholls and the rest of his unit, sodden to the skin, were piling on to a truck and pulling out, their job done – all told they had bagged the incredible total of twenty-plus tanks. Near Wormhoudt, General Heinz Guderian, commanding the German 19th Corps, dictated for the War Diary: 'The commander is of the opinion that further useless sacrifice must be avoided after the severe casualties which the 3rd Armoured Regiment has suffered during the counter-attack.'

The 2nd Warwicks, down to seventy men now, were withdrawing too – from an eerie world where the rain streamed sullenly and burning farms fountained red sparks to the sky. Never in his life would Captain Edward Jerram forget the German infantry searching for them along the hedgerows, the mocking cries of 'Hallo, hallo' like men who had lost a dog. Pushing their wounded in wheelbarrows, the Gloucesters moved out from Ledringhem, slogging silently for six and a half hours across open country.

But all these men were safe. Within hours the low-lying fields were a vast shining carpet of water. Those of General Guderian's tanks still operative were forced to hug the roads.

The front had contracted as Gort had prayed it might. Shivering, their uniforms black with moisture, another 300 men, all that was left of this rearguard, were moving north towards Dunkirk.

In London there was no escaping the facts. At 2.45 p.m., packed tensely on the green leather-padded benches of the House of Commons, 600 Members of Parliament heard out Prime Minister Winston Churchill in shocked silence: following a brave unequal struggle, the Belgians had thrown in their hand. 'Meanwhile,' Churchill warned, 'the House should prepare itself for hard and heavy tidings. I have only to add that nothing which may happen in this battle can in any way relieve us of our duty to defend the world cause to which we have vowed ourselves . . .'

He had told them the worst in just four minutes.

In the long stone corridor leading to Churchill's private office, the Premier's bodyguard, Detective-Inspector Walter Thompson, shook his head ruefully. Brave words bravely spoken – but to Thompson, eighteen days back, Churchill, in a moment of stress, had revealed a secret fear. Returning from Buckingham Palace after taking office, Churchill had paused for a second outside Admiralty House, where he was still quartered. Offering congratulations, Thompson blurted, 'I feel you've taken on a very heavy burden, sir.'

Tears in his eyes, Churchill answered gravely: 'God alone knows how heavy that burden is. All I'm afraid is it may be too late . . . we can only do our best.'

Then, as swiftly as always, the mood had passed. Straightening up, Churchill squared his shoulders. As he stamped ferociously towards his top-floor flat, it seemed to Thompson every footfall echoed defiance.

And this afternoon, leaving the House, the defiance was there still. In the long Cabinet Room at the rear of 10 Downing Street, Churchill, mustering the twenty-five Ministers outside the War Cabinet, told them plainly how bitter the future might be. Without emphasis, almost casually, he wound up: 'Of course, whatever happens at Dunkirk, we shall fight on.'

A split second's silence. Then, to the old bulldog's astonishment, they cheered . . . Minister of Labour Ernest Bevin . . . Lord Chancellor Sir John Simon . . . Minister of Food Lord Woolton . . . Minister of Supply Herbert Morrison . . . twenty-five sober politicians cheering as one, some pounding the table with their fists, others leaping up to slap Churchill on the back. The long room rang with their loyalty.

In great ways and in small, the mood was set – not only in Downing Street but all over Britain. Already Mrs Rosa Bishop felt she'd known no other world but Ramsgate Station; for thirty-six hours, ever since that strident chorus of 'Home on the Range' wakened her from sleep, she and scores of volunteers had ministered to each fresh batch of troops – brewing up urns of tea, carrying trays of chocolate, touring the mean back streets to beg bread and tea from working-class homes. Each night, with the help of a friendly railwayman, she slept in a locked carriage – unwilling to go home lest her husband, Sergeant Tom Bishop, passed through at daybreak.

Along the track to London, the railwaymen worked as hard . . . District Traffic Superintendent Percy Nunn, at Orpington, Kent, speeding through a train every four minutes for six hours on end . . . Dover's 200-strong Loco Shed team working twenty-six-hour shifts on bread and cheese snacks . . . so many trains coaling and watering at Redhill Junction that a simmering 300-ton mountain of boiler-ash choked the Loco Yard.

The spirit was universal – yet few divined as clearly as Churchill the hazards that lay ahead. For two days now, the men of Dunkirk beaches had inveighed bitterly against the Royal Air

Force. Where was the fighter cover they'd been promised? Why could Kesselring's bombers pound the harbour at will? Now the Navy were wondering too: in the small hours of that day Ramsay himself had called Churchill from Dover. The captain of the destroyer *Worcester*, Commander John Allison, was boiling at the lack of air-cover.

But Allison, seated in the admiral's bedroom, was startled beyond words as Ramsay extended the phone. Chilling in its implication, the Premier's answer ground out from the receiver: 'I can't provide you with *any* reinforcement from the Metropolitan Air Force because I must reserve them for the battle of the future.'

Chastened, Allison took his leave. Somehow it was like hearing the sober truth voiced beside a death-bed.

The R.A.F. were doing their best, but it was uphill work. At first, Air Ministry policy had been finite: at Dunkirk under-strength fighter patrols must cover the eighteen daylight hours non-stop. Within days the error was plain: as sixty-strong forces of Kesselring's bombers pounded the harbour with thirty fighters in tow, British losses soared frighteningly. Now Air Chief Marshal Hugh Dowding, Fighter Command's chief, made a top-level protest. If any of his aviators were to survive, his fighters must launch fewer patrols – but up to four squadrons in strength.

Even so, Dowding's pilots were still feeling their way. Trained to fly pre-war copybook attacks in rigid air-display formation, the fluid weaving tactics of the Messerschmitts and Heinkels had them dazed. Only that morning, above the target, Flying-Officer 'John' Petre of No. 19 Squadron had felt a shade uneasy; a star pupil of the R.A.F. College at Cranwell, all Petre's training had been to fly in line astern in formations of three.

Busy watching the two planes on which he was formating, Petre couldn't even peek to his rear to see if anyone might jump him. For the first time he wondered if this could be wrong.

Next instant he knew. Hard by a vast egg-shaped swarm of fighters, German and British, wheeled like a flight of bees in the summer sky; in seconds Petre had put his Spitfire on the tail of a Messerschmitt 109 harrying a British fighter. Suddenly fire ripped at his eardrums. Within inches of his ear, an explosive bullet tore into the dashboard, shattering his instruments. Flying glass peppering his knees, cordite pungent in his nostrils, he yanked instinctively at his stick, plunging into a spin-dive below the level of the swarm.

Then, shaken, Petre limped for home. The truly unnerving factor of the combat was that he never even saw the plane that hit him.

Whatever the pilots lacked, it wasn't courage. When the oxygen tube of his Hurricane failed, Flight-Lieutenant Robin Powell blacked out, hurtling 14,000 feet before coming to – but next day he was back at Dunkirk, fighting again. Squadron Leader Teddie Donaldson, closing a Heinkel, found his ammo exhausted; still, in manic fury, Donaldson rammed his Hurricane forward. His nerve gone, the pilot first jettisoned his bombs, then baled out minus parachute.

Eager to hit back, they took risks which in retrospect turned them cold. Of the Spitfire's two hours and fifty minutes' flying time, only twenty minutes' ops were feasible at full throttle, yet pilot after pilot, reluctant to break from combat, got back by the skin of his teeth ... with airscrew blades holed ... bullets through the front tyres ... control wires holding by a thread. Elevator controls severed, battery gone, Pilot-Officer Colin Gray of No. 54 Squadron took his Spitfire back to Hornchurch airfield, Essex, a perfect sieve of cannon holes. Later ground staff put the total at fifty.

And in Hornchurch's Flying Control, Wing Commander Cecil Bouchier, station commander, was forever talking down planes by radio telephone; with replacements taking up to two days,

Bouchier just daren't think in terms of a write-off. That day, as a pilot signalled, 'I can't get my under-carriage down,' Bouchier counselled, 'Loop very violently, lad – try and shake it loose. We can't even afford to lose a damaged aircraft.'

Within Bouchier's sight, on the tarmac, fitters were literally thumbing the metal back into bullet holes, rough-riveting cannon-tears on the spot. No wonder Bouchier later went on record: 'The coverage of the beaches at Dunkirk was infinitely more exhausting and exacting than any part of the Battle of Britain.'

As the day crawled, the chances of holding the Luftwaffe at bay dwindled perilously. After ten days' intensive ops some squadrons had to be withdrawn from the line. Down to half-strength, Flight-Lieutenant James Leathart and six planes of No. 54 Squadron flew north to Catterick, Yorkshire, for a well-earned rest. As they touched down, a senior officer, puzzled, hailed them: 'Which flight is this?'

Replying, Leathart might have spoken for the whole hard-pressed R.A.F.: 'Flight, nothing. *This* is a squadron.'

Over at Dunkirk Bastion Captain William Tennant closed down a briefing conference with a sombre reflection: 'If this goes on we shall all see the inside of a German prison camp.'

Tennant and his commanders had reason to be gloomy. Only five hours back – at the very hour Gort was urging General Blanchard to withdraw his forces to Dunkirk – two motorised divisions of Generaloberst Fedor von Bock's Army Group had raced across the Belgian coastal plain to Nieuport, the easternmost point of the whole Dunkirk perimeter.

What did this mean? To Tennant above all it meant the Germans might at any hour gain control of another lethal battery – the guns of Nieuport, which could bring a deadly hail of fire to bear on Ramsay's Route Y.

By a strange irony, Generaloberst von Bock, in his Brussels headquarters, felt every bit as gloomy as Tennant. Stubbornly he'd urged all along that Dunkirk was the key to the whole campaign – but now, after two days' delay, shorn of close armoured support, it was anybody's guess how the battle would go. Even two days back, Chief of Staff Hans von Salmuth had noted sourly in the War Diary: 'Obviously the largest part of the British personnel has already been transported off.'

At Army High Command headquarters there was the same pessimism. Bitterly Generaloberst Franz Halder complained: 'Thousands of the enemy are crossing the Channel under our very noses.' Again he urged Commander-in-Chief von Brauchitsch: 'If the tanks follow the coast road from Calais to Ostend they can cut the British off before they even reach the coast.'

Von Brauchitsch agreed, but word had come that the Führer was still adamant. Dunkirk was not to be attacked except with artillery fire.

Though neither Halder nor von Bock could know it, Dunkirk was still ripe for the taking. As yet there had been no time for Lieut.-General Alan Brooke's 2nd Corps to move north-east and form a last-ditch stand. The last barrier between the Germans and Dunkirk was being held by a thousand-plus force rushed there by General Sir Ronald Adam in charge of perimeter defence . . . the armoured cars of the 12th Lancers . . . the French 60th Division . . . above all, a mixed force of gunners, sappers and storemen fighting as infantry. From where Captain Tennant stood the chances looked slim indeed.

Closer still they looked worse. Eighteen hours back, Private Jack Atkinson, a non-combatant of 2nd Corps Ammunition Carrying Company, had been making for Dunkirk with high heart; now, as part of General Adam's scratch force, he and two other privates were guarding one room of a two-story house perched high above the canal at Nieuport. Cautiously, waiting until Corporal Ryan, who was in charge, had left the room, Atkinson confided a pressing problem to Private Cardstock: he had never fired a rifle.

Cardstock was reassuring. 'Oh, I have — once. I'll fire it for you.'

Passing it over, Atkinson was contenting himself with changing into dry socks when the room seemed to heave. With a mighty flash the world rained bricks and the window-pane draped neatly round Cardstock's neck. Horrified, Cardstock broke silence with a despairing heart-cry: 'Corporal — I'm *frightened*.'

For the first time ever one man had made the discovery thousands had yet to make — it was their war, too.

It was hard to envisage any graver plight — yet one man had premonitions that worse was to come. In his tented camp not far from Gort's headquarters in the sand-dunes at La Panne, Major-General Bernard Montgomery was just settling in, after a sixteen-mile journey to the perimeter, when one of his commanders, Brigadier Jack Whitaker, bounced in: it would be interesting to inspect the line between Furnes and Bergues, the twelve-mile-long canal that formed the outermost periphery of the Dunkirk bridgehead.

Montgomery, whose 3rd Division was to hold this line, was unenthusiastic. 'Jack, you go if you want to but I'm very busy . . .' Then, as an afterthought: 'And you're not to either — that's a job for battalion commanders.'

Whitaker persisted: to go in an armoured carrier would be safe enough. But still Montgomery shook his head; the needless danger appalled him. He urged Whitaker: 'In two hours' time you'll find them tapping up your front — in the meantime you've plenty to do.'

As so often happened, Montgomery was right. At 9 p.m. that evening two battalions of the Grenadier Guards were moving in to take over the old market-town of Furnes – a solid red-brick town bisected by a fly-haunted canal. The fearless commanding officer of the 2nd Battalion, Lieut.-Colonel Jack Lloyd, was minded to do the same reconnaissance that had appealed to Whitaker.

Along with his company commanders, Major Dermot Pakenham and Captain Christopher Jeffreys, Lloyd prepared to pace out the poplar-shaded tow-path that would be the 2nd Battalion's sector of the canal. Fifty yards behind followed Major Robin Bushman, commanding the company Lloyd had reserved for counter-attacks, and Lieutenant Tony Jones, Lloyd's carrier officer.

As an afterthought Lloyd told his intelligence officer, Captain William Kingsmill: 'You can see all you want to from here, Bill, no point in your coming along.'

Kingsmill, seeing no point either, knew a strange unease. All intelligence reports had stressed this northern side of the canal nearest to Dunkirk would be occupied by British troops. The French would be firmly entrenched on the southern bank. Yet there was no sign of the French at all. The only British in evidence were two truckloads of machine-gunners from the Middlesex Regiment who had just pulled up.

Suddenly, a passing sapper sergeant urged: 'Don't go any farther along – there are snipers.' But when five minutes had passed uneventfully, Lloyd decided: 'Well, we'll have a look, Bill. You stay.'

In the fading light Kingsmill watched them saunter the full length of the tow-path, allotting company sectors . . . three minutes . . . five minutes . . . they had reached the farther end now and were turning back. In that moment the war, after two days' respite, found them again. Three shots whiplashed as one across the stagnant water.

Open-mouthed Kingsmill saw all three men fall, then grabbed

a rifle from a nearby sapper. To Lieutenant Tony Jones he yelled: 'You work round, Tony – try and get them into cover.' Inch by inch he began to snake on his belly along the tow-path. Another burst – and from the crawling position Kingsmill saw all the machine-gunners sliding raggedly, untidily, sideways, but he could see now the red steep-pitched roof, lacking one tile, four yards away across the canal – a custom-built snipers' eyrie.

He raised his rifle, pressing the trigger. He did not stop until he had finished the magazine. A scarf of blue smoke hung above the scummy water but no answering fire came.

Back at La Panne, Gort heard the news in tight-lipped silence. Any comment seemed superfluous: von Bock's men were faring better than their commander knew. Now driving westwards like the plunging blade of a rapier, they had reached the edge of the last canal of all – only four miles from the beaches of Dunkirk and Gort's own headquarters.

CHAPTER FIVE

INTO HELL AND OUT AGAIN

Wednesday, 29th May
1 a.m.–12 p.m.

Sapper Thomas Marley had the shock of his life. From the moment Major Adams, his commander, had said 'Head for Dunkirk,' he was convinced that his pioneer company had somehow disgraced itself and was being banished to England.

Now, shivering in the pouring rain on Dunkirk beach, up to his waist in water as he man-handled stretchers into small boats, Marley was one of thousands who knew differently. It wasn't only his company that was going back. It was the whole Army.

Those pin-points of light pricking the darkness when he arrived on the beach the night before hadn't been fireflies, but soldiers – countless hundreds of them – drawing quietly on cigarettes. The dinning nerve-racking clangour, like a hammer pounding an anvil, had been the destroyers' 4-inch guns smashing back at the Heinkels and Messerschmitts. The soft uncanny sighing, like the wind through telegraph-wires, had been the moaning of the wounded that Marley now helped to succour.

'Lift me as lightly as you can,' a man told Marley matter-of-factly. 'I know I'm dying.' For Marley, as for thousands of others, this was the moment of truth.

On the bridge of H.M.S. *Wakeful*, peering into the drenching darkness off Braye Dunes, Commander Ralph Fisher felt tension mount slowly. Things had been bad enough when Ramsay's earlier message reached them: no time to refuel, 30,000 troops still to be taken off. Then, on the way over, *Wakeful* had had a hard time driving off a savage bombing attack; to Fisher, the strain of handling the ship with almost seventy bombs hailing down on them was something he'd never forget. The net result: a hole blown in the ship's side . . . one seaman killed and two gunlayers badly injured . . . the bleak knowledge that *Wakeful*'s ancient guns, with a 30-degree elevation, were little use against Stukas dive-bombing at 70 degrees.

Worse, Ramsay had signalled that E-boats, U-boats and German destroyers were making for Dunkirk – and on this trip, working off the beaches instead of the Eastern Mole, it had taken eight gruelling hours for *Wakeful* to load up.

But at last, with 640 soldiers aboard, Fisher was ready to go. The old destroyer's mechanism clicked into gear once more as the crew doubled to night action stations . . . Able Seaman Geoffrey Kester to the searchlight manipulators . . . Sub-Lieutenant Bill Mayo, junior officer of the watch, settling at the starboard wing of the bridge . . . Leading Seaman James Ockenden to the gun director.

Slowly, at a steady twelve knots, *Wakeful* churned northwards, heading for Route Y. Tonight the whole ship seemed as silent as the grave; for greater manoeuvrability Fisher had ordered all troops should be packed well below decks and there wasn't a Tommy in sight. And the crew, swaddled in oilskins against the rain, weren't talking much – that E-boat warning made for dry mouths and they knew that on this route they were skirting minefields all the way.

At 12.40 p.m., though, as the dazzling whiteness of the Kwinte Buoy split the darkness to the west, the tension eased a little. Ninety minutes' sailing time behind them now – the only sounds the steady pulsing of *Wakeful*'s engines, the rush of the wake creaming on an almost phosphorescent sea. In this aching silence, their ears alert for the drone of aircraft overhead, men still gave themselves up to random thoughts.

Leading Seaman James Ockenden mused about superstition: as he'd hastened to his action station a grateful Tommy had presented him with a jack-knife and Ockenden was glad now that he'd traded a penny in return. Sub-Lieutenant Bill Mayo dreamed of a hot bath – though his uniform was wringing wet he hadn't wanted to disturb the exhausted army officers who thronged his cabin by changing. Commander Ralph Fisher was thinking: That Kwinte Buoy light almost blinds you – anything could hide up there and you'd never see it.

The thought was pertinent – for as Fisher bent to the voice-pipe, bidding the helmsman take *Wakeful* up to twenty knots, he saw a sight which turned him cold. On the starboard bow what looked like two searchlight beams were streaking towards them across the gleaming water. At the gun director, Leading Seaman James Ockenden saw them too – a brilliant sizzling flash like a tube train rocketing through a darkened tunnel.

Thunderstruck, Fisher whispered, 'You don't mean to say those bloody things are going to go off when they get here?' His First-Lieutenant, Walter Scott, was admirably impassive. 'You know, I'm rather afraid they are.'

'Good God!' Ockenden heard Fisher yell then. 'Hard a-port.'

The helmsman lost no time – but it was too late. The first torpedo, missing by a hair's breadth, sliced like a razor clean across the path of the bows. Then, with a convulsive shudder, the second torpedo struck *Wakeful* amidships, fair and square, on the starboard beam.

With the rending blustering snarl of tortured ironwork, the old destroyer reared and broke clean in two — bow and stern canting upwards to the black water like the twin peaks of a skyscraper.

There was scarcely time to act, let alone think. James Ockenden heard a yell, 'Abandon ship,' got just two puffs into his life-belt before he was down the bridge ladder, breasting the black syrupy water. Sub-Lieutenant Bill Mayo, feeling the whole ship heel to port, lunged for the starboard rail, then found Fisher beside him.

Cheery as ever, Fisher joshed him, 'You beat me to it by a short head.' At the same moment both men felt the water like a slow chilling of the blood steal upwards past their loins. They struck out almost as one.

Few of the crew were so lucky. The force of the explosion drove navigating officer Wilfred Creak through the chart table screen like a bullet, killing him outright. Surgeon-Lieutenant Walker never made it either — to the last he was in the sick-bay attending the wounded gunlayers. The wireless mast, snapping like toppling timber, trapped Petty Officer Telegraphist James Thursten in the signals cabin.

By most reckonings, it took only fifteen seconds to finish off *Wakeful* — only a few, by strange quirks of fate, survived. Stoker Petty Officer Baker owed his life to the torpedo striking the boiler-room; the impact washed him clean into the sea and he came to, clinging to a coir fender. Able Seaman Geoffrey Kester had his life-belt inflated already but nearly lost out; as he jumped from the after-end of the bridge the signal halyards trapped him like the tentacles of an octopus below the dark boiling water. Minutes of pure terror followed until the ship somehow lurched and freed him.

Lungs on fire, he bobbed to the surface and struck out: he'd had more than his share of excitement now.

The troops on board never stood a chance. More than 600 of them below decks struggled in a cold Stygian hell of rising water: the old-fashioned port holes, nine and a half inches against the now-regulation twenty-two, were never wide enough to permit egress. One of the few to escape, Sergeant 'Sonny' Alderton, a pioneer, did so because he'd disobeyed orders; instead of going below to the rope locker in the lazaret he was nonchalantly enjoying a breather on deck, relishing the thought he was safe at last. Followed a blast like a tropic wind and a sheet of flame; he came to in the water remembering nothing.

But over 700 men were doomed – within fifteen seconds.

Now, as the sea came alive with desperately bobbing heads, thin cries echoed piteously in the night, to die as abruptly away. In the inky darkness more men were saving their breath to keep themselves afloat, struggling fiercely against an implacable three-knot tide ... Able Seaman Geoffrey Kester sharing a life-belt locker with Able Seaman Jackie Chivers ... Leading Seaman James Ockenden clinging to a tin biscuit crate with a man whose name he never knew. He, too, heard the cries of 'Help', but rated them unseamanlike. Instead, at intervals, he kept up a stentorian bellow of 'Boat ahoy.'

Ockenden was one of the few optimists who never doubted rescue was at hand; as he paddled steadily he congratulated himself on putting by enough money to send a survivor's telegram to his wife in Devonport.

Near at hand, Fisher exhorted those around him: 'Don't exhaust yourselves trying to swim for the wreck ... you'll go against the tide. We're on the route of a lot of other vessels ... we're bound to be picked up.' Fisher, a tower of strength, even had Sub-Lieutenant Septimus Percival-Jones in tow as he swam; the young officer had mislaid his life-jacket but Fisher didn't even feel the extra strain.

Sub-Lieutenant Bill Mayo was having a tougher time; seeing

the yellow-white light of the Kwinte Buoy flashing not far away, he wrestled to swim towards it, but all the time the tide was sweeping him farther south-west. A deeper chill seemed to invade his body along with subversive thoughts: it would be so easy to give up now. Only a brisk sense of family duty snapped him to sanity and kept him swimming: But Father only died last December – what would Mother do?

To most men fighting to keep afloat the minutes seemed hours – in fact it was little more than thirty-five minutes. Ockenden's first intimation of rescue was the white, red and green bow and steering lights of a ship dead ahead. A moment later he heard a voice – he thought Fisher's – roaring like an outraged air-raid warden: 'Put out those bloody lights.'

Now Ockenden told his erstwhile mate: 'Don't care whether those lights are English or German, that's where I'm heading.' Suddenly, as he kicked off, a whaler loomed from the darkness. Sailors from the minesweeper *Gossamer* were hauling him aboard.

Already *Gossamer*'s captain, Commander Richard Ross, hearing the cries of men in the night, had lowered his three whalers and a skiff. Now a new problem rose to plague him. From the water Fisher had hailed him: 'We've been torpedoed – the sub's still around.'

Privately Ross thought a motor torpedo-boat must have done the damage; strangely, he had received no U-boat warning. In any case there was nothing he could do. His whalers were lost to view in the darkness, picking up survivors – among them Sub-Lieutenant Bill Mayo.

By chance they didn't pick up Fisher at all. About the same time the Scottish drifter *Comfort* had arrived on the scene. Her skipper, John Mair, hadn't lowered boats, but on spotting heads struggling against the glistening water he had hove-to. At least four men – A.B. Jackie Chivers, A.B. Geoffrey Kester, Midshipman Patterson, Fisher himself – scrambled over her low gunwale.

At once hastening to the wheelhouse, Fisher gave Mair a swift outline of all that had passed. The old skipper didn't seem worried; placidly accepting Fisher's command, he set out on an unflurried search for those still afloat, stopping his engine every time the commander heard a cry from the darkness. Finally, with fifteen men aboard, Fisher decided: 'Let's head dead up-tide towards the wreck . . . there'll be more there.'

It was now 2 a.m. In contrast to the milling horror of the past hour, a strange calm fell over the waters. By now others had joined *Gossamer*'s boats . . . the minesweeper *Lydd* under Lieut.-Commander Rodolph Haig . . . the motor drifter *Nautilus* . . . the destroyer *Grafton*. Purposefully, feeling their way through the night, their whalers sought out *Wakeful*'s last survivors.

There was no panic, only a strange confusion; uncertain as to what really had happened, men were playing it by ear. From the bridge of *Lydd*, Lieut.-Commander Haig had seen flares and heard shouting: the pale light of an Aldis lamp gave one nightmare glimpse of men fastened like limpets to *Wakeful*'s bow and stern. As *Lydd* lowered a whaler and two Carley floats, *Gossamer* bulked from the darkness.

From her bridge, Ross ordered Haig: '*Gossamer* to *Lydd* – put out all lights and let go depth charge.'

Haig protested: he could do no such thing. He was too close to *Wakeful*'s wreck – a depth charge would kill those men still in the water. He hailed back: 'But what's happened – what is the situation?'

Infuriatingly, *Gossamer* made no reply. As magically as she appeared, she had gone: Haig, in *Lydd*, never saw her again that night. It wasn't until Able Seaman Fred Cawkwell brought the whaler alongside with twenty survivors that Haig had an inkling of what had happened.

In *Gossamer*, in fact, a blessed peace prevailed. Leading Seaman James Ockenden, one of the first aboard, had headed for the engine-room to don denims and dry underwear; now he was in the wardroom sipping a tot of whisky. He noted with mild astonishment that a soldier wrapped in blankets on the floor was actually having hysterics. Sub-Lieutenant Bill Mayo, numb to the core, had passed clean out after one gulp of brandy.

In the captain's cabin, Major Wilfred Wilkinson of the Manchesters awoke from sleep with a start. The voice-pipe was still connected and from somewhere he had heard Fisher shout, 'Get the hell out of it . . . it's still around here.'

The pitiful cries for help, the sound of scuffling feet, barely made sense until someone – he never knew whom – explained a ship had been torpedoed. Feeling this was the Navy's job, Wilkinson went to sleep again.

Much the same aboard *Comfort* too. On the seamen's messdeck Able Seaman Geoffrey Kester and his mates were snugly tucked up in the crew's bunks sipping cocoa, when Commander Ralph Fisher looked in – duffle-coated and dripping, binoculars still slung. Fisher, like most destroyer captains, was no man to maintain formal relations with ratings; accepting a mug of cocoa, he settled for a brief chat.

Aboard the destroyer *Grafton*, Commander Charles Robinson had no time for small talk; he couldn't make head or tail of what was afoot. He could see *Wakeful*'s wreck jutting from the water; now the minesweeper *Lydd* had signalled that *Wakeful* had been torpedoed.

At once, briefing *Lydd* to circle in case of submarines, Robinson ordered 'Away lifeboats.' Ten minutes passed without fresh bulletins.

The only object in plain view was now the Kwinte Buoy, winking steadily on the starboard bow. It was at this moment that Robinson saw, three cables distant on the port quarter, a small darkened vessel making steady tracks towards him.

Whoever it was, it wasn't *Comfort*; at this precise moment she was closing *Grafton* from starboard. Appalled to see her lying stopped, her rails massed with troops, Fisher had instructed Mair: 'They're English – I must go in and have a word with them.' At the same time he noted that Mair was bringing the drifter closer in than seemed prudent – hard against *Grafton*'s starboard quarter.

Now, from the foredeck, Fisher hailed *Grafton*: 'For goodness' sake, get moving – you'll get torpedoed if you lie stopped.' From the upper deck, someone – he never knew whom – objected: 'We can't go off – we've got a boat down by that wrecked ship.' Still Fisher urged: 'Never mind your boat . . . I'll pick them up. You move on.'

The tragedy was that Commander Robinson could never have heard – minutes later his Number One, Lieutenant Hugh McRea, who had seen the whalers off, saw the bridge's Aldis lamp flashing to the newcomer on the port quarter: 'Close and pick up survivors.' The one strange factor was that the newcomer didn't acknowledge – just kept coming steadily.

It was now 2.50 a.m. Within seconds their calm was broken, their vigil mocked. From the look-out on *Grafton*'s bridge came one frenzied yell: 'Torpedo on the port bow.'

If few saw it, hundreds felt the impact. Almost as one, two torpedoes slammed clean into *Grafton* – one slicing through the wardroom, killing thirty-five officers . . . the second tearing aside the stern like a child's toy.

On *Comfort*'s foredeck Fisher felt it too . . . a white livid flash . . . the little drifter soaring like a balloon from the sea . . . a roaring blinding cataract of water. Grabbing vainly for a rope's end, Fisher still lost his foothold; for the second time he catapulted backwards into the deadly sea.

Aboard *Grafton* nobody knew what was happening – but like a chain of small deadly explosions, fear ignited in man after man. Three times Driver Ernest Smith had woken in the hold, yearning for the comfort of a life-belt; he had just gained the deck and grabbed the last one as the torpedoes struck. It was a prescient move; he was blown backwards into the water and as he fell he trailed a long, long cry.

Sapper Thomas Marley, his dismal vigil on the beaches ended, was asleep on deck close by. He awoke convinced they'd struck a rock – then lay in a companionway where blast had pitched him, frozen with horror. The face of the man sleeping beside him had vanished in a mass of red seething bubbles.

And the crew knew as little. Able Seaman Wilfred Lodge, of *Grafton*'s gun crew, heard the explosion, then half the gun-deck seemed to shatter on his steel helmet; he went out like a light. Lieutenant Hugh McRea, hastening to the bridge to report to the captain, found only the sides left standing.

The Asdic Control . . . the binnacles . . . the fore-screen . . . the compass platform . . . all were a shambles of twisted metal. In the wreckage Commander Robinson and three of his crew lay twisted and still – whether they had died from a grenade or machine-gun fire McRea never knew.

Things were as bad below. Captain Sir Basil Bartless awoke to find the ship rocking violently and a strong smell of fuel oil; hearing someone scuffling in the darkness, he shouted, 'For God's sake don't light a match.' A pre-war actor, his next reaction was all pro – what would Gary Cooper do?

In the petty officers' wardroom, Rifleman Daniel Casey of the Cameronians started up from the mess-table; a sudden rending clatter had echoed from far below. At once a sailor tried to bar his way: 'That was only engines knocking, lad.' But Casey wasn't having any – a veteran of Colonel Gilmore's heroic bayonet charge, the dread of death was upon him. In seconds he was on deck, elbowing his way through a press of panic-stricken soldiers.

Now with revolvers drawn, McRea and his officers manned the

high points, quelling panic. Over and over McRea's voice boomed weirdly through the megaphone: 'Keep your heads . . . I say again, keep your heads . . . there is no danger of the ship going down if everyone goes for'ard.'

McRea hadn't yet had a chance to go below and check the truth of this, but until the screaming mob of soldiery was quieted there was no passage clear from bridge to engine-room.

It was as bad on all sides now: in the chill darkness, lacking directives, ships were feinting like combatants in a darkened room. The minesweeper *Lydd* had only completed one circle of *Grafton* and was heading west with her stern to the destroyer when the torpedoes sliced into *Grafton*.

Craning into the darkness, Lieut.-Commander Haig saw, about fifty yards away on the starboard beam, what he took to be a motor torpedo-boat. She was steering south-west, almost stern on to him.

At once Sub-Lieutenant Edwin Britten, on *Lydd*'s bridge, opened fire with the starboard Lewis-gun, raking the intruder up the stern. As the bullets struck home, her wheelhouse was engulfed in a cloud of fiery sparks.

But *Lydd* hadn't finished yet. A quick check with *Grafton* that the destroyer could keep afloat and Haig once more brought the minesweeper round, circling to starboard. If the Germans were still afloat they'd finish her off now.

Abruptly, dead ahead, they sighted her. Again *Lydd*'s guns were chattering, and now the *Grafton*'s guns under Lieutenant Leslie Blackhouse joined in, pouring fire at *Wakeful*'s killer.

Aboard *Grafton*, along with scores of others, Rifleman Daniel Casey let out a wild cheer: they were showing the Germans now.

It was a tragic error – tragic because the records show that the original raider, U-boat 269, was by this time well away from the scene. Instead, the battle of the Kwinte Buoy had become an all-British battle, the *Lydd*, vengeance-bent, joining fire with the stricken *Grafton* to wipe out *Comfort*, the unarmed drifter that had saved Commander Fisher.

And Fisher, though he sensed what was afoot, could do nothing to halt the slaughter. Afterwards he thought that the first explosion as the torpedoes struck *Grafton* must have washed Skipper Mair and his men from the foredeck – for within seconds *Comfort*, like a latter-day *Marie Celeste*, was drifting helplessly away from *Grafton*. Still clinging to a rope-fall, Fisher found himself being towed willy-nilly through the water. Over and over he yelled to be hauled aboard. But no answer came.

Fisher made a prompt decision: the tide was bearing *Comfort* south-west, too close to the Belgian coast to be healthy now. Abruptly, releasing the rope-fall, he kept swimming, watching *Comfort* veer slowly away.

Then, as the commander watched, a strange thing happened – strange because he still believed there was no helmsman aboard. From somewhere ahead firing broke out; as suddenly the drifter's engine cut out. Silently, on the dead calm sea, she came gliding back towards Fisher.

At first Fisher was jubilant. The drifter, he knew, wouldn't sink – and if she came within reach there were rope-falls trailing in plenty. Now, seeing her thirty yards distant, he made up his mind. He would swim to her, board her and get her engine going. He had actually reached her starboard bow and was grappling for a rope-fall when a dark rushing shape loomed monstrously overhead.

For the *Wakeful* survivors still aboard *Comfort* it was worse: they didn't even know their new-found ship now lacked a crew. Below decks Able Seaman Geoffrey Kester and the others were just drifting off to sleep when all of them were hurtled from their bunks into a torrent of swirling water.

Naked – for their clothes were still drying in the galley – they wormed frantically through a hatchway to the upper deck. At once a red-hot fusillade of machine-gun bullets sliced into them. *Lydd* was closing in.

It was the purest luck anyone survived: without warning, *Comfort* slewed round, broadside on to the vengeful *Lydd*. Able Seaman Geoffrey Kester and Sub-Lieutenant Percival-Jones only made it by belly-flopping behind the galley – both badly peppered with flying shrapnel.

As *Lydd* closed in, the pure horror of it struck home to Kester and the others. Their attacker was going to ram. At once they went across the deck in a flying dive, back into the icy water.

In *Lydd*, Able Seaman Samuel Sinclair, glimpsing the leaping figures, sang out, 'Stand by to repel boarders.' As Lieut.-Commander Haig's crew doubled to the rails, rifle-fire whined and cracked – so loudly that Fisher's frantic cry – 'For Christ's sake stop – we're all British' – went unheard. On the bridge, Britten kept the machine-gun going until the barrel was almost red-hot, emptying belt after belt at the leaping men, bullets raining on the water. Then, with a breath-taking, spine-jarring crash, *Lydd* tore clean into the drifter.

Fisher, his eardrums almost ruptured by the crack of splintering wood, sensed rather than saw *Comfort* heel over on top of him. Instinctively he dived like a shark – fighting to the surface yards away, gasping and spluttering.

It was only now that *Lydd*'s crew, swarming aboard the broken vessel to take 'prisoners', found only two survivors – and for the first time Lieut.-Commander Haig realised the enormity of what had happened.

Still convinced that a German raider had singled them out, Kester, Midshipman Patterson and Jackie Chivers clung shivering to *Comfort*'s drifting mast until a whaler from *Grafton* came to pick them up. But Sub-Lieutenant Percival-Jones wasn't seen again.

Help wasn't long in coming – though Fisher, swimming steadily for hours with only the tide-tossed dead for company, was almost gone with fatigue when the Norwegian tramp *Hird* took him aboard. Towards dawn the railway steamer *Malines* and the destroyer *Ivanhoe* closed in to take off the bulk of *Grafton*'s survivors. By now *Grafton* was listing heavily, the sea lapping greedily over her after-end. From a range of 500 yards *Ivanhoe* put three shells into her. Within minutes she sank.

Two destroyers and a drifter were gone within hours – and the Germans had hardly started.

Back at Dunkirk, nobody had an inkling as to how serious things were: at long last the Navy felt they had the measure of things. To Commander Colin Maud and the officers of *Icarus*, this Wednesday dawned as a perfect summer day, with the mist just clearing from the land – the kind of day to set a man thinking on river picnics and strawberries and cream. Only the inky pall of the burning oil-tanks wreathing far over the promenade, beyond the great sanatorium at Braye-les-Dunes to the beaches at La Panne, marred the silent beauty of the morning.

In the first milky light the beaches, at first, weren't visible. Sub-Lieutenant Edmund Croswell, aboard H.M.S. *Harvester*, couldn't even imagine why he'd been asked to take the ship's motor-boat in. But wading ashore at La Panne he did bump into a dapper brigadier with a party of troops.

'How many of you are there?' Croswell asked.

The brigadier was positive. 'Sixty-eight.'

Now turning to his signalman, Croswell made to *Harvester* what he later described as 'the most fatuous signal of the war'. 'There are sixty-eight survivors. About to evacuate them.'

In every ship it was the same. Most newcomers had been summoned so speedily from far-off places that the life-and-death signals routed to early birds like *Wakeful* never reached them. Even Captain Eric Bush, who had urged the need for small boats on Ramsay, had no clue as to the gravity of the situation.

Back off La Panne, on the bridge of the minesweeper *Hebe*, Bush was sipping cocoa as he asked Lieut.-Commander John Temple: 'What do you make of the dark shadows on the beach over there?'

Temple peered; with the dawn mist slow to clear, objects took shape only gradually, like printing a photograph. He shook his head. 'I can't think, sir, unless it's shadows thrown by clouds.'

'Impossible,' Bush answered. 'The sky's clear.'

But now as the mists parted every ship could see: on the bridge of *Icarus* men held their breath, sick at the magnitude of the task ahead. In huge dense squads they blocked the beach; queues of them wound like long black serpents from the sandhills; from Dunkirk nine miles east, to La Panne, piers seemed to jut every few yards a long way into the sea – human piers, the front ranks up to their necks in chill grey water, waiting patiently for boats.

In an instant, as the appalling truth dawned, Captain Bush summed it up for all of them: 'Soldiers – yes, by God it is . . . ten thousand of them!'

They came back across the bridges to Dunkirk, the beaten bloody men whose minds were not defeated. They bore noble names, as stirring as war cries – the Chasseurs d'Afrique, the Die Hards, the Grey Breeks, the Foreign Legion – and the tradition of bitter battles moved in their veins – Mons and Talavera, Malplaquet and Waterloo. No medals were struck for them, for this was an hour of shame, yet, by paradox, the conflict would figure in a score of regimental honours as amongst the bloodiest ever. This one they'd call 'Dunkirk'.

They came in ingenious ways . . . Private Haydn Mathias and his mates slumped awkwardly astride dairy cattle . . . Sergeant Bob Copeman, a Norfolk countryman, perched on a white hunter twenty hands high . . . Tom Blackledge and other Lancashire Fusiliers, in a lorry whose radiator ran dry. Without more ado, Blackledge and his mates solemnly dismounted, passed a watering can to relieve the needs of nature, gained power for a few extra miles.

And still they came, the strangest retreat a modern army ever undertook . . . on scooters and children's fairy-cycles . . . Trooper Paddy Kennedy and his pals in a Brussels dustcart . . . Bombardier 'Darky' Lowe in a tractor towing a Bofors gun . . . Lance-Corporal Syd Garner in a truck so festooned with men he could barely see the windshield for dangling feet.

Despatch Rider Bill Challen and his buddy, Peter Nicholls, journeyed in their officers' Ford Eight – Nicholls garbed in a captain's greatcoat, waving footsore Tommies aside with a lordly 'Stand back there, men.' But few officers travelled as cushily. Captain Jack Churchill of the Manchesters, a keen toxophilite, came on a bicycle, the bow and arrow with which he'd sworn to bag a German astride his handlebars. Lieutenant Stanley Pritchard-Barrett, of the Pioneer Corps, went on foot, leading a scant fifty men, ending like a khaki-clad Pied Piper with 250.

Captain Edward Bloom, with Hugo, the sledge dog by his side, marched as often as he rode in his staff car – even in full service dress and greatcoat on one of the year's hottest days. In anguish with the bones of his right little toe broken by blast, Bloom still didn't think it fair to his men to ride too often – and he had forgotten his need for a wash in caring for Hugo.

Often it went against the grain – but walking was in fashion. Private Mervyn Doncom of the Hampshires foot-slogged every mile, though the kitbagful of watches was tugging now. Private Walter Osborn of the Suffolks made it the same way – though still he urged his escort, Sergeant Frank Peacock: 'Straight up, Serge – why don't we stand and fight?' Osborn now had the fierce urge to become a fighting man again, to forget the stigma of close arrest and that letter to Winston Churchill.

The humour wasn't lacking – yet it was a tragic cavalcade. Not since Corunna, more than a hundred years back, had a British

Army fallen back like this – leaving ruin behind it, shocked and in defeat. At dusk, fevered with mosquito bites and nettle rash, they slumped thankfully on to the dry straw of barns or into ditches lined with boughs, too weary to hear the shrill-sweet song of nightingales. At dawn they waited eagerly, the steam rising from farmyard middens, for a more welcome note: the cackle of hens about to lay.

They were always hungry – so hungry that Driver Percy Case, of the Service Corps, retreating from Bailleul, remembers the 29th as the day he washed down mouthfuls of cattle cake with gulps of stagnant ditch water: that day he entered upon the nineteenth year of his married life. They were always tired – so tired that Private Ronald le Dube of the Loyals, plodding from Hondschoote to Dunkirk, kept awake only through the rifle of the man behind prodding him in the kidneys.

By day muffled explosions marked their progress and tall columns of pinkish dust spiralled to meet blue sky: behind them the sappers were blowing the bridges. In darkness they wound their way down a pergola of fire, so eerie that Brigadier George Sutton, a First World War veteran, was puzzled once by scores of seething orange Catherine-wheels on the horizon: the tyres of abandoned trucks, flaming in the night.

Often, until forced back to old skills, they were all at sea. In Driver Harry Owen's unit the canned milk ran out and they drank milkless tea for two whole days before one pioneer caught on: those abandoned cows with swollen udders were there for a purpose. Often they were in pain: their feet misshapen with huge blisters, they marched with their insteps bound in sacking or with the blood seeping through the soles of their boots.

Some knew such bewilderment that they trebled their own sufferings. Private Ernest Taylor of the 6th Green Howards marched for days lugging the unit's anti-tank rifle because another man had the ammo; it wasn't until he hit Dunkirk he found the man had long since junked it. Driver Oliver Clifford, a Service Corps man, walked miles with his feet in agony: it took a medical officer in England to break the news his boots were on the wrong feet.

Always the refugees blocked their way on the white dust-clouded roads, smelling of wool and poverty and garlic, and always they were harassed from the air . . . by the chilling eldritch scream of von Richtofen's Stukas . . . by the urgent crackle of machine-gun bullets . . . by the terrified screams of '*Allemandes*' as women and little children raced for cover – to Sapper George Brooks it was 'like a knife sweeping crumbs from a board'. They were harassed by leaflets, too: leaflets which said 'You have no R.A.F.', leaflets which said 'Your generals have gone home.'

Always the planes were moving towards Dunkirk: as Driver Bill Challen watched, a man went insane counting, as if on an abacus, ninety-seven planes.

Despite themselves they absorbed shameful skills that the years cannot blot out – for a man had to eat. Gunner Hugh Fisher recalls: 'God help me, I learned to pick dead men's pockets – but someone had always been there first.'

Most travelled as hard a road. Somehow, by sheer dint of tongue-lashing and taunting, Sergeant Sidney Tindle contrived to bring fourteen out of his twenty-four charges through to the beaches. Now, seeing their helpless apathy, a sudden anger seized the little Irishman; he ground out, 'I could shake the lot of you,' swinging away in disgust. Yet mingled with the bitterness, he knew, was the faintly pleasurable sense of his own superiority.

If it hadn't been for him, not one of these green kids would ever have made the coast. It was he who'd taught the survivors to duck beneath a topcoat when they lit a cigarette by night . . . to sleep in a circle, rifles at the ready, in case a fighter swooped low. Despite his refusal to feed them, it was he who found chickens in a backyard, plucked and cleaned them, building a fire in an old petrol tin.

And it was Tindle who had forced them to bury the warm pathetic corpses of nuns and little children caught in a machine-gun ambush. They had wept as they dug the grave – but Tindle, close to tears himself, had snarled, 'Get on with it now – tears won't win this war.'

But the little sergeant had the desperate urge to be done with his responsibility; even twenty years' peacetime soldiering hadn't equipped him for this. He wondered just how much farther the old soldier's veneer would carry him.

Some men had doubts as grave. For minutes after that first slashing burst of machine-gun fire had sent him slumping for the ditch near Comines, John 'Warrior' Linton was convinced he would fall prisoner to the Germans after all. Only the cheering voice of Lance-Corporal Norton across the road had spurred him to fresh efforts.

But the German machine-gunner had the road covered. What hope was there now of ever reaching the first-aid post at the farm across the way?

Four yards away from one another, the two men held a hoarse consultation. As Norton saw it, the one hope was the drain channelling the flood-water from the drive by the first-aid post to the ditch where Linton lay.

Norton confessed: 'But I don't know how wide the drain is – it's all bricks up my end.' Norton was on sentry-go, guarding the drive that led up to the farm: he could not leave his post to check.

Painfully, legs trailing behind him, Linton summoned strength to crawl the few remaining yards to the drain's entrance. Now his heart sank. A long way off, as through the wrong end of a telescope, he could see the green doors giving access to the farm. But the drain seemed too narrow to admit a man's arm, let alone his body.

But as he lay there, hurt, exhausted and left to fight his own battle, something of the old fire glowed in Linton's blood. He could die in the drain, trying to escape; he could lie there until the Germans came to finish him off. Was it for nothing they'd called him 'Warrior' at school . . . that first newsboy's job . . . the factory job in Birmingham, when sixteen-year-old Linton had backed the others against a sourpuss foreman and been fired for his pains . . . his decision to join the Army at seventeen, again to help the family budget.

All his life he'd struggled not to be a burden, nor yet to be left behind. Now he was fighting again not to be left behind.

Slowly, sucking down precious air, he inched his way into the tunnel. Belly-deep in slime, he lunged forward, eyes shut, fingertips pushing and scrabbling ahead. Then he opened his eyes and a terrible fear surged through him. He could see nothing, and the vile air seemed to engulf him in a spinning, stinking multicoloured vortex. Pain stabbed from his broken nails now and his fingertips were torn and bleeding.

He thought he would die there in the tunnel, sinking deeper until the black slime crept into his mouth and nostrils and choked him to death.

Then a foolish and blessed relief flooded through him for his bloody fingertips, probing forward, had met the outstretched fingers of Lance-Corporal Norton, and now Norton was helping him to work away bricks and plaster, his hands clamping tightly round Linton's wrists.

With one mighty heave, Linton came out of the drain like a cork torn from a bottle-mouth, bathed in evil-smelling slime, hands red-raw, legs crooked at a strange unwieldy angle behind him.

'Thanks, mate,' he managed to gasp but he had no breath to say more.

Now it seemed there was still a chance. He was near enough to the farm's green doors to hear voices from behind them. Slowly he began to scrabble his way along the cobbled approach; a medical orderly pelted to help but the Germans were too close. The farm was battalion headquarters as well as first-aid post and the Germans were seeking the range; as Linton struggled upright, red-hot mortar fragments were whirling past him at shoulder height.

'You're stopping me, mate,' Linton croaked to the orderly. 'I could get along better meself.' He had almost made the last few yards on his own steam when Lieutenant 'Leech' McCallum, the young fresh-faced medico, ran out to grab him by the wrists. Tugging, a deadweight on McCallum's epaulettes, Linton got there finally.

Then hours seemed to pass while he and three or four others lay in the barn on straw-scattered cobbles sipping gratefully at warm milk, while McCallum took three long flat wooden splints, padding them with bandages so that they would not chafe . . . a splint on each leg from calf to ankle . . . a shorter splint in between the legs . . . all three tightly lashed with webbing straps.

Linton realised now that he could no longer move at all without help and, though he pinned his faith in McCallum, who was young and strong and mixed easily with the men, a small ember of watchfulness glowed inside him.

Whatever he did he mustn't sleep – he must stay awake if need be to help himself when the time came. McCallum's offer of a morphia injection was firmly refused. McCallum said, not unkindly, 'You're pretty badly hurt, you know – do you want to take a chance?'

Linton agreed. If there was a chance of escape he would take it. He even agreed to suck on the morphia tablets McCallum gave him, explaining they would deaden incipient pain.

Now calling for a volunteer from headquarters to drive his 15-cwt. truck, McCallum explained his plan. The Germans were now 100 yards away. The truck was to take the few wounded that had got this far to the nearest casualty clearing station. There was just one hazard: it would have to drive clean through the German lines.

He stressed to the driver: 'The Boche are covering the road on both sides. Your only chance is to get out so fast they don't know what's happening.' The best plan, McCallum thought, was to rev up the engines well before the farm gates were ever opened.

They had to work fast now. First the back of the 15-cwt. truck had to be padded with blankets . . . Linton to be lifted in . . . Private Hawkins, who had a wounded arm, to sit beside him and support him in case he got thrown out at the bends. An officer from the carrier platoon with a stomach wound was huddled beside the driver.

The stretcher-bearers took up positions by the green double doors. 'You lucky so-and-so,' one ribbed him. 'Going back to England.' More formally McCallum added: 'Goodbye, Linton. Have a pleasant sea-voyage.' The truck's engine was roaring now. McCallum shouted: 'Are you ready? Right!'

The green farm doors smashed open. The stretcher-bearers leapt back. At once, as the driver changed up, the truck screamed forward like a bullet, bouncing Linton almost clear of the floor. As they hurtled down the cobbled approach, Linton thought for one sickening moment that the truck would overturn within sight of safety, but the driver wrenched the wheel over, hanging on somehow, and they were through. The Germans closing in on either side of the road couldn't open fire without hitting one another.

In England it was like a gradual coming-of-age. Everywhere men and women made ready to shoulder new burdens, though few as yet had any concept of what those might be.

At Gravesend, on London River, Ambulance Officer Charles Jackson and ten care-free volunteers heard an emergency job was on in France: there'd be a fast boat to race them over and ample supplies of dressings. Volunteer Arthur Purves settled his book-ie's bill in advance – you never knew – but most were optimistic. As Jackson and the others set off down river, Ambulance Chief Harry Fletcher pressed some pound notes on him: 'Just in case you run short . . . you'll need a drink over there when you're finished.'

Some literally talked themselves into trouble. At Portsmouth, the crew of the motor-vessel *Bee*, a 70-tonner of the Pickford Line, had word that the Navy were taking them over, but Engineer Fred Reynard, a chirply little sparrow of a man, thought differently. He quibbled so long with a naval sentry on the dockside that a voice rasped down the intercom: 'What is all that argument going on?' Minutes later Reynard was bustled before Admiral Sir William 'Bubbles' James, Commander-in-Chief, Portsmouth.

The admiral explained curtly that naval officers were comman-deering the boat for a hair-trigger mission, but Fred was obstinate. 'Beg pardon, sir, what do your young gentlemen know about Swedish engines? I've been looking after them since 1912.'

Still the admiral was dubious: 'We've no guarantee you'll get back – though we've no guarantee you won't. Ever been under shellfire?' A First World War soldier, Fred had the answer to that one: 'Ever heard of Gallipoli?'

James hadn't become an admiral without knowing when to sur-render: 'All right, I'll give you a naval officer to look after the navigation – but how about your crew?' Simply, Reynard replied: 'They go where I go'; already, returning to the *Bee*, his mind was made up on that point. He explained to Skipper Trowbridge, 'We're off to France.'

Trowbridge, with reason, exploded, 'You're talking daft'; the *Bee's* crew, really a team of removal men, had never sailed wider waters than the four-mile channel of the Solent between Ports-mouth and the Isle of Wight. But Fred wasn't even listening. There were five days' rations to collect, the engines to check over and Sub-Lieutenant Kindall, their navigator, would be aboard in no time at all.

Others heard more dramatically. On London River, within sight of the Tower, Skipper Lemon Webb was at the wheel of the *Tollesbury* wrinkling his eyes against the afternoon sun as the old sailing barge glided up-river at a peaceful four knots. Rust-coloured sails spread to catch the faint breeze, her green-painted ironwork a picturesque contrast to her sky-blue decking, the eighty-foot *Tollesbury* looked as she always did – a peaceful survivor of a more tranquil age.

If Lemon Webb seemed part of the barge the kinship wasn't fortuitous. Aged sixty-two, a soft-spoken, pink-cheeked veteran with twinkling blue eyes and a battered old trilby hat perched on his head, Webb had been one with the river all his life, mate of his father's barge, the *Why Not?*, at the age of twelve, a skipper himself by the time he'd turned twenty-one.

Sometimes, the *Tollesbury*, a 140-ton grain barge owned by R. and W. Paul of Ipswich, had set sail as far as Antwerp, but mostly Webb's life, for fifty years, had been as ordered as the Thames tides: Ipswich to Cory's Jetty, Erith, discharging cargoes of grain and maize, standing by for fresh orders, back again to Ipswich and the little cottage above the Orwell River, its garden a multi-coloured riot of the roses and sweet peas that Webb loved.

Suddenly, to the old skipper's astonishment, a naval launch cut a peremptory swath towards them down the shining river. The orders, bellowed through a megaphone, were peremptory too: 'You will proceed to Cory's Jetty, Erith, and not go past at your peril.'

A wave of the hand in assent, then Webb exchanged a puzzled word with mate Edward Gunn and Percy Scott, the nineteen-year-old deck-hand. But in a moment he had shrugged it off. He thought that uniforms made people *feel* more dramatic – it probably wasn't too much.

At the Erith jetty Webb learned differently. Along with other barges that Webb well knew – Skipper Harold Miller's *Royalty*, the *Doris*, skippered by his brother-in-law, Fred Finbow, *Barbara Jean*, his nephew Charlie's craft, the *Ena* and eight others – the *Tollesbury* was to tie up. Soon a tug would tow them all to Tilbury Dock Basin for further orders. Meantime, no one must leave the dock gates.

It was a picture to have stirred a painter to action – the barges with their russet-red canvas, sprit-sails soaring to the sky, the old men in their patched roll-top jerseys trading excited speculations on the quay, the sun dazzling on the oily water.

All except Lemon Webb – for he was not speculating. Two days earlier he had seen motor launches towing long strings of yachts and cutters down-river and guessed their destination. Now, in the space of minutes, he was resigned to what might be their ultimate fate. In defiance of orders, he walked calmly through the dock gates to the nearest post office and penned a postcard to his wife Mabel, at 133 Cliff Lane, Ipswich.

His message could hardly have been briefer: 'Commandeered. Rather afraid Dunkirk. Love. Lemon.'

Skipper Lemon Webb was speaking metaphorically but there were reasons to be fearful. In the German camp, at that precise moment, it seemed Dunkirk was doomed.

On the Army's side the high-level polemics had endured for three days now, with the top brass at daggers drawn. From Charleville, Oberst Günther Blumentritt, von Rundstedt's chief operations officer, sent a home thrust to von Kluge's Fourth Army. They seemed to be making no headway at all – at Wormhoudt and Cassel and Hazebrouck the British had fought too stubbornly. At once Kluge's Chief of Staff, Oberst Anton Brennecke, flew to their defence. How could you blame the tanks when they were halted one day, urged on the next – and now all this talk of a southern offensive to take their minds off the job? The Führer should postpone 'Plan Red' – and speed on to Dunkirk, whatever the cost.

From his Fourth Army headquarters, Château Bonne Etable, Béthune, Brennecke groused: 'Like the French say, order, counter-order, disorder – and that's what we've got now.'

For all that Brennecke still had acid truths for the Kleist Panzer Group's Chief of Staff, Oberst Kurt Zeitzler: 'There's an impression that nothing is happening to-day, that no one's any longer interested in Dunkirk.' And Brennecke laid it further on the line: the town and harbour must be bombarded, embarkation stalled, panic caused.

Now it was Zeitzler's turn to make excuses. They'd been forbidden to use tanks close in to the coast . . . if Kleist's Group attacked now they would want Sixth Army's help but the pampered infantry had been pulled out for a rest. Finally General von Kluge himself took over from Brennecke, ordering Kleist: 'All forces to the coast east of Dunkirk immediately . . . reach the coast without fail to-day.'

Then with a final as-you-were, the Army High Command cut in. From 2 a.m. on Friday, 31st May, the Eighteenth Army of von Bock's Army Group, six infantry divisions, plus motorised support, were to take over the Dunkirk Line. Von Rundstedt and Hitler had triumphed after all: the bulk of the tanks were to move south.

At Munstereifel, Generaloberst Franz Halder, hearing the news, made one last sterile appeal. He urged Commander-in-Chief von Brauchitsch: 'Every tank we lose and win one day is worth more than if we preserve every tank we've got and lose fourteen.'

But von Brauchitsch, characteristically, had turned his coat; he wanted no more humiliating showdowns with the Führer. He cajoled Halder: together with Hitler he'd been working out some useful hints for von Bock's infantry. Maybe they could land infantry units from the sea, in back of the British – or step up the chaos by firing ack-ack shells with time-fuses into the dunes.

Halder listened in stony silence; they'd pay steeply for this vacillation, he knew.

No such doubts, though, assailed the Baron von Richtofen. All morning in his St Pol headquarters, he had smarted under a constant stream of criticism from Goering – why weren't his 8th Flying Corps attacking Dunkirk as they should? But Richtofen, no man to spare men or planes – was adamant – cloud ceiling was down to 100 yards, they wouldn't stand a chance. Disgruntled, he scribbled a note in his diary: 'The Luftwaffe's supreme commander has the jitters over Dunkirk.'

Then, at 2 p.m. came the message for which he'd yearned: observation planes reported the Channel skies clearing fast. Nothing now stood between Dunkirk and von Richtofen's 180 Stuka dive-bombers.

The word passed swiftly. In a converted banana truck, on Beaulieu airfield hard by, Major Oscar Dinort, commanding No. 2 Stuka Wing, uncradled his field telephone, listened calmly as Chief of Staff Seidemann announced: 'Clear all decks for Dunkirk.' At once Dinort rang his three group commanders: 'Report to my truck for briefing.'

Both the calm and the setting were typical. While other officers lived out in billets, Dinort, a thoughtful hawk-faced man of thirty-nine, rarely strayed far from the job: the truck with a trailer hook-up had served as working and living quarters for three weeks now. A devout Catholic who neither smoked nor drank, Dinort was the first Stuka pilot to win the Luftwaffe's most coveted award – the Oak Leaf to the Knight's Cross.

As his commanders clambered into the wagon, Dinort looked them over affectionately . . . Hauptmann Hubertus Hitschold, his Skye terrier as always cradled in his arms . . . quiet, dependable Hauptmann Lothar . . . they'd been with Dinort so long now he styled them 'the old ducks', men he'd still take along when the weather was too murky to risk a neophyte's life.

Hunched over the briefing table in swift conference, Dinort barely glanced at the map. In a few weeks they'd come to know the Channel coast well enough. They'd shared the destruction of the port just as they'd shared a year's fiery baptism in the pre-war Stuka school at Graz . . . plant your bomb in a circle 150 feet in diameter or flunk out . . . practice dive after dive against live ack-ack . . . pit all your bodily strength against a room de-pressurised then flooded full of air.

In their time they'd seen dozens opt for a transfer after pulling out from their first dive at the regulation 2,000 feet: the men with weak stomachs, who crawled vomiting from the cockpit, the men with weaker nerves, whose bowels and bladders failed as one.

Methodically, Dinort flicked over points. Take-off at 4.45 p.m., as an element of the second wave. They'd reach Dunkirk around 5 p.m., which still left time for group commanders to brief their squadrons. Target, shipping – and the bigger the ship the greater the prize.

Without malice, Dinort warned: 'They say there are a lot of small craft around – leave them. We're after the big fish, carrying the most troops.' Then, shrugging, he amplified, 'We're not fighting a war in pigskin gloves.'

As a Catholic whose beliefs were a sore point with the Luftwaffe's top brass, Dinort's conscience had fought a long and silent battle over just this point: how did you reconcile religious convictions with total air war? On the point of resignation when even Luftwaffe chaplains couldn't help, he'd resolved his doubts finally through a precept of Luther's: a man must obey superior orders unless he finds them contrary to Biblical precepts – and that he can rarely judge.

And since Dinort had come to terms with fear and doubt, his

group commanders gave him an allegiance they'd accord few others. The man had the courage of a lion – yet hadn't he, time and again, tangled with von Richtofen on behalf of his crews if a mission seemed plain suicide.

More technicalities now. Height, as almost always, 18,000 feet – diving height to be settled over the target. Cruising speed 175 m.p.h. Of the Stuka's five bombs, the heaviest, the 250 kilo, was to be dropped first, on the choicest target. The four 70-kilo bombs to be loosed on the second run-in.

The rendezvous with their escort, General Osterkamp's 1st Fighter Wing, would be west of Dunkirk, hard by Mardyck.

Now Dinort checked: 'How about your crews? Any trouble there?' Though all three shook their heads he warned: 'Well, watch them. You know what I mean.'

No one needed telling. Each time a Stuka pilot dived he died a little, and every day the strain was stepping up. Pilots could go crazy, ramming their machines at the earth in a death-dive to end them all. Gunners might bale out without warning. Cravens might break from formation, heading ignominiously for home base.

As the meeting broke up, Dinort gave them his eternal pre-flight benediction: 'Dead soldiers don't fight, so sell your lives dearly – and remember, no hair falls from the head without God's will.'

Automatically, he checked his watch – forty minutes before he need change, so time for neglected paperwork. Settling at his desk, he knew no fear: he held a profound belief that God would protect him from British fighters and flak.

Briefly the thought crossed his mind: today is quite a landmark. We never tackled a shipping target until now.

At Dunkirk Captain William Tennant's staff had problems and to spare. Only 17,800 men had been lifted in the past twenty-four hours – a bare 25,400 since Tennant and his party arrived.

Already Tennant had seen welcome changes – but still the tempo was desperately slow. At the Eastern Mole a fifteen-foot rise and fall of tide made it doubly hard for troops to board ships at top-speed. That had meant dreaming up new devices ... the destroyer *Icarus* using water-polo goalposts for gangplanks ... the hospital ship *St David* rigging the boards used for painting the funnel.

And few ships could even gauge their own capacity. The destroyer *Winchelsea*'s First-Lieutenant, R. C. Watkin, jumping ashore, told piermaster Jack Clouston, 'We can take four hundred,' but Clouston was scathing. 'Come back and tell me when you've got a thousand.' To Watkin's undying astonishment the Tommies did squeeze in somehow.

And today, thanks to the surf on the beach, it hadn't been possible for Tennant's men to get the ships away with full loads before daylight. All morning Commander Hector Richardson had been sending troops to the Mole at the rate of 1,000 per quarter hour.

At Dover, Tennant knew, Ramsay was doing his utmost: every available destroyer the Admiralty could muster was slated for Dunkirk by now. In the night just past, over seventy ships had been ranging the nine-mile stretch of beach from Dunkirk to La Panne – destroyers, minesweepers, schuits – though small boats were still desperately lacking for inshore ferry work.

Faced with tragedies like the *Queen of the Channel* – the first ship to berth at the Eastern Mole, sunk soon after with 950 troops aboard – Ramsay had at first decided that lightly-armed ships like the cross-Channel ferry *Canterbury* must operate only after dark. But now time was of the essence: the risk must be taken.

This afternoon eleven ships lay at the Eastern Mole's seaward end, with the French destroyers *Mistral*, *Siroco* and *Cyclone* berthed inside the harbour: evacuation of French troops had begun this very day. The inshore waters, slicked with oil, dotted with jetsam and the bloated bodies of dead men, swarmed with craft — destroyers, ferry boats, tankers.

Close to 4 p.m., just as the old Western Isles steamship *Loch Garry* was clearing the harbour, the skies to the west seemed to darken. On the beaches men had a grandstand view. Private Arthur Yendall of the King's Own Royal Regiment thought of a pond in springtime swarming so thickly with tadpoles you couldn't even see the water.

Farther towards Dunkirk the sky grew darker still and all men held their breath: within minutes the bombers of von Richtofen's first wave had swelled into an inky cloud, sliding between the sea and the sun. As they fell with the light behind them, Sub-Lieutenant John Crosby, in *Oriole*, thought of 'black wasps diving from the sun'.

Lower and lower they came — so low that Private Charles Ginniver, up in the sand-dunes at Braye, saw one Stuka poise above a ship like a raised arm, raining its bombs clean down the funnel. Within seconds the Stuka, swerving from the mushroom of flame and smoke, had dipped lower still, the Channel water rippling on its wings in the sunlight. The aerobatics so moved Ginnever he forgot where he was: aloud he applauded. 'Oh, I hand it to you, Jerry — you're the best, the cream.'

Aboard the coaster *Bullfinch* Gunner Jack Saunders saw another plane snarl so close to the masthead the pilot's face was clearly visible — 'It was like a mask.' The screaming of von Richtofen's toy whistles chilled the blood: to Leading Seaman Charles Chaplin, aboard *Winchelsea*, the Stukas seemed 'to make a hole in the sky'.

In *Codrington*'s engine-room Stoker Arthur Rozier summed up the Dunkirk approach for all of them: 'Into Hell and out again . . .'

Now, in a long tilting plummeting dive the Stukas fanned out — over the harbour . . . over the nine miles of grey-blue water between Dunkirk and La Panne. At once all sound fused into an

ear-splitting crescendo . . . the pounding roar of the destroyers'
4.7 guns . . . the metallic panging of a Bofors . . . the scream of
bombs . . . the hammering of the 'Chicago pianos', multiple Vick-
ers guns firing 2,000 half-inch bullets a minute. Aboard *Mistral*
Lieutenant de Vaisseau Guillanton couldn't even make himself
heard; from now on every order had to be passed by messengers.

It was worst for the ships on the Eastern Mole; tight-packed
like pleasure steamers at a jetty, they didn't stand a chance.
Aboard the old fishing trawler *Brock*, First Mate Herbert Bidle
held his breath: nearby bombs had landed close to the trawler
Polly Johnson, wiping out the entire gun crew as they polished
their guns prior to a first blast at the enemy . . . whirling First
Mate Jermyn Greengrass from his own deck on to *Brock*'s
bridge . . . ripping away one side of his uniform . . . skinning his
body like a chunk of raw steak. As sailors and doctors ran to help,
Bidle, bending with a cigarette, essayed a note of comfort: 'Cheer
up, boy, we aren't dead yet.'

It was true, but there was still time. In the trawler *Calvi*, as a
bomb howled down the ventilation shaft, Skipper Bertie Spindler
was hurled across the bridge, the *Calvi*'s stem knifing sheer up
Brock's stern. But Spindler kept not only his balance but his head,
firing a piece of oily waste to burn the secret chart used for mine-
sweeping. Within minutes *Calvi* was sinking, Spindler and his
crew clambering aboard the *John Cattling* which lay hard by. Still
above the water, her masts and funnel protruding, *Calvi*'s white
ensign of battle streamed, a last gesture of defiance.

The Army was defiant too; aboard *Canterbury*, Captain Bernard
Lockey, the O.C. Troops, watched them keep coming, doubling in
tight-packed three-abreast ranks along the Eastern Mole. Helpless he saw man after man blow to smithereens. Even those who
got aboard made it narrowly; the bomb that burst behind Brigadier George Sutton sounded the death knell of the man behind
him. Scrambling into *Canterbury*'s saloon, Sutton knew the next

bomb was as close: a fine whirlwind of stone-dust seethed through the blasted porthole.

The destroyers carried a heavier armament than the trawlers – 4.7-inch guns against the trawler's single-shot 3-inch, but today nothing was immune. In *Brock*, First Mate Bidle, having seen his friend Greengrass transferred to the destroyer *Grenade*, was still glued to the bridge-rail when the Stukas came screaming for *Grenade*, three bombs plunging home, one going plumb down her funnel.

Within seconds the destroyer's decks were a nightmare sight . . . sailors floundering in a slippery film of blood and oil . . . a youngster trapped in the forepeak screaming for his mother . . . a soldier shouting, as he dived for the water, 'If this is your job, you can keep it.' At that moment, to Bidle's horror, the *Grenade* swung round, blazing like a pine-brand from stem to stern, jamming clean into *Brock*.

Again the presence of Tennant's party saved the day. Calmly, shouting to make himself heard above the din, Commander Jack Clouston briefed a trawler to take the destroyer in tow. For now *Grenade*'s mooring lines had parted and slowly, with the terrible majesty of a Viking funeral, she swung into the fairway out of control. For seconds only one thing seemed certain: the destroyer would sink, blocking the fairway in the very entrance to the harbour, and bring the whole evacuation to a standstill.

The trawler made it but only just. Next instant, *Grenade*'s magazine had ignited and with a violence few men have witnessed, 1,000 rounds of ammunition went sky-high. Hugging the quayside, Lieutenant Robert Bill, R.N., caught a glimpse of her weed-grown bottom and thought incongruously: *She* hadn't been in harbour recently.

Ten miles up the coast at La Panne, Lieut.-General Alan Brooke saw it, too, and held his breath – 'a colossal column of smoke like an atom bomb, then nothing but floating debris'.

But *Grenade* was still afloat; to the crew of the armed boarding vessel *King Orry*, steaming in later, it seemed her plates were ablaze even below the water-line. Seconds later it was the *King Orry*'s turn; a bomb, smashing through her stern, tore away her rudder and she drifted helplessly, heeling over. Then, with the inhuman screech of steel against stone, the rubbing strake on her port bow tore a yawning chasm in the Eastern Mole.

The long breakwater on which Tennant had pinned all his hopes was out of action. All contact between the landward and the berthing ends was cut off.

To the *Orry*'s Lieutenant Jonathan Lee it was an appalling sight . . . the harbour littered with blazing wrecks . . . the water lapping nearer and nearer the bridge, as the ship heeled feebly to starboard . . . a steward, his mind broken by bombing sweeping slivers of glass over and over from the wardroom floor. As water engulfed the bridge, Lee dived from the stern. Wreckage tangled the whistle lanyard and the whistle moaned pitifully like something dying as the *King Orry* sank from sight.

And other ships were catching it as badly: aboard H.M.S. *Jaguar* just under way, a sailor had handed Signalman William Brown a hunk of bread-and-butter, assuring him, 'You'll be in London by five tonight,' when a Stuka swerved at her in a kamikaze beeline . . . killing a score of officers and men who had scrambled in defiance of orders to her open decks. On the bridge Lieut.-Commander 'Beppo' Hine, blood streaming down his face, announced with cold calm hatred, 'The dirty bastards . . . abandon ship.'

It wasn't surprising that fear swept the beaches. Sheltered from the true nature of war by Gort's 'useless mouths' policy, thousands, for the first time, were seeing sights beyond all belief.

Some went entirely to pieces. Private Walter Allington, the big gentle man who sought to help every man as he'd helped that Belgian cripple, was aghast: he could do nothing now for the man who raved in circles, stripped to a loincloth, proclaiming himself Mahatma Gandhi. And at Braye Dunes, Sergeant Sidney Tindle's little band recoiled in horror to see their leader wild-eyed and quivering; the fear and the burden of leadership had proved too much. Overnight his hair was to turn snow-white.

A few were powerless to move. Private George Hill, of the Lincolns, lay flat on his face for more than an hour, not stirring; sand was in his ears and nostrils, a thin gritty film on his lips, but somehow he believed if he lay doggo the Stukas would think him dead and not machine-gun him. Private Charles Fenton lay with his eyes shut, living in a world of abysmal sound where planes burst like monstrous eagles into a closed room. The nightmare has stayed with him, sleeping or waking, for twenty sweating years.

As the sand quaked with the force of the bombing, smothering men whose foxholes were too deep, Driver Ernest Holdsworth saw sergeants hurl away their rifles . . . men roaming distractedly in circles clutching children's Teddy bears . . . officers weeping hysterically. Now an inferno of flame engulfed the harbour, molten metal dripping from the buckled cranes . . . waving an axe atop a truck's bonnet, a sergeant yelled, 'Come down and fight fair, you bloody bastards' . . . through the dunes a man ran wildly, crying like a lost soul, 'Lord have mercy on us, Christ have mercy on us.'

Vast columns of grey-white water geysered a hundred feet high and in the sunlight men were screaming.

It was enough to make the stoutest heart quail. On the beach at La Panne, Lieut.-General Brooke watched in horror as what seemed like the bodies of men flailed into the air amongst fountains of sand. Doubling to the beach in a temporary lull, Brooke breathed a sigh of relief: the soft sand had soaked up the bulk of the blast. The 'bodies' had been discarded greatcoats after all.

Major Oscar Dinort felt relieved too. At 5 p.m. his Stuka, flying at a steady 175 m.p.h., was fast approaching the Channel coast – and thus far the omens were good. In back of him, the first wave of No. 2 Wing, a tight formation of thirty planes, were spaced in rigid battle order, three breadths of the plane apart.

It had all gone smoothly from the start. No sooner had the 'Scramble' sounded than Beaulieu airfield, in a twinkling, looked like a stage-set at curtain-fall – everywhere ground crews were doubling to shift the dummy trees and bales of straw that screened the olive-green ranks of von Richtofen's Stukas. Between ops the airfield was for all the world like any other farm – and Dinort, a camouflage fanatic, flew daily recce flights to check that very point.

Then, too, there'd been the stirring send-off that Hauptmann Ulitz, the adjutant, laid on before each mission. As the pilots in grey-green linen overalls sprinted to their planes, the yellow-and-white flag of the 8th Flying Corps, embroidered with swastikas, was broken above the runway and a guard of honour presented arms. It was a touch of panoply that went to Dinort's heart.

Ahead the wind teased a black lazy plume of smoke across the horizon. Over the intercom Dinort asked his gunner, blond smiling Hauptmann Muller, 'All set?'

'All set, sir.'

To the west, sunlight glinted silver on a weaving body of planes: the Messerschmitts, lining up for escort. Dinort smiled faintly. He knew how their pilots hated working with Stukas: the dive-bombers went too low towards the light flak and the British fighters for comfort. Often he'd rib them: 'Why be scared? The British want to get home – they don't want to die for their country any more than we do.'

The Stuka purred on. Again Dinort switched on the intercom – then the words were stopped in his throat. He could see the other Stukas at work and their hits were registering truly ... the paddle-minesweeper *Gracie Fields*, her steering gear gone, veering in crazy circles at six knots until the *Pangbourne* took off her survivors and she sank . . . the 6,900-ton Glasgow cargo boat *Clan MacAlister*, the largest merchant vessel used at Dunkirk, afire aft in No. 5 hold, her combings burnt out and all her hatches collapsed, abandoned as she burnt . . . *Fenella*, with a bomb splitting her funnel, her engine-room mangled, lumps of concrete from the Mole tearing through her side below the water-line.

Dinort, of course, couldn't know that the British had destroyed their heavy ack-ack two days back, but it looked as if this was going to be a picnic all the way.

By radio telephone, he called up Hauptmann Hubertus Hitschold, first of his group commanders: '*Achtung, achtung*, Eagle to Condor, Eagle to Condor . . . *bitte kommen, bitte kommen* (please come in).'

His earphones buzzed with static, then: 'Condor to Eagle, Condor to Eagle, I am receiving you.'

'Stand by,' Dinort ordered. Split seconds were needed now to make the crucial survey, but as he lost height, orbiting at 10,000 feet, judgement was suspended. The sea, grey and wrinkled like a rhino's hide . . . the flak, white cottony puffs floating upwards from the destroyers' guns . . . planes wheeling and hurtling . . . and the scuttling specks of men on the paler sand, like an ant-hill overthrown. The spectacle held him mesmerised.

With relief he saw, dead ahead, what he judged to be a destroyer – all of 1,300 tons. 'Eagle to Condor, Eagle to Condor,' he called. 'Battleship dead ahead . . . both groups get ready.' He checked with Hauptmann Lothar's group: 'Stand by . . . await further orders.' Then Hitschold's calm voice: 'Condor to Eagle . . . understood . . . over and out.'

Now, as always happened, Dinort was no longer himself; in these moments he became one with the machine. Behind him, he knew, the first three planes of his group were jockeying for position, diagonally in line, wings oscillating gently to signal, diving-brakes on.

Fifteen seconds left. Taut with expectancy, Dinort's right hand shuttled from lever to lever, adjusting the nine cardinal precautions that ensured a pilot's safety . . . diving-brakes out . . . bombs fused . . . reflection sights on . . . tail trimmed for altitude . . . propeller blades in for perfect streamlining . . . acceleration off . . . water and oil-coolers off, too, the dive would do all the cooling that was needed.

Hastily he stuffed cotton-wool plugs beneath his earphones – sometimes the static threatened to burst your head. He swallowed once, convulsively, to ease pressure on the eardrums, contracting the muscles of his throat. He called for the last time: '*Achtung*, Eagle to Condor, Eagle to Condor . . . the battleship ahead of you . . . attack!' Then he pressed forward on the stick.

He felt the Stuka dip like a falcon ready for the stoop; to Gunner Muller, seated behind and facing the tail-plane, the sky seemed to tilt now in a monstrous giddying arc. Glued tight to the stick, Dinort felt pressure clamp his body against the safety harness. Then the Stuka was falling sheer, the others peeling off behind, faster and faster, pitched at 70 degrees, the air-speed indicator quivering like something alive . . . 280 . . . 290 . . . 300 . . . 310 m.p.h. Like avenging furies they streaked for the destroyer, the wind clawing at their wings with a pressure that would have wrinkled the thin aluminium save for those cherished diving-brakes.

Lower still, and faster. With third-dimensional clarity Dinort saw the whole scene now . . . the dove-grey mass of the destroyer, zig-zagging at 30 knots, rushing to meet him . . . white puffs of flak soaring so fast it was like diving into a galaxy of smoke-rings. Instinctively he opened up and the two forward machine-guns blared into life. It couldn't help much but he'd drilled his crews to do the same: enough flak and tracer flying around and the effect was strangely comforting You couldn't identify your own bullets from those which were aimed to harm you.

And suddenly everything was wrong. At 1,800 feet he should have loosed the bomb, but the ship was moving too fast: swerving in, he knew that this was no picnic, that he'd misjudged the angle. What chance did they stand when they'd never practised against shipping? Flak hammering at him, he thumbed the bomb button just in time; he felt the Stuka heave violently as 250 kilos of high explosive sped free. A giant spurt of water went skywards but whether he'd hit the ship he didn't know. At the same moment, from the corner of his eye, he saw another Stuka dash violently against the bosom of the sea. Another man had misjudged – and without hope of redress.

Then his stomach leapt to his throat for it seemed he was next in line; he was too low, agonisingly low, lower than the destroyer's mast level, seeing the toy figures of men scampering absurdly on the iron deck. This is it, he thought, by God, this is it, I'll never pull out now.

Despite the hazards of the raid, the bombers' totals were creeping. By 5 p.m. they had wrought further havoc still ... the Southern Railway ship *Normannia*, bombed and settled on an even keel at Mardyck, six miles to the west ... the *Lorina*, her back broken, sinking lower in shallow water ... the *Waverley*, ripped to pieces by twelve low-weaving Heinkels which rained bombs at her for a solid half-hour.

Yet everywhere the courage was matchless – as if men, faced with unimagined horrors, found relief in calm unflurried routine. Aboard *Jaguar*, the whole boiler-room was a sweating inferno of vapour, so dense that Engineer Officer Cyril Rothwell, hauling a dead man from the hatch, couldn't even get below to investigate. Yet Stoker Petty Officer James Carr saw every man out, then stayed for ten broiling minutes until all steam was shut off. Tied up in the harbour, in the *Angèle-Marie*, Officier des Equipages Auguste Brunet and his men shrugged silently at the racket, then went on unloading shells. One bomb would have blown them to kingdom come but it didn't occur to them to stop.

Aboard the burning *Clan MacAlister*, Chief Officer John Woodall, too, saw no reason for indecent hurry. A third of his crew was dead, scores of soldiers had been killed and wounded – but as the remaining troops scrambled aboard the minesweeper *Pangbourne*, Woodall went to his cabin and changed into his best uniform, fumbling around to locate the cuff-links his wife gave him as a wedding-present, and his old alarm clock.

Ordinary Seaman Stanley Lilley, of H.M.S. *Bideford*'s gun crew, showed the same spirit: as shrapnel punctured his back he felt the warm blood pumping through his serge jacket but he hung on, four-inch guns blazing, at last politely asking the officer of quarters, 'I've been hit, sir. Can I go below for treatment?' As soon as Surgeon-Lieutenant John Jordan had swabbed out the wound with iodine, Lilley volunteered for duty again. He was ecstatic when Jordan refused but it still seemed the thing to do.

Topside the spirit was the same: a bomb had torn away forty feet of *Bideford*'s stern, but as she listed in the water Commander John Lewes, her captain, leaning over the bridge-rail, yelled to Commander Haskett-Smith of *Kellet*: 'There'll be a hell of a row when Vice-Admiral Dover hears about this . . . I'm supposed to take a convoy out tomorrow.' Based on Gibraltar, *Bideford* had no right to be there at all, but Lewes, whiling away four days in Dover, had felt that Dunkirk was the place to be.

And the Army, despite the horrors of the journey to the coast, played up as well. In *Jaguar*, as the first frightened rush of troops surged from below decks, Engineer Officer Cyril Rothwell saw a Guards corporal, midway through shaving, lunge an ominously bulging towel to block their way: 'If anyone tries to get out, I'll shoot.'

The towel cloaked nothing more lethal than a safety razor, but the panic was quieted.

In the coaster *Bullfinch*, a high-hearted Tommy, rendering 'Land of Hope and Glory' on a bugle, whipped it from his lips as a mate panicked past him and knocked him cold – then resumed his paean without missing a note.

It was the same all over. Chef de Peloton Jean Demoy, finding the blind fury of the raid unbearable, suggested taking shelter to a British Ordnance Corps major, but the major, blandly manicuring his nails, refused – he must guard some mortars. Shepherding his fifty men to a cellar, Demoy returned during a lull to find his friend mutilated beyond recognition. Turning to his men he burst out, 'The British are brave and especially this officer – he died with his hands well-groomed but now, look, even his fingernails are blown to pieces.'

Aboard *Waverley*, Driver Albert Thompson marvelled. The old paddle-steamer was out of control and sinking by the stern, yet *Waverley* fought back at the swooping Heinkels with everything she had . . . her one twelve-pounder . . . Lewis-guns . . . the massed rifle-fire of 600 Tommies. Still officers and crew were rock-calm. Captain Patrick Campbell, an army officer, was in the captain's cabin changing into carpet slippers when the ship's surgeon looked in: 'Ah, I need those for the wounded.'

Without protest Campbell passed the slippers over – then, glimpsing the sea through the bulwark, he stuffed the hole with a smouldering mattress before changing into sweater and flannels. All the time the racket was deafening, the ship's hooter blurting 'SOS' in Morse, but Campbell, ascending, queued on deck as calmly as the rest until Lieutenant Sydney Harmer-Elliott signalled 'Abandon ship.'

Within minutes of the last man diving twenty feet from the rails, *Waverley* had gone, wallowing out of sight below the foam-churned water.

One man couldn't even take evasive action. Earlier that day Lieutenant Edwin Lanceley Davies, the florid forthright commander of the paddle-minesweeper *Oriole*, had arrived off the beaches with no motor-boat, only two Armstrong Patent lifeboats. By mid-afternoon, one lifeboat was already a write-off – grounded by sixty frantic soldiers battling into her.

At once Davies tried to use his other boat to pass a heaving line to the mast of a wrecked sailing sloop. That way his crew could move inshore to secure grass lines to the wreck – non-absorbent coir rope, which floats gossamer-light on the water, it would enable the troops to haul themselves hand over hand.

But by 3 p.m. Davies knew black frustration. No sooner was it made fast than the troops, not waiting for a grass line, put all their weight on it, striving to fight their way out to *Oriole* on the slack heaving line.

Insidiously the tide coaxed both troops and heaving line directly astern of *Oriole*, and many men sank like lemmings as they struggled.

Davies made a swift decision. If the troops massed in unending lines along the beach were to be saved, they needed a pier on which they could scramble to safety without drowning. But the only pier at Davies's disposal was the 432-ton *Oriole* – once the old Glasgow paddle-steamer *Eagle III* of the Williamson-Buchanan Line, whose white black-topped funnel had been known to millions of Clydeside holiday-makers.

Now Davies told Sub-Lieutenant John Crosby, who stood beside him: 'There's only one thing to do, Sub. I'm going to ground her until next high water – and all the others can send their boats to *me*.'

To Crosby it made rock-ribbed sense. The next flood-tide was over two hours distant, which gave them time enough. And already Crosby was wet through from diving without cease to unstrap the packs and haversacks of frenzied men drowning in the swift-running water.

Slowly, with infinite care, Davies brought *Oriole*'s head round until she was facing the beach. Next he ordered the bulk of the twenty-eight-strong crew aft – the bows must be raised as much as possible. Then, her paddles churning the water to froth, *Oriole* went for the beach at a roaring twelve knots, Davies keeping her full ahead until she jarred and came to a stop.

At the same moment seamen dropped two 7-cwt kedge anchors from the stern: two-third of the weight of a normal anchor, used for lighter work, these would ensure *Oriole* a quicker get-away once the tide had turned.

It was a gallant gesture. All that afternoon, more than 2,500 troops scrambled to the safety of ship's whalers over *Oriole*'s decking and stern – but though the Luftwaffe were pounding, Davies couldn't even hit back. *Oriole*'s armament was one twelve-pounder, one twin Lewis-gun – and reluctantly Davies had decided the twelve-pounder must cease fire.

He explained to Crosby: 'We're hard aground now – I think the stress might prove too much for her shell.'

Yet the average Tommy wouldn't have believed it possible. Sapper Stanley Bell, one of 200 exhausted men lying in *Oriole*'s companionway, heard Davies explain, 'Oh, I grounded her deliberately,' only suppressed a chuckle with difficulty. As if anyone grounded a ship deliberately – but what officer in the world, Bell thought, would *ever* admit he made a mistake?

Davies was making no mistakes. But now another problem bedevilled him: all around, troops were trundling engineers' collapsible boats down to the water on squat wheeled trolleys. Rolling the trolleys into the sea until the boats floated clear, they then abandoned them.

The trolleys were roughly nine feet high – a little more than the depth of water in which Davies had grounded *Oriole* – but what would happen when the ship refloated? With wind and tide the way it was, Davies couldn't manœuvre out one inch astern – and the trolleys were silted in the soft sand ten feet to either side of the port and starboard bows. To Davies one thing seemed inevitable: they would snarl up in the threshing surface paddles and slash them to knife-edged ribbons.

But Davies was lucky. In four chaotic hours not one bomb struck *Oriole* – and the damage done when the ship refloated at 6.30 p.m. was only slight. But one problem still remained: Davies had aboard only 200 Tommies, thirteen Army nurses. If *Oriole* had taken a risk like that it seemed right she should be filled to capacity.

Then Davies had a brainwave – what had happened to all those soldiers with the collapsible boats? Heading eastwards from Dunkirk, he soon discovered: without oars or sails the boats, dotted like cockleshells across the water, were drifting blithely with the tide – straight for the Nieuport guns.

Swiftly Davies veered to take them in tow – and only just in time. High overhead a flight of fifty planes came winging from Nieuport and all hell broke loose again – the stacatto bark of the Bofors guns hitting back, light flak starring the sky like black balls of cotton-wool. From close to Sub-Lieutenant John Crosby came an irreverent mutter: 'For what we are about to receive . . .'

But the bombs were near misses – forty yards distant to port and starboard. With 600 troops aboard *Oriole* steamed northwest for Harwich, blazing ships dotted like marker buoys to guide her.

Only two days later did Davies, feeling a pang of conscience, find time to let Ramsay into the secret: 'Submit ref. K.R. and A.I. 1167. Deliberately grounded H.M.S. *Oriole* Belgian coast . . . May 29 . . . objective speedy evacuation of troops. Refloated . . . no apparent damage.' And he wound up: 'Am again proceeding Belgian coast. Will again run aground if such course seems desirable.'

A skipper who puts his ship in jeopardy, Davies knew, normally rates nothing but a wigging – yet Ramsay's reply summed up the whole Dunkirk spirit: 'Action fully approved.'

★

Both *Oriole* and her skipper bore a charmed life. To thousands lining the beaches of Dunkirk it was plain that ship after ship was fated to make her last voyage this day.

None felt more strongly on this point than Major Oscar Dinort. For seconds after that perilous death-dive below the destroyer's mast-level Dinort had believed all was lost – and only the born Stuka pilot's instinct saved him.

Don't cut out slowly, this instinct was telling him – 'skying', the Stuka men called it. Cut out slowly and you'll never make it – the blood flies too fast from the head. And in obedience to instinct he yanked on the stick and with one sickening upward twist gained height. He climbed fast, curving to port so that the flak couldn't follow, then to starboard, gaining height all the time. His right hand was working overtime, robot-wise, reversing the controls he'd set for the dive . . . oil and water-coolers on . . . diving-brakes in . . . until at last, marvellously alive, he was 8,000 feet above the cheated sea.

From the time he'd sighted the destroyer to this moment had taken just sixty seconds.

But he was no man to give up easily. The problem you couldn't lick mentally or physically was the one that always brought the tenacious Dinort back for more. Hadn't he, at twenty-eight, established a double world record as a glider pilot? And at thirty-six, as a Luftwaffe research project, he'd tried again, keeping a glider aloft for thirty-one hours. After twenty-eight hours, he'd noticed, weird hallucinations possessed the brain – but Dinort, notebook on lap, had still contrived to keep track of them for the record.

He called: 'All planes, all planes. Prepare for new attack.'

Orbiting, his eyes swept the waters: so many ships that it rendered choice difficult, but a few, moving out from the long breakwater, seemed unscathed. Impartially, over the radio telephone, he doled out targets for his eager weaving wing: three-plus planes to a target was von Richtofen's decree, the naked sense of being singled out paid off in terms of panic. Dinort decided that he and his *Staffel* of three would try for the biggest of three ships just moving out. In a series of jinking lives – 'butterfly flying' to the pilots – he readied for the long bold run.

Below, Dunkirk harbour was a scene of horror. In the mine-sweeper *Ross* Yeoman of Signals Wilfred Walters felt sick with impotence: the telegraph was one frenzied crackle of plain-language Morse – E.A.B . . . E.A.B . . . the 'may-day' call which betokens 'Enemy are bombing.' But every signal went unheeded. Too many ships were in distress.

And more were destined to be. 'Eagle group, Eagle group,' Dinort rallied over the intercom, 'The largest ship in the mid-dle . . . attack.' Again he pushed the Stuka's nose into a 70-degree dive.

This time it went better but only just. In an instant, scream-ing towards the shimmering water, Dinort was aware of a fearsome sensation: the pilot following up had released his bombs a fraction too early. Now a great and awful fear seized him because for split seconds he was plunging to earth level with the other man's bombs.

At 1,500 feet, not a moment too soon, he jerked the bomb but-ton, swerving to port. He saw a vast mushroom of steam bellying from the heart of the ship but, curving upwards, there was no chance to see more.

All evidence suggests that the old Thames River paddle-steamer *Crested Eagle* was the target Dinort hit upon. In any case, scarcely had she embarked *Fenella*'s survivors and slipped her lines when she too was struck . . . one bomb falling aft, sparking a raging fire in the diesel-oil supplies . . . another near the engine-room, blocking the companion-way leading to the engines . . . searing Chief Engineer George Gladstone Jones and his men with blow-torch fire.

Yet strangely the engines kept turning – and the shaken chief engineer reported up the voice-pipe that all was still in order. Her captain, Lieut.-Commander Booth, replied: 'Right, keep her going – we'll see if we can get the fire under control.'

Not all were so philosophical. All over the ship ammunition splintered like fire-crackers . . . a barking dog ran hysterically along the decks . . . along with many *Fenella* survivors, Lance-Corporal James Harper thought once was enough. Seizing a cork life-belt, he hopped overboard, the churning paddles missing his head by only a quarter of an inch. Gunner George Goodridge, who'd been carried from *Fenella* with both legs broken, had the same instinct; his whole body a mass of weeping tissue from scalp to waist, the last thing he was to see for weeks was acrid sky-blue smoke filling the cabin as the *Crested Eagle* burned. He, too, made it to the shore, miraculously swimming even with broken legs, though destined for weeks of total blindness.

The *Polly Johnson*'s mate, Jermyn Greengrass, who had been transferred from *Grenade*, made it, too, with the help of others – only to spend helpless days in the dunes and three years in a prisoner-of-war camp.

Giving no quarter, the German fighters zoomed low as the survivors struggled to safety, machine-gun bullets 'crackling like frying fat' on the still water. But the twenty minutes a Stuka could stay above the target was up now. Calling up his planes, Dinort headed for home base, too early to witness the *Crested Eagle*'s end.

It was a harrowing sight. As Booth headed the *Crested Eagle* for the shore thousands stood aghast to see men on fire from head to toe, dancing like dervishes, their faces contorted, leap screaming into the sea. For the ship's plates were glaring white-hot: her deck beams, expanded by the heat, rising like a turtle's back.

Outside the fray it was hard to get the measure of things. Telegraphist Dennis Jones, of the sister ship *Golden Eagle*, was idly monitoring radio traffic ten miles off the North Foreland, en route for Dunkirk, when he heard the *Crested Eagle*'s telegraphist, Petty Officer Frank Godward, trying to raise Dover's Port Wall Signal Station. At once Jones was puzzled – Godward was using the Navy's cherished priority 'Immediate' – rated only by cases of extreme urgency – yet the very touch told him Godward was under stress. 'He might have been practising at signal school.'

Now Jones was listening with both ears – for the Dover station's response was no more than a peremptory 'Wait.' Again the telegraph crackled into life: another ship now, using the routine 'E.A.B.' of enemy air attack. This time Dover was curter: 'Wait.'

Chilled, Jones had the sensation of sitting in on a deadly game of cards: another ship was bidding now, slapping down the highest ace of all: 'I have a Most Immediate message.' Used normally only to announce the outbreak of war, the message went through Jones like a knife – but Dover's implacable 'Wait' went deeper.

It took only minutes – for Dover was clearing the air for an urgent message to Lord Gort – but still Jones waited in fascination. What had the *Crested Eagle* to say that rated an 'Immediate' and made the operator's hand shake like that? In a minute he heard it – the crippled ship's last message that made his blood run cold: 'I am on fire and going on the beach.'

Godward survived, though, narrowly: he had turned off all the switches in the wireless cabin and gone on deck to salute the captain on the bridge before he abandoned ship. Then, fully dressed, even to his spectacles, he jumped, feet first, fifteen feet into the dark oily water.

Back in the line there was still only blind faith. If you got to Dunkirk, you were sure of a boat and the Navy would see you through somehow.

As he jolted in the back of the truck towards Dunkirk these thoughts were foremost in the mind of John 'Warrior' Linton. And the chances seemed more than good – they had outwitted the German ambush, the truck was running well, Private Hawkins, sitting up beside him, was able to tell him what kind of country they were going through.

Some time after 6.30 p.m. they arrived at the barn.

As Linton saw it, the barn, set down in open country, had been some kind of dressing-station, but there were no wounded there now; the last ambulances were already revving up. As they lifted Linton from the truck a medical orderly told him, 'You were lucky to catch us. We're just pulling out.'

At first all seemed according to plan . . . Linton was lifted on to a trestle-table while a medical orderly gave him an anti-tetanus shot in the arm . . . then his stretcher was laid on the barn floor . . . soon another truck-load of wounded arrived. Overjoyed, Linton recognised old friends who had been wounded at the same time as himself – Sergeant Adams, Lance-Sergeant 'Ginger' Dawson. One by one the medical officer did a swift check before the orderlies moved them out into ambulances: Private Hawkins, the wounded officer who had shared the truck with them, Adams, Dawson . . .

Casually, glancing at Linton, the officer ordered: 'Move that man's stretcher up to the corner of the barn.'

It was then Linton knew with dreadful certainty that he was too badly wounded. He was being left to die. The barn was almost empty now; soon they would have gone. Suddenly, using all the strength of his lungs, he shouted.

As a tough medical corps sergeant came running, Linton rounded on him furiously: 'You bastards, you're going to leave me to die with the Germans.' Suddenly, his pent-up control snapping, Linton shouted, 'I'll haunt you to the end of your days.'

The sergeant wasted no time arguing. Within seconds he was back with a major. 'What's all this, my man?' the major led off, and then, when Linton protested: 'Haven't you been taught how to address an officer?' But Linton, swept by a scalding sense of injustice, was past all caution now.

'Don't use your rank on me, Charley,' he blazed back. 'I'm not going to be kept here to die. I didn't run the gauntlet of the Germans for that.'

But when the major, too, went, leaving only a young orderly to sit on Linton's stretcher, the corporal knew it was the last fling of the dice. He took a long look at the orderly's face. A nice kid, he thought, with a cunning born of desperation. I'll work on him.

Now, quietly, in a hushed monotone, he began to improvise – details of all the atrocity stories he had ever heard, details he couldn't even vouch for. How the Germans bayoneted their prisoners through both eyes. How they tortured you lingeringly first before administering the *coup de grace*.

It was quiet in the barn, so quiet that as he talked Linton could hear the birds singing; outside it was growing dark, darker inside the barn with the lengthening shadows. Still talking, he saw the young orderly's mouth give a little at the corners, sensed his hands beginning to shake. With a quick twist the youngster wriggled from the stretcher: 'I'll go and fetch someone.'

But Linton was quicker. 'Oh no, you don't, by Christ you don't.' With the terrible strength the cornered knew, he lunged out, grabbing the boy's wrist, pinning it to the floor. '*You* don't go. We're for the Germans, we two.'

And now both men were shouting, bawling at the pitch of their lungs, until suddenly an Army Service Corps captain, unshaven, grimy, appeared before them. 'What's up, lads?' Swiftly Linton explained – people had risked their lives to get him this far: now he was being left. The captain had just one question: 'Did you come from the rear-guard at the front?'

When Linton nodded an affirmative, the officer was final. 'Well, you're not being left here after all that duffy.' Calling for a medical orderly, he scribbled a brief note on a pad of movement orders. '*I'm* authorising transport for this man.'

Tight-lipped, the major could still say nothing; the Army

Service Corps, in charge of transport, had, in the same way as a ship's captain, the final say on who travelled in it. As the orderlies lifted Linton's stretcher towards the Service Corps' ambulance, he heard the captain say, 'This gives him priority on a boat.'

Inside Linton's head the word seemed to reverberate. Boat, he thought, he said boat. I really will make it after all.

Private Bill Hersey had much the same idea. For two days he had lived as in a nightmare, unwashed, unshaven, each jolting mile a purgatory. But now, suddenly as dusk was falling, everything was wonderfully right again. As Nobby Clarke swerved the Bedford into a farmyard whose name he never knew, Hersey espied a sight that set his heart leaping – Driver Johnnie Johnson's truck halted on the stone flags.

With one bound Hersey was down from the Bedford, scudding like a madman across the yard. He, too, was yelling as loudly as 'Warrior' Linton – but it was his wife's name that echoed from the old lichened rooftops.

Few men can have enjoyed a rapturous reunion with their wives in more off-beat surroundings – for at that moment Augusta's face, still surmounted by the steel helmet, appeared over the wall of the pigsty. The farmer had refused both water and lodging, and when the rainstorm burst it had seemed the driest place to sleep.

As Hersey recalls it, his first words were '*Chérie, je vous aime*' (I love you, darling.) His next were unprintable – a tirade of vituperation, which Augusta luckily couldn't fathom, at the farm-folk who had left his wife to this.

The tragedy was, the language barrier prevented both the young lovers from confiding how they really felt at this moment. Augusta could see that Bill was very angry indeed – but she did, by plucking at his sleeve, dissuade him from storming in to raise hell with the farmer. '*Ils ont peur aussi*' (They are frightened, too), she pleaded – and finally Hersey, with many grumblings, desisted.

On one thing, though, Hersey was adamant – Augusta was not spending one moment more bedded down with a strange medley of young piglets and orphaned refugee children. He coaxed her away from the pigsty into one of the unit's trucks – then, while Augusta pulled gratefully on his water-bottle and munched hard army biscuits, tried to shave with a cupful of precious water.

Puzzled as to why Augusta kept giggling at intervals, Hersey shrugged it off finally as delayed hysteria. It would have taken too long puzzling through that dictionary to work it out as a question. He knew only that he was tremendously proud of this young vital wife of his, who never seemed hungry or thirsty, or gave a hint of being tired, who always saw the funny side of everything.

More than just a wife, she was a companion, someone with whom you could share everything. Obscurely he knew that others like Nobby Clarke felt this too, and that if by appalling chance anything happened to him the rest of the unit would see her safely through.

Bill Hersey only half understood it, but Augusta wasn't just being brave. Her boyish impetuous nature, her bubbling sense of humour, had until now made all of it the greatest adventure on earth. She could still chuckle over the way she'd made that first casual inquiry about special licences – and the way the Town Hall officials at Tourcoing had asked in amazement: 'But who would want to marry an Englishman?' Their disgust when she'd answered firmly, 'I would,' had been much akin to the pursed disapproving lips of her relatives when she raced Bill from house to house to introduce him – it just wasn't done for a nice girl to marry by special licence, at twenty-four hours' notice. Yet still in a crazy world Bill symbolised the one certain stable force.

Perhaps her father was already in Bordeaux – or machine-gunned on the roads down, for who could say? And who knew when she would see her mother again? Her life now lay with this gentle, fair-haired soldier, her husband, who moved awkwardly, almost bashfully in repose but who, when angered on her behalf, became at once a cold implacable avenging angel.

This was the way God had ordained it. You would not eat the better nor sleep the better, nor know more peace of mind if you questioned why, but if you accepted it with a tranquil heart all at once you seemed to laugh the better.

Her meal over, she settled blissfully into the crook of Bill's arm. Soon both were asleep in the back of the truck and nourishing, like 'Warrior' Linton, the same thought: 'Soon, very soon, we will reach the coast and then there will be a boat.'

The fate of the *Crested Eagle*, beached but still flaring like a furnace in the night, meant one thing to Captain William Tennant. Somehow embarkation must be accelerated still more, before the Germans struck again. Yet at 9 p.m. on this ill-starred Wednesday, it seemed almost as if Ramsay had called off the evacuation altogether.

By now Tennant was dropping on his feet. Pacing the Mole in his old blue Burberry, the silver symbol 'S.N.O.' still gummed firmly to his steel helmet, the only nourishment he had taken in hours was a cigarette tin filled with tea, brought by a solicitous rating.

It was hours since he had slept, too; the air in the dungeon-like Bastion, lit only by the bizarre flickering of candles in wine-bottles, was as hot and fetid as a zoo. After a brief attempt to catch forty winks on the stone floor, Tennant had given up: someone else had wanted the floor space.

Somehow he had contrived a shave, but the starched white collar Colonel Whitfeld had envied was less than ship shape now. There was only one thing for it: tomorrow he would have to turn it inside out.

Away from Dunirk all through the air-raid, conferring with Gort at the perimeter, Tennant had known only one fleeting moment of comfort – the moment when Gort, glimpsing the Stukas dive in to strafe, took cover in a ditch. Thankfully, Tennant had dived after him. If a First World War V.C. sought shelter, the Navy lost no face following suit.

But what worried Tennant most as the minutes crawled was the total absence of ships. Now, at 9 p.m., the flow of destroyers and personnel ships to the Eastern Mole should have been as non-stop as traffic on a summer highway – yet to date only four trawlers and a yacht had shown up.

The yawning gap the *King Orry* had torn in the Mole meant the seaward end of the pier was cut off – but it was still possible for troops to embark from berths nearer the shore.

Only that day Commander Jack Bickford of the destroyer *Express* had given Tennant cast-iron proof of the Eastern Mole's value: from the beaches it took *Express* an average six hours to load up. From the Mole, just twenty-five minutes.

Yet still as the hours passed the ships just weren't coming. Had Ramsay decided against the Mole altogether? Had some personnel ships journeying by Route Y come to grief under the Nieuport guns? At 9 p.m. Tennant didn't know what to think. Even dispatching signal after signal he could get no reply.

At Dover Admiral Ramsay was equally in the dark. At 7 p.m. a report apparently stemming from Tennant had plunged the admiral and all his staff into an abyss of despair.

As much as any of Tennant's party, the men behind 'Dynamo' were bearing a fearful brunt. First, the grinding travail of the Netherlands evacuation . . . Calais . . . Boulogne . . . now four non-stop days and nights of Dunkirk, with the officers in the massive 'Dynamo Room' coping with a peak 1,800 signals a day, collapsing exhausted beside their chairs for a swift three-hour cat-nap. So dead to the world were they that Cypher Officer Rosemary Keyes, doling out signals, had to pick her way over serried ranks of inert bodies.

Already that day, in a brief letter to his wife Margaret, Ramsay had written: 'Flesh and blood can't stand it much longer . . . no one can foresee what to-morrow will be like.' And now had come not only Tennant's shattering message but an identical report from Gort's La Panne headquarters to the War Office.

Neither left any room for doubt: Dunkirk harbour had been so badly mauled by that afternoon's bombing that the entry was a graveyard of sunken ships. Though the pier itself was undamaged, the messages stressed, the only evacuation channel left was the old and burdensome one: by whaler from the beaches to the ships lying offshore.

Yet at the same moment Tennant and his senior officers at Dunkirk were eagerly awaiting ships that did not come.

What had happened? By a bitter stroke of irony, neither Tennant nor his commanders even knew these signals had been sent. A junior officer of Tennant's party, his mind unhinged by bombing, had somehow made the nine-mile journey to Gort's headquarters to blurt out a garbled tale of disaster to Gort himself.

Separated from Tennant at the Bastion by miles of burning rubble-streets, Gort's staff could have been on another planet for all the check that was possible. The message, passed in all good faith by Commander James McLelland's naval signals unit at La Panne, was accepted by Gort as Tennant's own view of the situation.

Worse, at 8 p.m. that night, the First Sea Lord, Admiral Sir Dudley Pound, had taken two decisions vitally affecting the evacuation's final outcome. The first could prove helpful – though in no way superseding Tennant, Rear-Admiral Frederick Wake-Walker, massive fair-haired descendant of Hereward the Wake, had sailed with a party of eighty to take charge offshore along those twenty-five miles of beaches.

But the second decision, as Ramsay saw it, could prove nothing but disastrous. From tonight on, the eight most modern destroyers in the evacuation fleet were being recalled from the fight. On this one day three had been sunk and six damaged — and the destroyers' first duty was to protect Britain's sea lifeline.

Even in the knowledge that the fifteen old destroyers left could lift only 17,000 men in the next twenty-four hours, Ramsay had to agree.

But still bulletins from Dunkirk were vital. From Dover to Dunkirk, the wires hummed with frantic signals, seeking information . . . to Tennant, asking for urgent clarification . . . to Captain Eric Bush, afloat in *Hebe* . . . to Admiral Abrial, pleading for a full report.

Meanwhile Ramsay accepted with anguish that only one step could be taken. At 9.28 p.m. his Flag Officer, Commander James Stopford, signalled irrevocably: 'All ships approaching Dunkirk will not repeat not approach the harbour. Remain instead off the eastern beach to collect troops from the shore.' Von Richtofen had triumphed after all.

Inexplicably neither Tennant nor Ramsay ever received the other's signals. As midnight came and went without fresh news, Ramsay sent word to Commander Conrad Alers-Hankey, in the destroyer *Vanquisher*, to set sail for Dunkirk on an urgent confirm-or-deny mission.

But for ten thousand men who might have made good their escape from the Mole this night there wasn't the solace of knowing the worst or grappling with a decision. There was only the celestial beauty of a night seared by red and green tracer . . . the gentle blinking of Aldis lamps far out to sea . . . the unearthly blasting of the destroyers' sirens and the shrilling of the whistle buoys . . . the pitiful cries of the wounded . . . the patient glow of a thousand cigarettes, like the lights of a Japanese garden.

CHAPTER SIX

LIKE SOUTHEND WITH THE OLD WOMAN

Thursday, 30th May
1 a.m.–3.30 p.m.

General the Viscount Gort had just one resolve at dawn on Thursday, 30th May. Whatever came to pass, no hardship should befall his troops that he himself wouldn't share.

On the Wednesday night, bidding farewell to two old and trusted friends — Lieut.-General Henry Pownall, his Chief of Staff, his military assistant, Lord Munster, both slated to return to England — Gort had been more moved than they'd ever seen him. His voice unsteady with emotion, he assured Munster: 'You can tell them back in England that nothing on God's earth will make me come home . . . I'm going to stay here and fight it out to the last round.'

Though Gort had never been more sincere it was still an anxious prospect. By Thursday midday, close on 200,000 men were cramped inside the Dunkirk bridgehead — but of the divisions slated to hold this last line, only Major-General Harold Alexander's 1st Division was in real fighting trim.

At Furnes, the triple tragedy that had overtaken the 2nd Grenadiers was all too typical. With Lieut.-Colonel Jack Lloyd and two of his company commanders killed outright by snipers, Major Richard Colvin had taken over the shattered battalion — yet ammo was so short that the fifty guns of the field regiment supporting them were down to six rounds each per day. And north of the town, defences were thinner — Major Robert Riddell's 4th Berkshires were down to just one company. Eager sappers, blasting a bridge too soon, had stranded more than 160 men on the German side of the canal.

It was small wonder that Gort's headquarters this day issued a situation report ranking high in the annals of military double-talk: 'The situation is obscure but thought to be improving.'

Worse, through no fault of his own, Gort was now embroiled in a bitter quarrel with Admiral Jean Abrial, French commander at Dunkirk. Even now, like General Georges Blanchard, Abrial had received no finite instructions on evacuation from his Government; to the best of his belief the British, like the French, had been ferrying their untrained base troops out of harm's way. Now it came home with stunning impact: the British were quitting *en masse*.

But Gort, a fighting soldier, had no taste for high-level political entanglements. This was a question for the British and French Governments to unravel between them. Bluntly he told Abrial as much.

In his headquarters at Bastion 32, Abrial was beside himself. To Captain Harold Henderson, British naval liaison officer, he burst out: 'Who does this Lord Gort think he is? If necessary I will close the entire port and place him under close arrest.'

All unaware of this, Gort, at La Panne, had as always sought solace in the hour-by-hour routine of running an Army . . . seizing a megaphone and organising troops into queues like any beachmaster . . . not only co-opting the 23th Infantry Brigade's quartermaster, Captain Nibbs, into perimeter defence, but giving him personal tuition in the use of a Bren-gun.

At Bastion 32, though, Captain Henderson had to act fast. Beseeching Admiral Abrial to do nothing hasty, he called Admiral Ramsay in Dover. He pleaded: 'Look, the evacuation's been on for days but nobody's told the admiral a thing.' And he stressed further: not only should Abrial's Government bring him up to date but French troops, too, must have an equal right to get away.

He summed up: 'Suppose French troops tried rushing British boats? There'd be the most ghastly international incident and we've got to avert it.' To his undying relief Ramsay agreed wholeheartedly. From now on the Admiral himself would take up the cause with Winston Churchill.

Still smarting at the injustice of it, Henderson hung up. To man the French section of the bridgehead, Abrial, he knew, had only two divisions – his infantry reserves so meagre, the crew of the torpedo-boat *L'Adroit* formed the sole garrison of the western Fort Mardyck. Nor would he easily forget Abrial's pained rebuke: 'You owe loyalty to your country, yet you are a member of my staff – couldn't you summon enough loyalty to tell *me* what was going on?'

Another man, for different reasons, was smarting too: at St Pol airfield, General the Baron von Richtofen could hardly believe his ears. After the promising start the Stukas had made yesterday, his observation planes reported the worst news yet. A cold grey marrow-damp fog was rolling in across the Channel.

At once von Richtofen rang Major Oscar Dinort at Beaulieu airfield: Dinort and his entire wing were to strafe Dunkirk without delay. But within the hour Dinort was back, his bomb-load intact. The fog was impenetrable. The losses would have been bloody.

But, von Richtofen insisted, the weather at St Pol was

beautiful. When Dinort, to mollify him, agreed to take off again, von Richtofen was icy: 'I expect no less of you.' Even when Dinort returned a second time, the baron couldn't credit it: 'The sunlight here is perfect – I can't believe it's as bad as that.'

Silkily, Dinort played the trump card he'd been withholding all along: 'May I suggest then that the general flies with us to check?' No coward, he thought privately the Stukas needed a whole lot more practice against shipping targets.

There was no answer to that one; grumbling, von Richtofen retired to his office. Soon enough the weather *must* clear – and then they'd see. So far as Lord Gort and his army were concerned, he hadn't even started.

On the Kentish coast, almost overnight, the people had become adult. If Churchill's sombre prediction of 'hard and heavy tidings' began it, the sights now before their eyes had hardened that resolve. Within days or hours the grey-white cliffs of Dover might become the front-line.

The newspapers kept to the known facts – security decreed it that way. On page six, *The Times* headlined: THE KING'S SALUTE TO THE B.E.F.: 'OUR HEARTS WITH YOU IN THIS HOUR OF PERIL.' The *Daily Express* bannered: B.E.F. FIGHTS DOWN NARROW CORRIDOR TO DUNKIRK. On the spot, newsmen like the *Herald*'s Reg Foster knew differently: making a routine call from a pub parlour, Foster had a major in security burst in on him, arms tight-folded as he monitored every word.

Foster, of course, had no green light to tell his readers that no one could now leave or enter this zone without a military pass, that all letters were censored, that within days 48,000 school children were to be evacuated from the coastal area.

Some still wore their rose-tinted spectacles. Aboard a bus taking Belgian refugees for screening in Dover's Town Hall, Deputy Chief Warden George Youden was tallying his passengers when a car back-fired. At once a Belgian woman, nerves frayed, struggled from her seat crying 'Air-raid!' Majestically, Youden took her to task: 'Madam, calm yourself – we don't *have* such things.'

Few had such faith. The port, unlike Dunkirk, stayed clear of fog – but despite the warming sun on the old chalk cliffs, the gulls swirling above the town, they lived in a climate of disaster. Farther inland, amongst the pink-and-white apple-blossom, old trucks and farm-carts straddled the fields to ward off glider landings, and the Local Defence Volunteers, a new force 250,000 strong, made ready to repel the men who had crushed Gort's Army with an armoury of pitch-forks, golf-clubs and poachers' shot-guns.

Everyone knew that down at the harbour stokers running amok with strain had been carried from their engine-rooms laced in strait-jackets; that sailors, ordering black coffee at Miss Dora Woodward's Creamery Café, collapsed in coma on the table before the waitress even brought it; that manager George Evans at the Grand was making up beds in the corridors, even in the baths, for sleep-drugged naval officers.

They knew, too, the troops were in bad shape, filthy, footsore, many badly wounded: at the Union Street Emergency Hospital, Dr Gertrude Toland and her team were working round the clock, an operation per half hour. At Dover's Marine Station, Traffic Controller Leslie Annand and his colleagues worked as hard, speeding a trainload of dog-tired Tommies Londonwards every twenty minutes. Not all had their hearts set on the journey. At the Dover Hippodrome, the deep-drinking soldiers who packed Mrs Edith Chaplin's bar at every show needed forcible restraint from getting in on Prince Mikado's lion-taming act, where the grizzled beast's parlour trick was to wolf a chunk of raw meat from the bosom of an almost nude girl.

The privileged saw worse signs. Stoker Arthur Parry, enjoying a rare breather off H.M.S. *Halcyon*, noted what looked like small wooden wedges eighteen inches thick packed round the base of every dockyard crane. To Parry's query a sailor was direct: 'Gun cotton – if Jerry comes this lot goes sky high.'

Parry gulped. He had been to Dunkirk and back – yet things must be worse than even he had thought.

To Mrs Rosa Bishop at Ramsgate Station, disaster scaled down to the size of her own world. For two days and nights now she had not left the station and gradually all the faces had blurred into a flickering unreality. British faces, tired and unshaven, French faces, dark and lean, drawing on Caporal cigarettes, Moroccan faces crowned by gaily-coloured head-dresses, all eager for cups of tea – but never the face of Sergeant Tom Bishop.

These men were near breaking-point, she knew – hadn't an officer warned her, 'If the air-raid siren goes, get out of here – it'll be holy massacre.' But Mrs Bishop had stayed – spending all her Army allowance, bar the rent money, on chocolates and tobacco for the troops, trudging to the pillar-box to post their letters, bedding down in her railway carriage each night.

Early on she had accepted that Tom might be landed at another port. Meantime she must see to it that other women's husbands and sweethearts had the care she could not lavish on him.

But that morning, seeing a soldier in tears on the platform, her faith had taken the hardest knock yet. She had urged him, 'Haven't you something to be grateful for? You're home and alive.' But the man's reply drifted back despairing: 'All my mates the Germans didn't bomb or shell were machine-gunned.'

For the first time cold fear touched her heart: 'Supposing Tom never comes back – that's the end of my world.'

To Lieutenant Bill Tower, R.N., freshly arrived from Liverpool, it seemed that life was just beginning: it wasn't to be a boring depot job after all. Instead, with several score other young officers and as varied a collection of civilians as ever conned a chart, the fair-haired young officer was attached to the Small

Boats Pool under Commander Eric Wharton in charge of a motor landing-craft.

The little fishing-port, seventeen miles north of Dover, had the low quays which these small craft needed; already Tower had seen them jammed almost stem to stern on the shimmering waters of the inner harbour – salt-stained East Coast trawlers, fast Army motor-launches, sleek cabin-cruisers, lifeboats.

To the iron-willed young officer, this was a chance in a thousand: all his life he had believed that in a future war small craft would do great things. In some ways the skipper was closer to his engine; there wasn't any problem that he couldn't get down to and tinker with himself. Vital and quietly sure of himself, Tower loved tinkering with things: not only with 'The Top', his prized blue Renault, but with the rattle-traps that had been his only transportation before sister Penelope gave him the Renault as a present – like the old jalopy christened 'Popeye', which he had bought for thirty shillings down.

Small craft, too, called for the quick-thinking that Tower embodied; once, when his braces broke at a country house-party he had ingeniously fashioned a pair by shortening a picture cord in the bedroom. All his last leave he had been talking about the advantage of small craft and now the chance had come his way; as soon as could be he must write home and tell his parents, the rector of a Hertfordshire village and his wife, that he had pulled it off. And Penelope, too, he mustn't forget her. The Towers had always been a united family – friends and relations had called them 'The Joyous Four'.

Now, clustered with the others in Ramsgate's Naval Base, Tower heard the officer-in-charge issue final instructions. They could draw rations but not all would draw charts, for Wharton had few charts to give them. Rations were on a bare-bones scale – a few tins of corned beef and petrol cans of water. There was much to do and little time to do it in.

Wharton, dapper, capable, took over for a last pep-talk. 'The need to get back trained troops to train others is paramount – remember that above all. Now off you go and good luck to you – and steer for the sound of the guns.'

As Tower and the others moved out towards their craft, they caught the commander's meaning. Dull, menacing, like distant thunder, the sound of the guns had drawn closer, reverberating over the water, shaking the windows of the quiet lace-curtained hotels on Ramsgate's promenade. Three hundred of them, speaking as one, rumbling with the anger of thwarted gods, as they lined the last perimeter of all: the immortal, unyielding guns of Dunkirk.

Now from every port the boats were moving out, bent on a crazy, incredible rescue . . . from Ramsgate and Margate . . . from Dover, Folkestone and Portsmouth . . . from Sheerness and down the tidal rivers . . . their wakes planing like a sickle through wet grass . . . frail streamers of smoke trailing to the sky . . . a fleet almost a thousand strong.

There never had been an armada like it. The destroyer *Harvester*, built to fulfil a foreign contract, with all its gun-laying instructions in Brazilian; the *Count Dracula*, launch of the German Admiral Ludwig von Reuter, scuttled at Scapa Flow in 1919 but salvaged years later; the armed yacht *Grive*, where the captain, the Hon. Lionel Lambert, took his own personal chef; the *Canterbury*, the bejewelled ferry-boat of the cross-Channel run, with memories of Princess Paul of Yugoslavia and Delysia; Arthur Dench's *Letitia*, the little green cockle-boat from the Essex mudflats, breasting the waves like a sea-gull.

And still they streamed across the waters: the Thames hopper barge *Galleon's Reach*, built to pack in not men but the muddy spoil of dredgers; Tom Sopwith's yacht *Endeavour*; the Fleetwood fishing trawler *Jacinta*, reeking of cod; the Yangtse gun-boat *Mosquito* bristling with armament to ward off Chinese river-pirates;

Reiger, a Dutch *schuit,* redolent of onions, still hung with geranium pots, with mighty bunks for mighty men; the Deal beach-boat *Dumpling,* built in Napoleon's time, with a skipper seventy years young.

As the cockle-shell armada fanned out towards Dunkirk, even seasoned naval officers felt a lump rise to their throats: absurd yet magnificent, it was without all precedent in the world's naval history. On the bridge of the destroyer *Malcolm,* the navigating officer, Lieutenant Ian Cox, was moved almost to tears to see the oncoming fleet led by, of all craft, the *Wootton,* the old Isle of Wight car-ferry, wallowing like a sawn-off landing-stage through the water. His voice shaken by emotion, Cox burst out to the seaman beside him with the classic lines of Shakespeare's *Henry V* before another assault upon the coast of France:

> *And gentlemen in England now a-bed*
> *Shall think themselves accurs'd they were not here,*
> *And hold their manhoods cheap while any speaks*
> *That fought with us upon Saint Crispin's day.*

As with the boats, so with the crews. The rich and the famous, the poor and the unknown, as motley a bunch as ever set sail made up this mercy fleet. The Earl of Craven, third engineer in the rescue tug *St Olave* . . . a Dominican monk in a reefer jersey skippering the yacht *Gulzar* . . . 'George', the salty bos'n of the contraband control vessel *Ocean Breeze,* still wearing a privateer's golden ear-rings below his steel helmet . . . Captain 'Potato' Jones, 67-year-old skipper of the *Marie Llewellyn,* famed for running Franco's blockade through the Spanish Civil War.

Age was no barrier: though skipper Charlie Alexander didn't know it yet, 14-year-old Ronald Pridmore, the galley-boy, was sheltering below deck in the tug *Sun IV,* determined to show there were other proofs of manhood than shaving. Lieut.-Colonel

Charles Wharton, coming down from Oulton Broad in Suffolk, felt the same: they had rejected him for re-enlistment at sixty but still, though wearing carpet slippers for comfort, he'd show them this was an oldster's war too.

Neither race nor colour had meaning for this was an international fleet – a true United Nations . . . Californian-born John Fernald skippering one of the twelve lifeboats towed by the tug *Racia* . . . Dick Jacobus Hoogerbeets, a young shipyard plater from Ijmuiden, aboard Motor Boat 74 . . . Chinese Steward Ah Fong rushing tea to Captain Lewes on the bridge of *Bideford* . . . a crew from Stornoway with their own Gaelic interpreter in the minesweeper *Fitzroy* . . . Fireman Ali Khan shovelling as if all life depended on it in the stokehold of *Dorrien Rose*.

The mood was unique too – the grim gaiety of the gambler staking all his chips on the last spin of the wheel. Bouncing towards Dunkirk in Motor Boat 67, a First World War veteran with a compass twenty degrees out, Lieutenant Courtney Anderson, R.N., almost carolled with joy; only a bottle of malted milk tablets donated by his mother-in-law stood between the crew and starvation, but today it was good to be alive.

Spotting an old friend, Lieutenant Chris Dreyer, ferrying a brigadier back from Dunkirk in Motor Boat 102, Anderson couldn't resist yelling: 'Excuse me, can you tell me the way to Dunkirk?'

Dreyer, playing up, jerked a thumb: 'Back there, you can't miss it. It's burning.' As the brigadier turned crimson with horror, both skippers collapsed in unholy glee.

Not all the outsiders had signed T 124 – the form that made them Royal Naval volunteers for a month – for they prized their independence too much. Some in any case were there despite official qualms: Stewardess Amy Goodrich, the only woman to be awarded a Dunkirk decoration, swore that so long as the nurses sailed in the hospital ship *Dinard* she'd sail too. Most were entitled to £3 for their services but few bothered to collect. They were sworn to one single improbable purpose: the rescue of the British Army.

Their callings were as varied as their garb. Engineer Fred Reynard, who'd talked an admiral into letting his crew take over the motor-vessel *Bee*, wore an open-necked shirt, V-necked sweater, blue dungarees. Wilfred Pym Trotter, a Bank of England clerk, wore much the same, though he'd reported as for any city stint – bowler hat, pin-stripe trousers, umbrella. Dr Basil Smith, a peppery little chartered accountant who skippered the *Constant Nymph*, wore a padded golf cap, a lounge suit and a cork lifebelt so thick he had to stand a foot away from the wheel. Raphael de Sola, one of London's wealthiest stockbrokers, wore the full rig of the Royal London Yacht Club: blue gaberdine raincoat lined with red flannel, yachting cap with the club's insignia.

Aboard the *Tollesbury*, Skipper Lemon Webb was garbed more prosaically: old sailcloth trousers and jersey, shapeless trilby hat still perched on his head. He wasn't dressing up for this show.

Ever since sending that postcard to his wife, the old bargee had felt curiously resigned: almost the worst part had been the waiting. First the tug had to tow all the barges from Cory's Jetty down to Tilbury Dock Basin, then there was food to be taken aboard, then another long tow to Southend. But at last, bound from Southend to Dover, Webb could see the great armada streaming out into the mists beyond the North Foreland. He nodded quietly to himself: he had been right after all.

A man who'd lived all his life by the river code, Webb was still a mystery to his mates. His seamanship was as good as any man's on London River – going back to the time when a barge ferried straw stacks fifteen feet high and the skipper steered by instinct and the shouted instructions of the mate aloft. Yet Webb rarely stayed long for a yarn in The Bull or the Union Jack on Quay Street, Ipswich. Just the swift order of a round for his crew, then back to his pinks and rambler roses – often without a sup of beer.

Stocky and imperturbable at the wheel, Webb thought that if something tremendous lay ahead it couldn't be a whole lot tougher than the life he'd already known. In the days when there had been 9,000 barges on London River, and every small cement works up the Medway River in Kent had its own fleet, Webb had lived close to the breadline – walking every inch of London Docks, soliciting orders to see where he could get booked quickest. Though he'd seen history in the making, carrying maize for the old horse-buses, load after load of red bricks that built West London's suburbs, he'd never earned enough to ride.

In the worst times he'd lain awake till the small hours, waiting for the flood-tide, sacking wound round the anchor chain so that the barges moored alongside, their skippers sleeping blissfully, wouldn't hear him go. Experience, using the lesson of an empty belly, had taught that the early barge caught the cargo.

One stone jar of salt pork must last a barge's crew three weeks then – so Webb thought they'd be better victualled on this trip. The naval ratings at Southend had at least put aboard cold meat, hard biscuits, petrol cans of water.

Incredibly, the old barge was as well equipped as any craft destined to make this trip. Despite Captain Wharton's efforts at Ramsgate, despite all that Rear-Admiral Alfred Taylor, 'Dynamo's' maintenance officer at Sheerness, could do. Craft after craft was moving out with scarcely enough gear or provisions for a leisurely cruise up an estuary.

Aboard the motor yacht *Constant Nymph,* Dr Basil Smith and two stoker ratings were already off Dunkirk – ferrying load after load of French troops to the Dutch *schuit Jutland.* The excitement staved off hunger, which was as well – the Navy had given them a sirloin of beef and a sack of potatoes but the little boat boasted only a two-burner Primus.

In the Clacton Lifeboat, Wilfred Pym Trotter faced the same problem. There was just one way to make tea: wedge a kettleful of water, tea and milk, in the boat's funnel and wait until the dubious brew boiled.

It was the same in boat after boat. From the Admiralty's Small Vessels Pool to Ramsay's own staff, the Navy had worked like beavers to muster the small craft at all. Boat-builders Jack Powell and his brother Pat had been two of a team working non-stop at Sheerness to make the craft serviceable — in the grim knowledge that a full forty per cent had never put to sea.

Now, en route for Dunkirk, both Powells saw the shape of things to come. In the motor yacht *Reda* the engine control gave out before Dover was even lost to view: thereafter Pat Powell's petty officer had to work the old remote control engine by hand. In the twin-engined *Cordelia*, Jack Powell was at his wits' end; the cabin-cruiser was leaking at the seams and only one engine deigned to function at all.

And the small craft under naval control fared no better. Sub-Lieutenant Alfred Weaver had no sooner left Ramsgate than the *Quijijana*'s engine caught fire; dousing it with the extinguisher, Weaver ploughed on, but the minute he sighted Dunkirk the old yellow-funnelled pleasure launch began shipping water. Finding the bilge pump inoperative, Weaver and his crew had to bale desperately with their service caps.

For the first time Weaver saw the brass plate affixed to the bulwarks — 'Licensed to ply between Chertsey and Teddington' — and understood. That stretch of the River Thames, he knew, measured only fourteen miles.

The armament was primitive. Aboard the yacht *Chrystobel II*, a rich man's plaything, Lieutenant Hubert Wigfull had one Lewis gun — but the only sturdier weapon was an 1890 saluting gun geared to an angle of forty-five degrees. And other ships, moving out with less protection, faced a grimmer ordeal. The cargo boat

Roebuck, still on the Channel Islands run, had been unloading daffodils and new potatoes in Weymouth Harbour when the order came to set out. The old ship wasn't even degaussed — her hull wound with electric cable as protection against magnetic mines — yet Captain Wilfred Larbalestier moved off without question.

In the personnel ship, *St Helier*, Captain Richard Pitman had no contact with the outside world at all; after several gruelling trips, twenty of his crew had walked out so that now, half-way to Dunkirk, he didn't even have a wireless operator. After a despairing prowl round the wireless cabin, Pitman, sending for engineer Dick Dougal and second mate Frank Martin, experimentally touched a switch. Promptly a blue flame danced like a will o' the wisp across the cabin; the three men gave up. Without benefit of radio the *St Helier* steamed on.

The pitiful shortages might have made any man lose heart. In the tug *Sun IV*, the 'ample supplies' of dressings promised to Charles Jackson's Gravesend ambulance team just hadn't been forthcoming: even the surgical scissors turned out to be nail scissors. Without more ado they stripped off their underclothes, began slicing them into bandages. Not to be undone, skipper Charlie Alexander rummaged through cupboards and drawers. Soon all of them were shearing methodically through towels, pillow-cases, even the skipper's shirts.

Now the small craft drew nearer to the shore. The full impact of Dunkirk plunged home.

The twenty miles of fog-shrouded beaches were a bedlam of sound. True, Army and Navy, working together, had conjured some organisation from chaos now; in Bombardier Jack Boxey's queue, every man, like Galahad during his vigil, had to kneel on one knee to avoid cheating. Yet still the long lines of men wound into heart-rending infinity across the hard pearl-grey sand, moving so slowly that Corporal Bert Parks, Royal Corps of Signals, slept all night in his queue. When he awoke next morning, it hadn't even budged.

And the queue system had altered subtly now; the horrors of bombing had left fewer men with a taste for the oil-scummed water. Now there were fewer queues of men three deep into the water, more queues eight-deep stretching only to the water's edge.

From the first, evacuation from the beaches was a nightmare job – no more than 98,000 men were taken to safety that way during the entire mercy mission. Despite Britain's maritime prowess which made the evacuation possible at all, the landlubbers' lack of know-how gave the small boats headache after headache.

A few learned elementary skills: queueing in the water it was politic for non-swimmers to unfasten their battledress lest the sea, ballooning into it, carried them off their feet. You stayed anchored to the next man by what Private George Hill of the Lincolns remembers as 'the Dunkirk clasp' – right hand pressed into the other man's left, left hand gripping his shoulder.

But there were moments when even queuing took all of a man's fortitude – to Lance-Corporal Guy Cobbett the most alarming factor was awaking in the water after a fitful night's doze to find the man ahead of you had slipped quietly from sight. Sapper Alf Bate recalls a worse – the moment when the tide turned and the floating bodies of the dead nudged importunately at those still standing their ground.

For all with eyes to see, the seeming nearness of the ships made things worse still. From the decks of the destroyer *Impulsive* Stoker Walter Perrior watched a slow-motion horror: men in full kit, rifles held above their heads, wading towards the ship. On and on they waded until at last the waters quietly engulfed them. It was in the *Medway Queen*'s whaler that yachtsman Richard Brett found the calmest man of all: the blind man who took his hand and followed him with silent trust into deep water.

The sore straits the troops were in drove men to epic feats. Two hundred yards from the Kentish beach-boat *Gipsy King* twenty-nine-year-old fisherman Harry Brown saw a pontoon with a dozen soldiers almost swamped by a hail of shells; at once he told skipper Alf Betts, 'I'm going to get them.' As shell splinters whipped the water to white froth, Brown, a grass line coiled round his waist, dived over the side and struck out for the threatened Tommies. Then, securing the rope to the pontoon, he shouted to Betts for a tow. Every man aboard was saved.

Along with Betts, crew member Fred Hook stood and marvelled: married two days back in Deal, Kent, he had literally been rousted from his honeymoon bed and could scarcely believe he was here at all.

Time and again the Navy struck the same problems; brushing aside all caution, the troops scrambled so fast into boats the crew couldn't even handle the oars. In the minesweeper *Westward Ho*'s whaler, Telegraphist Harold Marsh struck a typical impasse: no sooner had the whaler reached the beach, breasting a heavy surf, than twenty Tommies in full kit sprang at her like a boarding party.

In a thrashing flurry of foam the whaler overturned; kicking themselves clear, Marsh and a ship's officer worked like beavers to secure the boat, baling frantically with steel helmets. Already the soldiers had sunk like bullets without hope of rescue, tugged down by kit now heavier than water.

Even now Marsh and the officer had to wade into the sea up to their necks to push the whaler out and refloat her. Then, sodden and empty-handed, they pulled painfully back to the minesweeper.

And Sergeant Sidney Tindle, white-haired and shattered by the incessant bombing, was a case in point. Struggling towards a whaler he felt the deadly current tweak at his legs and suddenly the little Irishman was swooning with fear. As the sailors shouted 'Come on, Serge,' Tindle was screaming: 'I can't . . . I can't move another yard.' Once the boat crept in towards him, he seized the gunwale in blind panic.

The whaler was rocking dangerously with a score of lives at stake: there was just one thing to do. Hauling off, a sailor hit him so hard his teeth smashed like pipeclay. Then, the old sweat was dragged aboard.

The more sea-wise troops were dumbfounded by the sights they saw. From a vantage point in the dunes, Sergeant William MacDonald Murray laughed himself sick; doggedly, cursing like the Middle Ages, six men were sweating like demons, not budging their rowboat an inch. It took a naval launch's party, coming alongside, to explain the boat was anchored fore and aft. Not far away, Gunner Albert Collins watched other tiros labouring to row a boat stern first.

Some found their mistakes only by trial and error: Private Alfred Williams and Corporal Tom Colduck of the South Lancs found their own rowboat, but while Williams rowed with his rifle, Colduck used his steel helmet. They veered in steady rippling circles until a lifeboat picked them up. A few made it on their own steam: Lance-Corporal Frederick Clarke and three others hauled out to the destroyer *Scimitar* in a canvas boat with just two inches of freeboard left.

As yet, not every man had reached the beaches. Caked with sweat and grime all those not needed for perimeter defence wound their way through the shattered stinking port of Dunkirk . . . through the ruins of the Place Jean Bart . . . the Boulevard Jeanne d'Arc . . . past the high empty shell of the church of St Eloi. Above the thunder of the guns, the scream of distant bombs, came a steady crunching like dry ice: the boots of a thousand men grinding broken glass to a finer powder. The breath of the raging fires was a torment felt a full mile away.

It was a port of bizarre contrasts: a toyshop, its front blown away, displaying the bright dead stares of wax dolls; a French citizen in a doorway, propped bolt upright by a stake of glass; a lone soldier smashing every glass in a deserted estaminet, muttering over and over 'No drink – then no glasses . . . '; men queueing patiently for a brothel in an underground cellar. Among the yellow-white dunes of rubble the smell of Dunkirk blanketed the warm air: an unholy compound of smoke and stale beer, putrid horse flesh and rank tobacco, cordite, garlic and rancid oil.

Others would remember it as a port of unearthly sounds – the frenzied braying of an ambulance's jammed klaxon, driven far out to sea at low tide and abandoned, the blood-chilling screams of French cavalry horses, wheeling and cantering as the guns thundered, the steady sound of chopping as countless million pounds' worth of equipment was destroyed, the far keening of bagpipes somewhere in the dunes at Bray.

Above the scene for thirty miles loomed the black pall of the oil-tanks at St Pol, 11,000 feet high, a mile wide, two million tons of oil roaring as one. To Chief Engineer George Tooley, aboard the *Maid of Orleans*, it looked 'like doom itself'.

A few found grounds for optimism. Glancing at the inky smoke that mingled with the fog, almost blotting out the land, ambulance officer Charles Jackson, in *Sun IV*, felt his spirits soaring: 'Good old Navy, look at the smoke-screen they've put up.'

It was a scene to make the bravest tremble – yet perversely, to Augusta Hersey it was the most wonderful sight she had ever seen. Since that off-beat reunion with Bill Hersey in the pigsty they had never been apart for an instant; at last it seemed their luck had changed.

No sooner had the convoy made its first stop next day than they found a friendly farm. Down to bedrock themselves, the farm folk had still insisted on sharing what little food remained equally. It worked out at one slice of dry bread per person – but Bill and Augusta Hersey, munching in silence, felt suddenly close to tears.

Nor did their luck end there. Somehow 'Nobby' Clarke had found time to explain to Bill the rudiments of truck driving – though

Bill had got in no more than half an hour's practice, it was better than nothing. Again on the second night they'd paused to sleep, a German mobile side-car had passed, spraying the wood with a deadly fan of bullets. Pressed up against Bill, Augusta heard the bullets crackling against dry branches, but the Germans didn't pause to investigate.

Today they had arrived in the little village of La Panne, once beloved of painters, within sight of the sea. They had been bombed all the way but Augusta laughed merrily – the bombs missed them every time. At La Panne they had even found a small seaside boarding-house with trucks parked near it; in no time Bill Hersey was rummaging through one in search of food while Augusta and the others watched with interest.

Suddenly, with a shrill whine, a shell burst a few hundred yards away. Lightning swift, Bill Hersey leapt from the truck, landing on a chain fence with a thud that drove all the breath from his belly. In a red mist he looked up and saw Augusta still standing there calmly. '*Couchez, couchez!*' (Lie down!), he roared.

But Augusta, choking with laughter, could only respond: 'I am not a dog.' Watching her from close at hand, Captain Harry Smith shook his head perplexed; never had he known a woman like this one. All around the world was breaking up, yet still Augusta Hersey could find scope for laughter.

In the end it turned out Bill's search had been unnecessary for the hotel kitchen laid on the largest meal Augusta had seen in days: roast beef, roast potatoes, cabbage and thick gravy. Even Bill lost his air of preoccupation, explaining to Augusta: 'This is how one eats in England.'

But Augusta was too happy to care: all she knew was, they'd reached the coast in safety. It couldn't be long now.

In truth the Herseys were luckier than they knew. The food dumps Gort's planning staff established in the Dunkirk perimeter had been stored for the fighting men holding the line to the last. But for the 50,000 men now cramming the fog-bound beaches patiently awaiting boats, no planning had been possible: the shattered railhead, the ruined port, the jam-packed roads, meant supplies were cut off. As the hours wore on, thousands lining the beach or lying up in the dunes were as near starvation as they had ever been.

Goaded by empty bellies, men went to desperate shifts: anything the jaws could masticate was fair game now. Lance-Corporal Syd Garner of the Leicesters and his mates fell on a 14-lb. chunk of corned beef soaked in diesel oil and carved it up with their bayonets. Gunner Douglas Hammond's unit had just three baked beans apiece, though Hammond rated one extra because he'd found the tin. Cutlery, even plates, were a luxury. Private James Wilson of the Sherwood Foresters, serving up sausage and tomato from a field-cooker, piled it on the hands of senior officers who gobbled like hungry dogs.

Others just took what came. Lancashire Fusilier Tom Blackledge chose a calorie-plus diet: greengage jam washed down with Scotch whisky. Corporal Leslie Hannant's victuals were less appetising still: cough candy and Italian spring onions. Inland, on the canal line, Private Joe Brasted of the Suffolks wasn't doing much better; his staple fare was cream biscuits and pickled gherkins. Even officers went short on mess privileges – Captain Geoff Gee and Lieutenant Richard Everard of the Leicesters breakfasted on chocolate and tinned asparagus.

Many weren't that lucky. Private Mervyn Doncom, of the Hampshires, after eating his iron ration in defiance of orders, had brought along the kitbagful of watches in lieu of food. Now, in disgust, he cast it aside, chewing the leather strap of his steel helmet in a paroxysm of hunger. Sergeant Leslie Teare found comfort in tobacco: a non-smoker until then, he now chain-smoked eighty a day.

Such hunger brought out the worst in men at times: near the

sea shore Captain George Anderson watched a hundred men fight like wolves over a loaf of bread. But more often it saw the best in them: Private Ernest Taylor and others of the 6th Green Howards unearthed a cache of a dozen eggs, voted unanimously to make an omelette so that each man there had his share.

A few found consolation in dreams. Lieut.-Colonel David Marley and officers of the 10th Durham Light Infantry planned a menu to top them all: champagne to drink, of course, but *hors d'œuvres* or smoked salmon to begin with – and was Sole Mornay tastier than Lobster Cardinal? (They survived to eat the latter choices in England.) Fusilier Arthur Wescombe of the Inniskillings had homelier tastes: eyes shining, he dreamed of a pan of scouse, traditional Merseyside meat-and-vegetable stew, back home in Liverpool.

Close by, Sapper William May saw a group of shell-shocked men quietly plying imaginary knives and forks. In the last resort there was always make-believe.

To most, thirst was the nagging desert torment. Cracked lips filmed with sand, they roamed blindly from the queues and into the ruined suburbs, seeking anything to assuage parched, dust-dry throats . . . sucking pebbles . . . scavenging rain-water from the gutters of houses with their tin hats . . . drinking deeply from lavatory cisterns. To Private James Wilson, his time in Dunkirk held one moment of pure ecstasy: the day he lit upon a ruined kitchen, a saucepan of scummy water in which an egg had boiled on top of a stove.

True, Ramsay's ships and the French Navy were unloading petrol cans of water to quench the thirst of the thousands, yet it was but a drop in the ocean. Y.M.C.A. canteen driver Hereward Phillips had stayed in Malo-les-Bains dedicated to the principle that the Englishman must have his cup of tea somehow: now he was brewing it for them the hard way, hauling it laboriously bucket by bucket from brackish back-garden wells, boiling it up with tea and condensed milk, thirty gallons at a time.

Some swilled down anything that came to hand. Private John Feaveryear of the West Kents, quaffing a bottle of Worcestershire sauce, felt as if he'd swallowed a live coal. Signalman John Butchard took a hearty swig from a wine bottle, then coughed up a mouthful of disinfectant. A few came close to breaking. Private Bob Frater, an ambulance orderly, seeing a corporal in the Service Corps pulling on a water-bottle, approached as humbly as a mendicant.

'Give us a drop, will you, Corp? Just a sip.' The corporal jerked a scornful thumb at the gutted town. 'I got it back there – and that's where you can bloody look for it.'

Before he knew what he was about Frater had pounced like a puma, knocking the corporal senseless. He took a long deep pull, feeling the coldness strike to his belly. Cruelly, he upended the bottle until the water was a dark spreading stain across the sand. Then he walked away.

In this inferno of stench and sound, the only means of escape by the small craft working slowly inshore, despair might have been excusable. Yet strangely, everywhere, men were retaining not only self-respect but a precious sense of humour.

Private Sidney Morris, bitterly ashamed of a three-day growth, carefully put aside the box containing his little boy's aeroplane and used the sea as a shaving mug. The razor rasping over unsoaped bristles was agony, but he felt better shortly. Staff Sergeant James Wilson, finding a dripping tap in a basement, lay on his stomach in the darkness shaving centimetre by centimetre as the moisture seeped down his face. Captain Robert Gordon of the Royal Ulster Rifles experimented and found the perfect pre-shave lotion: a beaker of piping-hot gin.

And north of Poperinghe, Lieutenant Bernard Stapleton stopped short in amazement: his company of the Royal Warwicks wouldn't even consider facing the folks at home until the camp barber had worked them over. Squatting on logs in an orchard, white sheets spread, they yarned while the barber snipped merrily away.

As yet, few men had any yardstick by which the shame could be measured. Many were still unaware this *was* a final retreat. The officers hadn't told them for few knew either. While the truth remained at Corps level, unknown even to some brigade commanders, many still saw the beaches in holiday terms: baking sands, the Channel gleaming like a blue-grey brooch, the chance to make hay while the sun shone.

With a cheery flow of huckster's patter, a sergeant stood waist deep in water palming cards and coins; close by in the dunes Private Sidney Morris, refreshed by his shave, hugged his little boys' plane and listened to the brassy lilt of a harmonica concert. Farther up the beaches Sergeant John Roper watched four Royal Engineers stunting on motorcycles. Not far away a soldier on a chestnut farmhorse went through the motions of a Cossack circus act, hand on hip, right leg bent, bowing to the brisk crackle of applause.

Private Sidney Grainger revelled to see other men happily bathing and splashing one another; they didn't even disturb twenty-two men, who had somehow found stumps, bat and ball, playing cricket a few yards away. Each time a lone fighter swooped to strafe they scattered solemnly, taking up positions again once danger was past.

Near Sapper Joseph Hicks, a newcomer spying men digging for sand eels, took thought of the famous English East Coast resort and burst out: 'Like Southend with the old woman.'

It seemed less of a holiday to those still on their way. With every hour traffic chaos was worsening: Gort's original order to destroy all but essential transport never really specified when, where, or how much. In the confusion almost all the transport of the French 3rd Corps passed within the perimeter. And many had their own ideas on the subject: Major-General Dudley Johnson, bucking the order, brought in enough transport to keep an entire battalion of his 4th Division mobile.

Many control officers had no clearer picture. At the Pont-aux-Cerfs Bridge, approaching the Dunkirk perimeter, Brigadier Thomas Wilson was shocked to see an overwrought staff officer brandishing a revolver, ordering all transport to be taken off the road and burned. Wilson got his staff car through just in time, but the Brigade's Signals and office trucks weren't so lucky. Thereafter Wilson, whose 3rd Infantry Brigade covered three miles of front, had to issue every order in writing – or visit each unit in person.

Much the same at the Houthem bridge: as one staff officer waved all transport through, the next man on duty ordered everything to be burned – even the 4th East Yorks' medical truck. The irate M.O., Dr Joseph Reynolds, was left only with his pocket hypodermic.

Worse, at Watten and Les Moeres, the French had opened the lock-gates, flooding the flat grey land for fifteen miles, a wet spreading fan three miles wide that in places lay fifteen feet deep. Though it was to prove a vital factor in holding the Germans back, it decreed that the men pressing towards the perimeter could move only on the high cambered roads: to Gunner Jack Saunders it seemed like one mighty traffic jam submerged half under water.

And to further the chaos for a multitude of reasons was all too easy: again and again the rattletrap laundry vans and milk floats which had served the B.E.F. as transport broke down at vital road junctions and stayed there. Moving up from Cassel, Gunner Hugh Fisher had a grimmer experience: a road block so dense that the only way north was up the tailboard of one truck, through the driving cabin, on to the tailboard of the next. Fisher thought it no wonder one driver had fallen asleep at the steering wheel, but he gave him a comradely shake as he scrambled through: 'Wake up, mate.' Then he was stopped dead, his stomach heaving, by the black fly-crusted hole in the man's forehead.

Confusion or no, orders had gone out; for miles circling the perimeter, red-armleted military policemen were signalling every vehicle in sight into appointed fields. The rich sweet smell of petrol was strong on the air as truck after truck took fire, a mighty funeral pyre of 60,000 vehicles, smoke spiralling to meet the high dark pall of burning oil.

To many the sense of waste went home with an impact no other sight could match. Private Sidney Morris and his mates waded into the shining red and black B.S.A. motorcycles, puncturing the engine cases with pick axes, strewing sand in the oil and petrol tanks. Each bike bore an inscription, 'Cynthia' or 'Daphne', after a favourite girlfriend. The men cried as they worked.

In another field, Hugo, the sledge dog, sat patiently by while dapper Captain Edward Bloom and his men wreaked an orgy of destruction on the twenty-six vehicles of their convoy – punching a large hole in the sumps . . . smashing the radiators . . . starting up the engines and jamming the throttles wide open until they seized into a molten mass . . . smashing the rear-axle casings with sledge-hammers . . . puncturing the petrol tanks . . . mangling the steering columns.

On all sides now men went to work with the fierce energy of vandals . . . Private Auguste Vercin of the 74th French Artillery personally broke up eighteen trucks . . . Sapper Sergeant Douglas St Croix claimed a bag of thirty-eight . . . Lance-Sergeant Edgar Plunkett and his men pulverised seventy vehicles in two hours flat. Nearby a brigadier taking farewell of his men, seemed to set the keynote: 'Every man for himself . . . good luck . . . burn, smash, anything that belongs to Britain.'

At this crucial hour, it seemed one man's brainwave might turn the tide. Early that day Major-General Harold Alexander had been appalled by the transport choking every approach to Dunkirk. At his Braye Dunes headquarters, Alexander mounted a bicycle, trying to force a passage through the chaos to Gort's H.Q. at La Panne.

After twenty minutes he gave up; even a bicycle couldn't inch its way through this. Imperturbable as ever, Alexander returned to base, wrapped himself in a blanket, then lay down and went fast asleep on the kitchen floor.

He awoke with the idea that bid fair to solve the whole problem. The prime factor holding up the Navy was that the troops were so near yet so far – but, now, calling for his Commandant of Engineers, Colonel Dad Perrott, Alexander propounded a novel solution. Why not a pier of trucks driven as far into the sea as might be? Troops could advance along them to meet oncoming whalers without risk of drowning?

Perrott was all agog. He promised: 'We'll put it in hand.'

Within hours it was under way. At Braye Dunes, Sapper Bill Searle was one of scores sitting grimly at the wheel of a 30-cwt. truck careering down the beach and far into the sea, until the water had almost reached the windshield level. In a jolting groaning line other trucks, moving nose to tail, rattled behind him.

Sapper after sapper took up the task now . . . Sergeant Reg Toates of the 250th Field Company sawing planks into 18-inch widths . . . other men scavenging for timber in abandoned beach houses, then lashing it to the truck: roofs with wire . . . the jetties, twenty-plus trucks in length, taking shape little by little.

Soon, along gangways three planks wide, the troops were moving – and the signalmen turned to, as well. At Braye Dunes, Signalman Frank Robinson, at the landward end of the jetty, was operating with two lines of cable and two field telephones, forced to press the receiver to his ear with both hands to shut out the unholy din.

At the seaward end, with the tide three-quarters out, Leading

Seaman Lionel Perry loaded the troops aboard H.M.S. *Codrington*'s whaler, twenty-seven at a time, as deftly as a turnstile attendant. From time to time he signalled Robinson: 'All right . . . stop them coming through now.' To the seasoned Perry the innovation was a godsend: as the men filed past he could see the naked fear in their eyes. Even at jetty level water was an alien element, distrusted and feared.

Though John 'Warrior' Linton couldn't know it, it was the traffic jams that were impeding his own journey to Dunkirk. When the friendly Service Corps captain had fought his battle for him back at the barn Linton's heart had soared: he was going to make it after all. But within hours of his boarding the Service Corps ambulance there had been disquieting complications.

It had been well past midnight, when the ambulance had stopped though Linton was wide awake – for the first time his legs were throbbing abominably. The driver, doubling round to the tailboard, explained they'd arrived at a Casualty Clearing Station.

Here Linton could not only get treatment for his legs; there would be medical officers with power to implement the movement order.

As stretcher-bearers loomed from the darkness, the driver ordered them, 'Take him into the church.'

Linton was shaken. 'Church? I'm not dying, what's all this?' The orderly reassured him: it was in the church that treatments were done.

As they lifted Linton from the ambulance an astonishing sight confronted him. In the night the truck had halted on a road, and the dark outline of the transept lay beyond, the vaulted porch illuminated dimly by two hurricane lamps. The churchyard and the fields beyond were packed with wounded – almost 600 men, Linton thought. Many were smoking; firefly lights pricked the darkness. In the opal light of the trucks' headlamps stretcher-bearers were hard at work, with busy cries of 'Stand clear there . . . mind your back.'

Actually it was the Church of St Blaise at Crombeke in Belgium, twenty miles south-west of Dunkirk. The unit, Colonel Tristram Samuel's 10th Casualty Clearing Station, had moved in there with 1,000 wounded that very day – in the hope of somehow moving their patients northwards to Dunkirk.

But Linton knew only that the church was as dark as a crypt; though two candles burned like votive lights on the altar, the nave lay deep in shadow. The pews had been moved out to make room for stretchers. Later dawn glowed softly through stained-glass windows that were still intact.

Time passed with agonising slowness. There was no food and little water; though doctors and nurses seemed rushed off their feet, Linton's only treatment was a cigarette doled out by a passing orderly. Lying in the midst of a group of wounded turbanned Moroccans, the young corporal felt an appalling ache of loneliness.

He wondered now whether he'd ever get home – back to his brother Bob's house where he had spent all his leaves once their parents were dead. He wondered if Joyce still went there as often – she was his sister-in-law's niece and Bob always said that when 'Warrior' was on leave you couldn't keep the girl out of the house. She was a petite redhead who hated snakes and Linton had loved to rib her about the massive snakes that had crawled across his legs on active service in India.

In truth they had been no longer than worms but Joyce's squeals of fright always made him feel oddly protective.

All at once Linton's heart leapt. Across the long stone nave he saw an officer carrying a steel helmet with his own regimental colours – yellow, black and red. But when he importuned a passing orderly, 'Tell that officer there's someone here wants to see him,' the man was shocked. 'I can't get *him* – he's a colonel.'

Linton, remembering the life-and-death hours on the railway embankment near Comines, felt a stir of pride. 'He's all right – he's in *our* unit.'

Now Colonel Ernest Whitfeld picked his way across the stretchers, a thin, dark, cheerful man who never shouted even when angry. All his battalion knew he had refused promotion earlier on to stay and command them.

Linton remembered his commander's elbow had been shattered in the fighting, and now he asked with pathetic trust: 'What are the chances, sir?'

'Good – very good,' Whitfeld answered. 'I take a pointer – while there's something coming up the line we can be taken out. There's still plenty coming up, Linton, we'll be all right.' Just as in the barn, Linton felt better already. There *was* still a chance after all.

In England, Admiral Sir Bertram Ramsay felt the same way. There *was* a chance now – and though it was the slenderest of chances, Ramsay had done his best. For the architect of 'Dynamo', lonely and remote as ever, had faced a bitter problem.

Despite the rise in that day's liftings – with each of the old destroyers between them lifting 9,750 – it still wasn't enough. In swift estimate Ramsay saw the true nature of the problem. A signal from Gort had indicated the perimeter could not be held 'for long' – whatever that might mean. At a pinch the destroyers could lift maybe 17,000 men that day. The personnel ships – say another 9,500. Yet all the small craft between them couldn't lift more than another 15,000 – making 43,000 in all.

Yet all the estimates had it that 55,000 men now awaited embarkation.

At 2.30 p.m., alone in the long chalk-walled office, the sun striking through the iron bars of the balcony, Ramsay lifted his red secret telephone, calling the First Sea Lord, Admiral Sir

Dudley Pound, in London. It was a closely guarded decision – his Chief of Staff, Captain Vaughan Morgan, wasn't even aware the call was planned – but somehow Ramsay knew that the modern destroyers must return to play their part.

No man stood in as witness on the bitter dispute which followed – but Ramsay, cold, implacable, ruthless, was always a man to go out on a limb when his heart was in a cause.

By the time he hung up he knew that he had won; within the hour he was retailing the way things had gone to his senior 'Dynamo' Staff Officer, Captain Michael Denny: 'I've made it plain that if I don't get those destroyers back I'll continue in command – but I assume no responsibility at all for the outcome of the evacuation.'

At 3.30 p.m., aboard H.M.S. *Harvester* in Sheerness harbour, Commander Mark Thornton scanned a signal which made his eyebrows arch: 'Proceed to beaches east of La Panne to embark troops.' Other destroyer captains – *Icarus*'s Commander Colin Maud, *Ivanhoe*'s Commander Philip Hadow – reading the same message, ordered up a full head of steam. The new-type destroyers were back in the fight.

CHAPTER SEVEN

JUST THE ODDS
AND SODS, SIR

Thursday, 30th May
3.30—12 p.m.

As the last of Gort's troops filtered back inside the Dunkirk perimeter a strange despondency fell upon the beaches. The miles of gutted transport, the blasted guns, their barrels flayed like peeling celery sticks – for many these were still the first signs of how tough things were.

Incredibly the gravity of the situation had never penetrated until now: still men thought in terms of *their* division, *their* unit, falling back. Trooper Patrick Browne imagined his 4th Royal Tank Regiment was returning to England for a refit; the firepower of those 'I' tanks never had been right. Lance-Bombardier John Barnard, a gunner, nourished the same belief – though blowing up all the artillery first seemed a drastic measure. Sergeant Robert Jack, twenty years a regular, shared his belief with a thousand others: the Navy would ferry them all to the south of France to attack the unsuspecting Germans from the rear.

Only the few knew better. Lance-Corporal Thomas Nicholls,

of the Worcester Yeomanry, still aglow at the thought of his first German tank, had just arrived in Bergues on the perimeter when he spotted the unit's old sweat piling on to a coast-bound truck. Remembering the old soldier's fighting words of three days back, Nicholls challenged him: 'Hey – what about the thin red line?'

The old hand was withering: 'The hell with the thin red line – I'm off!' Only then did Nicholls understand.

Staff Sergeant Frank Chadwick, an ambulance orderly, had it straight from the shoulder: from nowhere a padre approached him and his mates with a macabre suggestion: 'I expect you all realise things are extremely serious . . . I think if you'd permit me I'd like to read the burial service.' Though there wasn't a dead man in sight, no one could answer him, let alone dissent.

It wasn't truly surprising. The concept that Britain could suffer defeat rang strangely on ears attuned to a hundred years of imperial fanfare – and even at top level rumour piled on rumour. At Notre-Dame-des-Nieges, within the perimeter, Lieutenant Wilfrid Miron, 139 Brigade's Intelligence Officer, heard shattering news: the Allies had advanced 240 miles into Germany, as far as Koblenz, with the R.A.F. destroying 1,000 German planes. At Bulscamp Lieut.-Colonel Peter Jeffreys, commanding the 6th Durhams, had a note of cheer for the War Diary: 30,000 Marines had stormed ashore to take over Dunkirk. (The Marines' active 1939 strength: 12,390 men.)

The Rev. Hugh Laurence of the 6th Lincolns debated whether to tell the men: on the highest authority he'd heard the Canadians were relieving them next day. (In fact, Canada's General Andrew McNaughton decided six days earlier that the Dunkirk bridgehead was too congested for his 1st Infantry Brigade to operate at all.)

The things men were toting back shows how prone to optimism they were. Most took thought to the future: Private David Minton of the Hampshires, intent on starting his own barber's shop after the war, had a sackload of fifty hair-clippers. Bombardier Sidney Huntlea had a barometer culled from a gutted house; it hangs still on the wall of his Newcastle home. Captain Morton Fisher of the Cameronians regretfully junked his new warm woollen underwear, but hung on to his fishing-rod. Private Sidney Morris hugged that aeroplane for his little boy.

Others had weightier pickings. At the perimeter's edge Private Herbert Stern of the Service Corps saw men wobbling wildly on bicycles, radiograms and refrigerators strapped to their handlebars. Sapper George Lawson, ex-vaudeville entertainer, lugged a tea-chest full of puppets. On the beach at La Panne, a man hastened up to Sub-Lieutenant John Crosby of the *Oriole*: 'Can you take my motor bike, mate? It's only done 280 miles.'

A few had posterity in view. Second-Lieutenant Anthony Noble of the Lincolns thought of swimming for a ship, then decided against it; salt water might harm the fine German Schmeisser machine-pistol he'd picked up for the Regimental Museum. Bandsman George 'Jekyll' Hyde of the Royal Sussex Regiment thought the locale itself worth commemorating. He carried some Dunkirk sand in an envelope.

Few had a souvenir as grim as Driver Rowland Cole: eight bullets which had wiped out eight spies in a firing-squad party in Tournai. Cole had prised forth each one with a jack-knife, a private memento that war was hell.

And to thousands Dunkirk still remains the symbol of the most duty-free tobacco they ever saw: few men but didn't have upwards of five hundred tucked away in bandoliers, haversacks, even inside their steel helmets. On the perimeter at Nieuport, Major Edward Poulton of the Royal Fusiliers halted a non-com. 'Sergeant, can you spare a cigarette – I've run out.'

But when the sergeant pressed a two-hundred carton on him, Poulton drew the line. 'No, no, keep some for your-self – I'll just take two packets.' With the casual generosity of a cocktail party guest whose cigarette case is full, the sergeant urged: 'Please keep the carton, sir – I've got ten thousand.'

Scores of men had pets, too: it took more than the carnage raging on all sides to efface the British love for animals. Captain Edward Bloom had Hugo, the sledge dog . . . Lance-Corporal Eric Stocks still had 'Tippy', the dachshund, peeping from his pack . . . others were wading into the sea with caged canaries perched high above their heads . . . one man, stark naked, clutching a black-and-white rabbit in a basket.

Some men just failed to make it: those who saw him have never forgotten one unknown soldier who lay dead on the beaches at Braye Dunes. From his open battledress spilled a gaily-coloured cloud of little girls' gingham frocks: the father of a family detained on his way home.

Few men knew a deeper despair than Lieut.-General Alan Brooke. Despite the appalling losses of the past few days, 38,600 of his 2nd Corps were safely inside the perimeter – and these men, Brooke had no doubt, had saved the B.E.F. Yet now in their hour of crisis, Brooke brooded on appalling news. He must surrender command of his Corps and return to England – and all his eleventh-hour pleas to Lord Gort were of no avail.

Polished cavalry boots propped on his desk, tilting backwards in his chair, Gort, too, had seemed almost numb with despair. Staring sombrely at Brooke, he could only ponder: 'I wonder what view history will take of the events that are happening now.'

Moving on to Major-General Bernard Montgomery's tented camp in the dunes hard by, Brooke was engulfed by an overwhelming pity for his doomed Corps. Obsessed by the belief that he was betraying them, he groped his way through final orders . . . Montgomery was to succeed him as head of the Corps . . . Brigadier Kenneth Anderson of 11th Infantry Brigade to take over from Montgomery . . . Lieut.-Colonel Brian Horrocks of the Middlesex Regiment to replace Anderson.

Abruptly, the grief breaking in his body like a wave, the dark poker-faced Commander of 2nd Corps burst into tears, laying his head on Montgomery's shoulder.

And Montgomery, who had known Brooke as friend and mentor for fourteen years, found himself groping for words of comfort: Brooke was needed back in England, a new Army must be reformed to replace the B.E.F. But as Brooke left, heavy-hearted, for a last luncheon, Montgomery knew none of his nostrums had helped. Drunk with fatigue, Brooke was ferried out to the destroyer *Worcester*, to find another old friend, Lieut.-General Sir Ronald Adam, already aboard.

As the *Worcester* steamed towards Dover – temporarily grounding on a sandbank at 24 knots – Adam had no sense of being privy to history. Out of touch with the fighting beyond Dunkirk, he had asked Brooke to bring him up to date. The exhausted Corps Commander, collapsing into the bunk of the Captain, Commander John Allison, had passed over a small leather-covered pocket-book. At this moment Adam was the first outsider ever to scan the historic Alanbrooke Diaries.

Though Brooke hadn't fully realised it, Gort, too, was steeped in gloom. Early that morning Gort's aide, Lord Munster, arriving in London, had sped post-haste to his old friend Winston Churchill, at Admiralty House. Pyjama-clad, in an ornate black-and-gold dressing-gown, the Premier had just finished breakfast – but his prime concern was Munster's own plight. After wading out to a ship's whaler the night before, the young officer was sopping wet. Churchill, ringing for his valet, at once ordered clean underwear for him.

But Munster, remembering Gort's farewell speech, urged that there was no time to lose. He insisted that the Commander-in-Chief was bent on sacrificing his own life and the only man with power to save him from himself was Winston Churchill.

No man to deviate from cherished routine, Churchill was set

to take his bath. He inquired quizzically: 'I trust you are not overburdened with modesty, my young friend?' When Munster said he was not, Churchill was overjoyed: in that case the young peer could sit in on his ablutions.

Now, clad in long woollen underwear that enveloped him like a sack, Munster perched on the edge of the bath while Churchill, wallowing happily in the steamy water, heard him out in silence. Munster will always recall with affection: 'He only needed a pink celluloid duck to make the picture complete.'

And though Churchill, he felt, would have done no less than Gort, the old warrior saw the point: for the Commander-in-Chief to die at the head of his men was a wanton waste of life. At once, growling, 'We must put a stop to this,' Churchill trundled back to bed – and there, propped up against the pillows, he penned a positive 200-word order.

By early afternoon, he assured Munster, the War Cabinet would make the memo official and Gort would have heard the word: he must nominate a successor and return home.

At La Panne, a handful of these words burnt into Gort's brain: 'No personal discretion is left you in the matter . . . on political grounds it would be a needless triumph to the enemy to capture you.'

Yet Churchill's order stressed, too, that the present perimeter must be defended 'to the utmost'. A commander who knew the meaning of fear and yet had crushed it down within himself, Gort found the whole concept of deserting his Army more bitter than gall.

Before that afternoon's Corps Commanders' conference, Montgomery found him silent and alone in the drawing-room of the little blue-shuttered villa, staring pathetically into space. Apart from Brigadier Oliver Leese, his acting Chief of Staff, who was telephoning in the cellar, the whole headquarters seemed deserted.

Yet a flash of the old 'Tiger' Gort seemed to return as Montgomery entered: 'Be sure to have your front well covered with fighting patrols tonight.' Fond though he was of Gort, Montgomery found it difficult to hold himself in check: this was a matter for brigade commanders, yet to the last Gort was fascinated by the minutiae of running an army.

An unswerving realist, Montgomery, like Brooke, had foreseen disaster from the moment the pitifully equipped Army moved into France: to him 'the war was lost in Whitehall, years before it began'. But somehow Gort had believed the fighting spirit of his men would make it all come right. To him the whole nightmare campaign savoured of dishonour as much as defeat.

Other men were close to breaking too. As Gort's conference wore on, Montgomery saw shrewdly that General Michael Barker, commanding 1st Corps, was frayed to the point of hysteria. Nominated by Gort as his successor, the final winding-up of the evacuation side by side with the French now fell upon Barker's shoulders.

But no sooner was the conference over than Barker, storming into his headquarters like a caged lion, cried to the heavens: 'Why has this responsibility been thrust upon *me*?'

It was left to Montgomery, purposefully lingering for a chat with Gort, to change the Commander-in-Chief's mind. Briskly explosive, like a good-natured school-teacher, he urged him: 'Look here, you've seen the state Barker's in – he's finished, done. Put in Alex, for heaven's sake . . .'

Moments of wavering indecision – but Gort agreed finally. Driving to the Dunkirk Bastion, he lost no time in breaking the news to Admiral Jean Abrial, the French Commander: the British, under Major-General Alexander, would defend the perimeter to the last shoulder to shoulder.

Ever irked by the tortuous secrecy of the past week, Abrial still recognised fighting talk when he heard it. At once, Commander

Harold Henderson, British Naval liaison officer, recalls, he pressed a button, calling for champagne. 'We must drink to this – this is not only talking like an ally, this is acting like one.'

By a stroke of misfortune, though, Gort had had no time to brief Alexander; soon after he left Abrial, the general himself arrived at the Bastion. To Alexander's astonishment, Abrial now advanced on him warmly, expressing his appreciation of Alexander's gallant gesture.

Henderson never forgot the bitter scene which ensued: the weird candle-lit dungeon, Abrial standing frozen-faced with anger, Alexander repeating over and over: 'I've no idea what you're talking about – and I've had no such instructions. My whole idea is to get my men out of here as fast as possible.'

With sinking heart Henderson watched the French naval staff exchange significant glances: what deep and perfidious game were the British playing now?

If the men at the top knew such moments of pure confusion, it wasn't surprising the rank-and-file were all at sea. The whole complex ebb-and-flow of the evacuation was too mighty a concept for any man to grasp. First that disastrous message to Ramsay, after the great air-raid, had written the harbour off for good and all . . . then Tennant's tense vigil at the Eastern Mole, waiting for ships that never came . . . the almost total lack of liaison between Bastion 32 and beaches . . . the hazards of ship-to-shore communication along twenty-five miles of sandy dunes.

No one was more confused than Augusta Hersey. At first, arriving at La Panne, it had seemed all their troubles were over: now, within sight of the sea, there must surely be a boat. Yet at the eleventh hour, the cruellest fate had intervened: an officer had appealed for volunteers to drive relays of troops from the La Panne rear-guard to embarkation points hard by Dunkirk.

At once, Bill Hersey, fired by inexplicable quixotry, stepped forward – omitting to mention that his truck-driving experience consisted of half an hour's instruction from his mate, 'Nobby' Clarke.

Though it would have needed too much dictionary work to explain it, Hersey always a man to live for the day, felt volunteering was the only thing to do. Now he'd got Augusta to the coast he couldn't doubt all would go well. And to help others in worse plight seemed akin to a prayer of thanksgiving.

But time had been too precious to make Augusta understand. Instead of making tracks for the beaches with Bill she was lying on the concrete floor of a garage in La Panne, one of a motley company of civilians and bone-tired soldiers, fitfully courting sleep. The suitcase she had so carefully packed seemed a mockery now. What good was a brand-new linen tablecloth, leave alone soft silken underwear, when your husband insisted on risking his life for others and vanishing into the blue?

For the first time since the perilous journey began she knew a pang of despair: the heady sense of adventure that had thus far sustained her had as suddenly evaporated. The other civilians in the garage, lost in their own problems, were unsympathetic too. Who was the 'Bill' the woman dressed like a soldier kept asking after every hour of the day?

The trouble was that the system, envisaged by G.H.Q., tidy enough on paper, couldn't cater for a score of unforeseeable factors: an abundance of ships when troops were hiding-up in the dunes, long unending lines of troops when no ships were in sight. The plan for carving the beaches into neat divisional pockets took no account of the thousands cut off from their units who arrived to find themselves nobody's responsibility.

To hundreds it seemed they had full scope to please themselves. Bombardier Charles Reading, one of Major-General Montgomery's anti-tank gunners, arrived in Dunkirk to find the nearest report centre a spawning heap of bricks, the town a rabble of leaderless soldiers. A Montgomery man to the last, Reading plumped for organisation: hiking six miles to Bergues on the perimeter, he talked himself into three days of rear-guard action. Capitaine François Saguard, an infantry officer, felt the same motivation; he and his men also set out for Bergues, armed with three anti-tank guns bequeathed by friendly Britons. When a passing brigadier challenged their right to British weapons, Saguard referred him to Admiral Abrial; solemnly the brigadier inscribed the name on his visiting card, promising to pay the Bastion a social call.

It was the same all along the beach: impeccable traffic control for a hundred yards, a seething disordered mob hard by. Major Alex Grant of the Royal Sussex, reaching the dunes with the remnants of his unit, was stupefied by a military policeman's barrack-square salute: 'Forty-fourth Division, sir . . . to your left, *if* you please.' For Private Fred 'Chippy' Williams, of the Royal Warwicks, arriving with a random assortment of fifty other troops, the welcome was less clement. Passing from group to group along the shore, Williams found only sour looks: 'Find your own unit, chum . . . not here.'

Sheltering in a bandstand from a deluge of rain, Williams and his tatterdemalion party met up with a brigadier: 'Don't worry, men, an armistice will be arranged. Now, who are you?'

From the ranks a voice grumbled: 'Just the odds and sods, sir.'

'But who is the N.C.O. in charge?'

'Not a stripe between us, sir.'

Promptly the brigadier told Williams: 'Well, you're a corporal from now on. March these men down to the beach.'

Nothing loth, Williams did his bidding, but the dizzying promotion got none of them any farther. It was two more days before a chance encounter with a naval officer wrote them a ticket home.

Not all were so stoic. Lance-Sergeant Billy Mullins, an anti-tank gunner, rejected by five queues, snipped off his shoulder-flashes, then joined a sixth, announcing '4th Royal West Kents' — a

battalion in his own brigade. Miraculously it was the open ses-
ame; soon, huddled in a whaler, Mullins was pulling blissfully for
the destroyer *Winchelsea*.

Bombardier James Cole, cut off from his unit miles back,
marched confidently up to a Provost Captain on the Mole with a
bolder ploy: as the only known survivor of the 30th Field Regiment he classed himself as the Officer Commanding. His brashness
won him a passage on a Ramsgate-bound collier.

Even entire units met up with total chaos. Lieut.-Colonel
Maurice MacEwan's artillery regiment, the 58th Medium, arrived
at Braye Dunes two days earlier, were allotted the serial number
Two; soon, though, troops were pouring in so fast the embarkation officers changed their minds. MacEwan's Regiment must
march six miles west, towards Dunkirk, and seek a fresh embarkation point. Farther on the crowds were so dense, the gunners
couldn't have bulldozed their way through, but they did rest
there consoled by a new serial number – 26.

In fact MacEwan made private arrangements to embark 500 of
his men by hailing boats from the minesweeper *Kellett* – but
thirty-six hours later, with 230 men still to embark, the local
embarkation officers presented blank faces. They had no knowledge of serial number 26 – that belonged to some other unit. As
a concession they allotted MacEwan's men No. 33 – last on the
list.

And still the nightmare continued: on the same beach the gunners struck no less than three other units claiming serial 33. A flip
of the coin decided the issue. MacEwan's men, losing out,
marched gloomily to the back of the queue. Then, within hours,
hearing serial numbers had been abolished, they broke away –
plodding steadily in the direction of Dunkirk, lost in the shuffle
of other troops who had got the idea first.

Farther on it seemed the gunners were in luck: on this section
of the beach, at Braye, serial numbers were still in force. They

drew serial seven. Again, though, fate took a hand: another artillery regiment triumphantly flourished the same serial. The spun coin went against them: the 58th retired to the back of the queue.

It was to be sixteen hours before MacEwan saw the last of his men off – again on the do-it-yourself principle of his officers wading shoulder deep into water, calling up whalers like doormen questing a taxi.

A few embraced desperate stratagems. At La Panne, an outraged private in the Green Howards stormed up to Major-General Harold Alexander: 'You look like a big brass hat – perhaps *you* can tell me where we get a boat for England?'

Though his staff officers bristled with anger, Alexander was imperturbable as ever. 'Follow that lot there, son.' In tribute the private flashed back: 'Thanks a lot – you're the best pal I've had in 100 kilometres.'

The cavalier approach was in keeping. For many officers – and troops too – a bitter truth was dawning: the true qualities of leadership, rather than the rank and birth that had dominated the Army hierarchy hitherto, would see this war through. For thousands, Dunkirk would mark a sombre milestone in military history: as the rank-and-file realised that officers could equally show the yellow streak the old idols were tumbling, and for ever.

In the dunes, close to Driver Harry Owen, an officer cringed in terror, clutching a champagne cork in his hand. Each time an aero-engine sounded he popped it deftly between his lips – bombblast exerted less pressure on the eardrums if your mouth was open. Twenty years after Owen recalls with disgust: 'He looked like a bloody goldfish.' Sergeant Bob Chapman, a gunner, pelting to help an officer he thought was hurt, knew a kindred emotion. Unharmed, the man was blubbering frantically: 'It isn't fair, I've a wife . . . a wife and little girl.'

In a foxhole close to Private Sidney Grainger of the Ordnance Corps, a senior officer, paralysed with dread, explained over and over to all who'd listen that he couldn't venture out to comfort his men; he must guard a basket of eggs. Approaching, Grainger saw no eggs at all – only the man's hands hovering protectingly over nothingness.

Offshore, aboard *Hebe*, Captain Eric Bush, R.N., was as disenchanted as any private soldier: a dinghy manned by a young Army lieutenant had pulled selfishly out to the minesweeper. As the officer scaled the accommodation ladder, Bush upbraided him: 'This isn't the way for an officer to behave . . . go back on shore and look for your men.' Colouring, the man stepped back into the boat, casting off the painter. When Bush looked next he was rowing unrepentantly for the next ship astern.

Inevitably, morale broke down all over: even officers whose conduct was impeccable missed death by inches. Second-Lieutenant Clive Le Couteur of the Worcestershire Yeomanry swam out with another officer to tow in three rowboats for the men of his unit. By the time his colleague returned with the troops, Le Couteur was down to one boat. Silent watchful men, grinning wolfishly, rifles trained on his heart, had annexed the boats for themselves.

That Briton should turn with naked savagery on Briton showed how bad things were – yet as the screaming tension mounted it happened time and again. Private Joubert Rolfe, of the Royal Norfolks, was clambering from the Mole on to the paddle-steamer *Royal Daffodil* when a major, claiming he was out of turn, tried to force him back. As the major, past patience, drew his pistol, Rolfe brought his loaded rifle level with the officer's throat: 'Just try it.'

Only a naval officer saved the situation, shouting like a sorely taxed school-teacher: 'Put those bloody things away, both of you, and get on board.'

Not always was disaster averted. As Private Fred 'Chippy' Williams watched from the sand-dunes, a military policeman, his brain demented, broke through a cordon, haring for a boat.

Coolly, a major took aim and shot him down. Not far from Private James Wilson of the Sherwoods, a major suffered the same fate; as he thrashed wildly through the water, bypassing the queue and almost capsizing a ship's whaler, the officer in charge drilled him between the eyes.

But for scores of officers who deserted their men without compunction, thousands more saw them staunchly through. Aboard the *schuit Reiger*, alongside the Mole, Lieutenant Alex Tyson, R.N., was touched to the core: a party of fifty men led by a subaltern had halted twelve feet above the little Dutch barge. But Tyson saw one thing at a glance: the men were in no shape to scramble down the narrow iron ladder leading to the deck, still less wearing full packs.

Dead-beat though he was, the subaltern had seen it, too: as he ordered: 'Front rank . . . one pace forward . . . jump,' man after man leapt automatically to obey, catapulting like circus artistes on to the barge's wooden deck. But only when the officer had jumped, to be carried insensible to the wheel-house, did Tyson grasp the full measure of his sacrifice.

His boots surrendered to a hapless private, the subaltern had marched scores of miles in sea-boots. Now the soles of his feet were nearly innocent of flesh. The naked bones, white and polished, glistened under the binnacle light.

And others showed equal charity. All through the 'Phoney War', Major Valder Gates, a Service Corps officer, had engaged in bitter conflict with the bulk of the men of his unit – but at last the turning point had come. The son of Plymouth Brethren, Gates's straight-laced childhood had made him recoil against religion into a limbo of unbelief – until the boredom that had settled like a blight on his unit at Lievain, in the Pas-de-Calais, brought a new sense of responsibility. Appalled at the roaring turnover of the brothels and estaminets, Gates declared war on sin and sloth; church parades, route marches with 56-lb. packs, became the order of the day. Little love was lost between the handsome ramrod-backed commander and the unit other troops nicknamed 'Gates's Guards'.

Then came the retreat – and from the point where they ditched their transport, Gates's men faced a swinging 15-mile march to La Panne. Though other units fell by the wayside, Gates's men, non-combatants all, stood the test.

From that moment Gates knew a subtle change of heart. He felt not only responsible for his men, determined to wring the best from them; he loved them too. Each night at the head of a queue he waded to his neck to meet the few boats that came in, saw away as many as he could, returning sodden to lie up in the dunes.

Now, shyly, one of his sergeants approached: 'On behalf of the others, sir, I'd like to say this. When you started those church parades and put us on the square, we thought that a lot of baloney. Now we've seen the rabble here, we're proud you had the guts to go through with it.'

Suddenly an aching affection for all mankind swept over Gates in a torrent – not for his own unit alone but for all those left without leaders. The immortal words of the twenty-third psalm flashed through his mind: '. . . though I walk through the valley of the shadow of death I will fear no evil, for Thou art with me.' If his men were to wait much longer they needed a greater solace than discipline. Jumping to his feet, Gates cried: 'Down on your knees, men – and the padre will pray to Almighty God to have mercy on us.'

As the Rev. William Curtis said a prayer, Gates surreptitiously glanced round and felt his heart stir. Not only his own force, 500 strong, but hundreds more were kneeling in the dunes, an unending vista of bared heads as men bent in silent worship. It seemed to Gates then that all his years as an unbeliever fell away.

Other officers were as zealous in their fashion. At Malo-les-Bains, Captain Edward Bloom, still in charge of 380 men and

Hugo the sledge dog, was in search of an embarkation officer; he and all his men had shaved and washed at a churchyard well, and to the normally fastidious Bloom they now seemed ready for the journey. But threading through the packed crowds on the dunes, Bloom found only a brigadier who did things by the book.

Before finding a space for Bloom's troops, the brigadier wanted a nominal roll in triplicate – a pink form used under peacetime conditions. All the dapper little captain's protests met the same reply: 'I must have those forms.'

Bloom could find no nominal rolls, but at last entering an empty house he did find a toilet roll. Stretched out on his stomach on the floor, Hugo beside him, he laboriously penned a roster of every man in his unit – then returned it to the brigadier.

As the senior man exploded: 'Captain, are you mocking me?' Bloom was poker-faced. 'I have carried out your orders to the best of my ability, sir, but I have no carbon paper.'

Minutes of huffing and puffing – but Bloom won. The toilet roll, duly inscribed, carried all of them – Bloom, his 380 men and Hugo – on to Dunkirk.

To Admiral Frederick Wake-Walker, the burly fair-haired descendant of Hereward the Wake, newly arrived on the scene, it seemed no one was still within an ace of approaching Dunkirk's most vital problem.

Slated to take overall charge offshore – though in no way superseding Captain William Tennant – the Admiral had already arranged that Vice-Admiral Gilbert Stephenson should take over La Panne; Vice-Admiral Theodore Hallet at Braye-les-Dunes; Wake-Walker himself to relieve Captain Eric Bush off Malo-les-Bains and Dunkirk.

A new broom bent on sweeping clean, the admiral was to prove himself a ball of fire. Within twenty-four hours he had transferred his flag a record six times: from the destroyer *Esk* in which he made the trip to the minesweeper *Hebe*, from *Hebe* to the destroyer *Windsor*, thence to Motor Torpedo Boat 102, to the minesweeper *Gossamer*, over to H.M.S. *Worcester*, on to the destroyer *Express*.

But the big problem that had struck Tennant hit Wake-Walker too: the prime need *was* for more small boats. Though ships' motor-boats and launches were towing off the whalers, they couldn't work too close inshore; the engineers' pontoon crafts, which the soldiers paddled out to the ships, as often as not floated away empty. As for the destroyers, they'd no sooner loaded up than their whalers went with them. Boats' crews were gun crews – no one wanted to be left without them.

Still the clouds hung heavy and swollen, warding off von Richtofen's attacks – but how long could the weather, any more than the inland defence line, hold firm?

Berthing was a problem, too. At the East Mole, following Wednesday's havoc, Wake-Walker located only four berths out of sixteen at which personnel ships could tie up. Yet the picture was in some ways brighter. At 6.30 a.m. Ramsay, hearing the report of the destroyer *Vanquisher*, had signalled urgently: Could ships use the Mole again?

At 8.30, Wake-Walker signalled back: Destroyers *could* use the Mole again. Troops were waiting and the ships should come in one at a time.

Once he had landed at Gort's H.Q. at La Panne, where Second-Lieutenant Thomas Nuttall of the engineers still stoutly maintained the undersea cable link with England, Wake-Walker saw the difficulties all too well. Hour after hour the messages flooded in; at 5.49 p.m. a query stemming from Dover had asked about the urgent need for ships off La Panne. By 7 p.m., when Wake-Walker saw the signal, four destroyers and a minesweeper were working off this beach. The situation was too fluid for any man to keep pace.

Now the First Sea Lord, Admiral Sir Dudley Pound, signalled from London: were boats along the beaches being distributed to the best advantage? Wake-Walker groaned: aside from pontoons and a few landing-craft, whalers were the only craft that could get inshore at all. At all times the beaches they worked depended on the anchorage of parent ships.

So far as he could, Wake-Walker was keeping a parity between beaches, but he was hog-tied by lack of swift transport. No sooner was he off one beach than ships were arriving at another, loading at the expense of the one he'd just left.

And over dinner – despite Tennant's presence as support and Gort's unruffled charm – the admiral just couldn't feel at home. Already, after three attempts to land in a whaler, his trousers were saturated . . . he had no business to be an extra mouth at table, robbing them of tinned fruit salad . . . worse, the Army's whole attitude now seemed one of blind dependence.

As the four senior men chewed over the problem Gort's views became plain. The Army against great odds had fallen back to the sea. It was up to the Navy to get them off but the Navy was doing that much too little about it.

Carefully, keeping his temper in check, Wake-Walker made his point. Even though 53,823 men had been taken off that day, 29,512 from the open beaches, further large-scale embarkation would be slow, difficult, dependent on the weather. His own view, akin to Tennant's, was that the vast bulk of the troops cluttering the beaches must move westwards and come off from Dunkirk.

Now Brigadier Oliver Leese chipped in: at rock bottom the whole stumbling-block was the ineptitude of the Navy. Replying, Wake-Walker's words cut like a stock-whip: 'You have no business or justification to talk like that . . .'

It was a tragic meeting – tragic because the tempers of the four men grouped round the dining-table by the french windows overlooking the sandy beach were almost at snapping point . . .

because the real point at issue was the rout of an old proud nation . . . because Gort's last bottle of champagne, which they now shared, was in most ways too symbolic.

At 10 p.m. when he took his leave, Wake-Walker had few hopes of the way things would pan out. Already Admiral Sir Dudley Pound had promised Gort that if the cream of the rear-guard – 5,000 men – withdrew from the line within twenty-four hours, the Navy would get them away.

Apart from the rear-guard, Wake-Walker knew, there were tens of thousands still to come – and the prospect of taking off the rear-guard as they fell back on a jam-packed beach with the Germans in hot pursuit was a daunting one.

In the end, it needed the combined efforts of Wake-Walker, his flag-lieutenant, Lord Kelburn, Gort and Tennant, to launch the admiral's pontoon towards a destroyer. But within minutes the boat capsized; Wake-Walker and Kelburn floundered in the water.

As they waded back to empty out the pontoon the Navy couldn't resist the last word. Espying Gort still lingering on the shore, Wake-Walker hailed him jovially: 'Another example of naval ineptitude!'

The admiral couldn't know it then, but all his worst fears looked like being justified.

At Furnes, four miles inland, key stronghold against the whole German advance, the Guards had held out under murderous shellfire for two days now, but it was a bitter battle of attrition. Already many of the old timbered houses were ablaze. Clouds of acrid, yellow-brown smoke eddied through the narrow streets, mingling with the choking plaster dust from toppling buildings.

In the most dangerous zone of all, inland from the canal to dead centre of the town, Major Richard Colvin's 2nd Grenadiers were barricaded in their buildings with orders to live and fight and if need be to die there. Only ration and stretcher parties had free passage in this last no-man's-land: his padre's white steel helmet clamped firmly on his head, the Rev. Philip Wheeldon of the Coldstream crawled into the front line to hold communion in cellars, even in ditches.

It was a town of tensions. Every smoke-filled street and alley was alive with sharpshooters – yet time and again, when the Guards moved in to investigate, they found no trace of any enemy. Search as he might, Captain Edward Gage of the Coldstream could locate only women and children huddled in the basements. Major Robin Bushman of the Grenadiers, tip-toeing with revolver at the ready to a darkened upper storey where signal lights had been reported, met up with a bat and an owl.

On Colvin's decree, every civilian in the town was confined to the crypt of the Church of St Walpurg on the Grande Place – yet still the defenders had the feeling that eyes watched them everywhere.

Each time Brigadier Jack Whitaker, commanding the 7th Guards Brigade, held a conference he stressed anew Montgomery's orders; somehow Furnes must be held. If the Germans crossed the canal in strength the whole Dunkirk bridgehead would cave in like a walnut clamped in a nutcracker.

Eagerly Colvin and the other commanders agreed, anxious to get the conference over with as soon as might be. For safety, Whitaker convened his briefings in a slit-trench dug through a manure heap with a straw and dung roof for camouflage. In this he squatted cross-legged facing them, like the cox of a rowing eight, but to his battalion commanders the stench and the droning flies were a cruel torment.

Once already the Germans had crossed the narrow canal on barges and the armoured carriers of Colonel Arnold Cazenove's 1st Coldstream had beaten them back: the whole canal was so choked with abandoned barges that Major Robert Riddell of the Berkshires tried to scotch further attempts by creeping out at night like an Apache and setting fire to them. But the attempt fizzled out – there was all too much steel in the barges' superstructure.

Down to rock bottom with his company of eighty, Riddell had been forced to put even batmen and cooks in the firing line; he himself had shot and roasted a pig for his men, hacking off sizzling hunks of pork with a clasp-knife. Tonight at 10 p.m. he knew every one of his men hugging their rifles in the shallow ditch lining the canal was battling a terrible inertia, punishing their bodies far harder than any machine.

Suddenly Riddell stiffened. From his cellar headquarters, close to the dark water, he had heard voices calling. Listening intently he could distinguish them now. German voices – on the British side of the canal.

CHAPTER EIGHT

IT MAY SEEM STRANGE, BUT WE ARE...

Friday 31st May
1 a.m.–12 p.m.

As the pale sunlight of Friday morning flooded the iron-balconied stern-walk of Dover Castle, Admiral Sir Bertram Ramsay was close to tears. Beside him his senior 'Dynamo' Staff Officer, Captain Michael Denny, could find no words either.

At this eleventh hour things were as bad as they had ever been – so that Denny, after four thorny days and nights, had the weird feeling that he wasn't here at all, but floating disembodied like a yogi above the troubled waters of Dunkirk harbour.

Until a few moments ago, Ramsay's plans had seemed set for fair weather. After an all-out twenty-four-hour effort he had planned to close down Operation Dynamo for good and all on the night of Saturday, 1st June – by which time the last 4,000 men of the British rear-guard would have been taken off.

Now word had come from the Admiralty, indicating that Ramsay's earlier petitions had borne fruit. For days, impressed by Commander Harold Henderson's pleas from Dunkirk, Ramsay had urged the French must be granted an equal chance to make a last-minute getaway. As scrupulously fair as he was exacting, this thought had come close to obsessing Ramsay; in the 'Dynamo' Room, Lieutenant William de Quincy never forgot how the admiral burst out: 'It's vital they should be brought off if we're ever to have any relationship with the French again.'

And it seemed Ramsay had won the day. By Winston Churchill's own command, French troops must have the same chance as Gort's army to board British ships.

What did this mean? To Ramsay, chewing it over with Captain Michael Denny, one factor had been at once plain: the ships, in the next twenty-four hours, must gear themselves for an even greater effort. Only thus could the French stand a chance – yet with no news forthcoming of twelve personnel ships and hospital carriers still making the round trip, Ramsay had been forced, at 9 a.m., to postpone further sailings.

The gruesome thought had crossed his mind: the missing ships, concentrating in the narrow waters off Dunkirk, might have met with the same fate as Wednesday's ill-starred convoy. In fact the ships were merely delayed, but Ramsay couldn't know that then.

Worse was to come – for within two hours of reaching Dover in the *Worcester*, Lieut.-General Alan Brooke and General Sir Ronald Adam had strode into Ramsay's office. One glance at Ramsay's schedule and Brooke, who had known the admiral for twenty years, had started up in distress.

He exhorted Ramsay: 'Look here, can't you alter this plan at all? I've just come from Gort's conference and he asked me to impress that it'll be days before the troops are clear. If you can't carry on, it'll be fatal to the B.E.F.'

Ramsay had seen the need all right – but a more bitter blow had been in store. At Dunkirk, a report from the beach party at Braye-les-Dunes stressed, the wind, which they had watched like augurers all that week, had risen to a gently insidious Force 3. As the surf rose in the shallows the weary men of the little boats could no more fight against it than the dog-tired Tommies.

Gradually boat after boat broached to and grounded. By 8 a.m., as the tide fell, they lay like beached driftwood all along the wind-swept sand – while the men of Gort's Army watched impotently from the dunes.

Ramsay was right to be worried: rarely had ships or men taken such a beating. In the *Maid of Orleans*, three trips to her credit, 3,600 men already lifted, Purser Sidney Mason Springgay felt as hard-pressed as any man alive. No sooner had the ship tied up that morning than a naval officer warned them: 'You're under half an hour's notice again.'

Springgay groaned: at such times it wasn't even safe to walk down the quay. Dover's eight cross-Channel berths were now jamming in eighteen ships at a time, packed in tiers three-deep, and to inch them out at all was a tricky business calling for both time and tugs.

And by now, every approach to Dunkirk harbour was a navigator's nightmare, a forest of sunken masts and superstructures. Easing the ship into the Mole, the previous night, the *Maid*'s captain, Gordon Walker, had growled: 'It's like a bloody fly crawling on a hob-nailed boot.'

As the ship grew dangerously overloaded, with 1,400 troops sardine-packed below decks, an Army officer urged Walker: 'If we get hit we shan't stand a chance with this lot.' Walker, a handsome sardonic veteran, retorted: 'But if we get hit we shan't stand a chance anyway – let's take all we can.'

Already troops had been packing the *Maid of Orleans* to the very rigging – and Walker knew there wasn't a life-belt aboard for any man-jack of them.

At Dover engineers from the base-ship *Sandhurst* had hourly proof of how tough things were: the destroyers' auxiliary engines, which were made of cast-iron, fractured even by bombs dropping 100 yards away. H.M.S. *Malcolm*'s bow, curved like the spur of a fighting cock, after collision . . . the Polish destroyer *Blyskawica*, the sea plainly visible through a rent in her forward hold . . . Diver Walter Davis, of the Harbour Board, working a twenty-four-hour day nine feet under the murky water, unsnarling wires from propeller after propeller, plugging cannon holes with wedges and tow . . . other repair men patching trawlers' condensers with sand and gravel . . . caulking leaks with oakum, mattresses, even axle grease.

Time and again Repairs Officer Weston Smith, boarding a ship for the crucial twenty-minute inspection that decided her fate, had just one warning for her Chief Enginer: 'Touch it light – it's a dockyard job.' The implication was plain: one bomb dropping fifty yards from the ship meant the finish.

As the damage mounted, the men closest to Ramsay knew only a miracle could save the Army now.

But some men were in the mood for miracles. At 9 a.m., at the very hour Ramsay knew his deepest despair, Skipper Lemon Webb, moored alongside the quay at Dover, had already been roused from his bunk in *Tollesbury* by a stentorian hail. A naval commander, moving from barge to barge, was seeking volunteers for Dunkirk.

The barges would be towed in the wake of a tug, but the crews still had the option of saying whether or not they went too.

Rubbing the sleep from his eyes, Webb caught doubtful murmurs of assent along the quayside. At first Skipper Horlick of the *Beatrice Maud* said flatly, No. His barge had no towrope. Mate Albert Catchpole of the *Ena* thought they might as well go; an old skipper had once prophesied Catchpole was born to be hanged, not drowned. Now Webb's own mate, Edward Gunn, chimed in: 'Well, if we was caught we shouldn't be taken prisoner, should we?'

Puzzled, the naval officer asked, 'Why not?'

Appalled at such ignorance, Gunn replied: 'What, and us in civilian clothes with no papers nor nothing?' In the end the naval officer was giving up, just walking away, when Webb hailed him: 'All right, Skipper, we're with you.'

Gunn, quite satisfied, now replied: 'Of course, if *you're* going I'll stop with you and all.' It wasn't that Gunn or any of them had any sense of fear, but as British working men they thought it needful to make their point. This was a voluntary show.

Shortly the naval officer returned with final orders. The five Ipswich barges were to be towed to Dunkirk and abandoned. The *Aidie* and the *Barbara Jean* – nephew Charlie's ship – were to be partly loaded with Government stores, including sixty tons of T.N.T. apiece. The *Tollesbury*, the *Doris* – skippered by Webb's brother-in-law, Fred Finbow – and the other barges were to carry rations only.

It was a vital mission. All along the perimeter now, food, water and ammunition were perilously low, but to discharge cargo in Dunkirk harbour itself was impossible. Even beach-work was fraught with danger, but broad-beamed shallow-draft barges like the *Tollesbury*, built to lie on the Suffolk mud-flats, took the ground upright, and carried for their sail area the smallest crew of any sea-going ship. And their wooden framework rendered them immune to magnetic mines.

On Webb and on others like him much of the safety of the rear-guard depended now. And hearing this Webb nodded, satisfied: how could you say no at a time like this?

Even when grounded the barges would serve as improvised piers, from which the soldiers would be transferred, by small boats and launches, to larger transports lying in deep water.

This point above all clinched it for Webb. Twelve years skipper of the *Tollesbury*, he loved every inch of her sky-blue decking; her rust-coloured sails spread to the breeze warmed his heart like no other sight on earth. There wasn't any detail of her routine in which he hadn't some say: even the beef puddings and suet rolls, the crew's staple diet, were made by Webb himself, just handed to deck-hand Percy Scott for final galley-work.

If Britain had need of the barge he loved, well and good, but Webb would be in at her death or know the reason why.

At 2 p.m., as the tug *Kenia* took them in tow, the naval officer had a last word of comfort: 'You'll have an air umbrella all the way.'

Two hours later, steering grimly in *Kenia*'s wake, Webb laughed outright. An air umbrella, right enough – a fearsome outspread umbrella of German Messerschmitts and Heinkels, roaring low, guns chattering, bombs triggering vast whale-spouts of water. Clinging to the heavy mahogany wheel, Webb gritted his teeth: if it was worse than this closer in, he reckoned he'd seen the last of 133 Cliff Lane and Mabel.

At Dunkirk things grew hourly worse: it seemed to Captain William Tennant it was just a matter of hours. The Force 3 wind that had freshened up the surf, bringing inshore work to a stand-still, was fast banishing the haze that had cloaked the water.

Now the Germans' 10.5 centimetre guns commanded by Major Hans Sandar found the range of the harbour; all morning the docking berths rocked under a screaming whining hail of shell-fire. At Furnes, Major Robert Riddell's Berkshires just couldn't cope; it took a savage counterattack by Major Richard Colvin's Grenadiers to dislodge German infantry who had forded the canal by night – though not before a Grenadier truck unsuspectingly tried to deliver rations to the building they'd settled into. Worse, at the eastern end of the perimeter, by Nieuport, the German guns, moving up to the line of the Yser River, were straddling the beaches of La Panne. Three hundred tantalising feet out of reach, the observation balloon spotting for them floated mockingly in a clear blue sky.

In despair, Tennant wondered how this would affect the troops now.

Up at La Panne, Gunner Hugh Fisher was one of thousands who saw what was happening: in the slit-trench he shared with Gunner Harry Randall, Fisher flinched suddenly as a banshee wailing burst inside his brain. Along the water's edge for three-quarters of a mile, shells were falling, tall plumes of sand whooshing to the sky.

As Fisher watched, the gunners were bracketing closer inland; at twenty-five-yard intervals the tightly-sown barrage came howling – nearer and nearer to the crouching troops. Abruptly men were scrambling from their trenches, abandoning cover and pelting wildly inland – among them Fisher and Randall.

As they ran the air buzzed with bullets and on all sides men were falling. Appalled, Fisher saw the import; he yelled to Randall: 'We're plumb daft, Harry – we're running into them.' Less than a mile away German snipers with telescopic sights were picking off Tommy after Tommy.

Tensely the two men waited – then as the next shells came screaming, both counted three, then hit the sand face down. Doubling cannily back towards the water's edge, they saw the shells falling still farther inland. Quick-witted, Fisher and Randall had survived – but the twisted khaki-clad forms ranked almost regimentally across the dunes, showed the measure of the tragedy.

The sea churned with blood and froth, flecked white with the splinters of bursting shells, but still the men of the little ships worked dazedly on.

Not all were heroes. At 3 p.m., en route for Dunkirk aboard the minesweeper *Niger*, Commander St John Cronyn was mortified to see a whole flood of little boats making speedy tracks for Dover – without a soul aboard save their crews. Promptly Cronyn signalled Admiral Ramsay: 'Number of little ships are returning empty.'

Though Ramsay signalled back indignantly: 'Arrest any little ship returning empty,' Cronyn shrugged his shoulders. In mid-Channel, under non-stop air attack, that seemed scarcely feasible.

But scores who'd never heard a shot fired in anger stuck it gamely out. Engineer Fred Reynard had been up half the night, making plans for this moment, in the motor vessel *Bee*; by common consent even young Sub-Lieutenant Kindall deferred to Fred, a survivor of Gallipoli. Convinced *Bee* was too high out of the water for weary troops to scramble aboard, Fred persuaded Mate Harry Downer to jump over the side and see if he could get back unaided.

Since Downer barely made it, Fred found the solution – sawing up the 26-foot ladder with which they scaled the sides of bigger ships in Portsmouth Harbour. Now with the *Bee* grounded the crew were doing yeoman service, the two halves of the ladder suspended at either side of the bows.

Their only protection against the hail of shells was Sub-Lieutenant Kindall's revolver, but every man was too busy to think about that.

It was the same in every little boat. Skipper Albert Grimwade and the crew of the oyster dredger *Vanguard* didn't even have steel helmets; as they ferried troops to the armed yacht *Grive* they shielded their heads with enamel bowls, balers, even zinc buckets. Minute by minute the near-misses splashed closer. Dr Basil Smith, gruff little chartered accountant, had *Constant Nymph* so close in to the shore he thought for a moment he'd hit a wreck. From the stern-sheets, Stoker Meakle, three months' naval service, announced dispassionately, 'That was a shell, sir.'

Smith roared back, 'The hell it was,' then mentally chided himself. He was in the Navy now; the correct reply was 'Very good.'

Aboard the cutter-rigged cockle boat *Endeavour*, one of six that had come from the Essex mud-flats, Convoy Signalman Eric Marsh, a nineteen-year-old naval rating, hit the deck as a curtain of shells descended, seeking cover behind a sandbag; briefly he glimpsed the Eastern Mole, rearing above them, at low tide, like a liner's hull. When Marsh looked again, he saw in consternation that the Mole had receded. Skipper Fred Hall had the *Endeavour* heading for Dover.

At once Marsh stumbled aft. 'What are you *doing*?'

Skipper Hall argued: 'We can't go through that – it's suicide. We can't be expected to.'

Sadly Marsh shook his head. 'It may seem strange, but we are.' Patiently he explained the situation: naval discipline just wouldn't permit *his* returning empty-handed, yet *Endeavour*, while free to please herself, could hardly let him off in mid-Channel.

The first shock past, Fred Hall saw where duty lay. Within seconds *Endeavour* was heading back for the Mole, one of a six-strong fleet that ferried 1,000 men to the safety of the *schuits*.

The little ships had reason to be fearful. Their job done, Arthur Dench and the crew of his little green cockle boat, *Letitia*, were on their way home to Leigh-on-Sea, Essex, just clearing Dunkirk harbour in tow of a trawler, when Dench spied his nephew, Fred Osborne, engineer of the cockle boat *Renown*. 'We've broken down,' Osborne hailed, but his uncle reassured him. 'Give us a rope and we'll tow you.'

Soon, with 18 feet of rope securing *Renown* to *Letitia*'s stern, the three boats were gliding up the Belgian coast, cheating the tide. The night was so peaceful Dench sent his crew – his nineteen-year-old son Jim, engineer Tom Meddle and deck-hand Ken Horner – below for some sleep.

What followed was stark horror. In the darkness Dench never saw the mine that blew *Renown* to smithereens – though for one hair-raising moment he 'heard something scraping' against *Letitia*'s side. Then, with an explosion like Judgement Day, the night split apart – so violently that the decking was cleft beneath his feet, trapping him in the sprung planking. As he wrenched free, tiny slivers of wood from *Renown* came raining 'like a million matchsticks' from the sky.

The crew, bursting on deck, found Dench still clinging vacantly to *Renown*'s tow-rope, though it was almost a day before they knew what had happened: the shock had bereft him of speech.

Yet more and more craft were joining the fray – so many that Captain de Corvette de Toulouse-Lautrec, on the bridge of *Siroco*, thought instinctively of the Champs-Elysées in the rush-hour. The naval pinnace *Minotaur* manned by teenage sea-scouts from Mortlake on the Thames River . . . the Belgian fishing smack *Cor Jesu* . . . Corporal Leslie Fowler's R.A.F. seaplane tender, five times machine-gunned at low level . . . the London Fire Brigade firefloat *Massey Shaw*.

On the beaches north of La Panne, Major Hans Sandar could scarcely credit it; a lean, disciplined artillery officer of the S.S. Totenkopf Division, he at first stopped aghast as the little ships bobbed within range of his 10.5 centimetre guns.

Then, appalled by the unorthodoxy, he burst out: 'What are the British trying to do – turn this into a circus or something?'

Circus or no, they were tough performers – and few worked a longer stint than Ramsgate's lifeboat *Prudential*, one of the two Kentish lifeboats manned by civilian crews. For thirty non-stop hours *Prudential* plied between beach and destroyers . . . packing in 160 men at a time . . . towing other boats that had broken down . . . her seven wherries battling the lively surf . . . bringing off a peak total of 2,800 men. Once, as they struggled ashore in the darkness, a voice called, 'I cannot see who you are. Are you a naval party?' When Coxswain Howard Knight had defined their status, printed legend records a high-sounding tribute: 'Thank you – and thank God for such men as you have this night proved yourselves to be.'

From where Lifeboatman Jim Hawkes stood, though, the

benison was both informal and salty: 'Thank God you've got such bloody fine guts.'

Admiral Frederick Wake-Walker, aboard his ninth flagship, the destroyer *Keith*, would have been the first to agree — but more than guts was needed now. Above all, the Admiral needed patience: loaded to the gunwales with troops, scores of little boats were moving out, all set for a see-the-conquering-heroes-come return to England. To the admiral it was an all too human reaction, yet at dusk the sloops and minesweepers were due. If the little boats departed in triumph, the whole concept of the inshore ferry-service would break down.

Now, with *Keith* veering in majestic circles, the admiral sought to restore order from chaos — his flag-lieutenant, Lord Kelburn, roaring through a megaphone: 'Do not go . . . discharge your cargoes and hang on . . . to all little ships, you are still needed.'

In the heat of the *mêlée*, many thought to find their own way home. Bombardier Victor Allport set blithely off, paddling as if possessed, on a wooden locker. Private Arthur Yendall saw another man without concern set sail on a door. From the dunes, Private William Nightingale of the Ordnance Corps, watched men bobbing happily away on rafts made from barrels. In the minesweeper *Ross*, Yeoman of Signals Wilfred Walters watched in silent admiration: a soldier sitting in a motorcycle's inner tube was propelling it with his rifle.

Others escaped by a hair's breadth. Private Fred Shepherd of the Bedfordshire and Hertfordshire Regiment never saw the shell that spun him in a soaring parabola into the water: as he floated unconscious, a sailor from the *schuit Oranje* skewered a boat-hook through his battledress and swung him inboard. Private Leslie Carran of the Cheshires, spying a minesweeper's rowboat off Braye, struck out for thirty flagging yards, then knew one moment of pure agony as the boatswain hauled him over the gunwale by his hair. It was the first — and last — time he ever swam.

One man was rescued against his will. To Petty Officer Alfred Brinton, drifting helplessly off La Panne beach in a defunct assault landing-craft, life seemed as black as night. First, as a senior instructor at Hayling Island, Portsmouth, he'd known the cold comfort of sending his craft and ratings on ahead . . . then days of chafing without a boat . . . now, after fixing a transfer his craft had broken down after one spell of inshore ferry-work. In despair Brinton hailed another landing-craft towing a small motor yacht named *Rosaura*.

Sub-Lieutenant William Tower, her skipper, was a stranger to Brinton, but the Petty Officer felt an instant kinship. As Tower hailed briskly, 'What's wrong, coxswain?' Brinton confessed, 'Blooming old engine's broken down, sir.'

'Can you get it going again?'

'No, it's seized up, useless. How about giving us a tow, sir?'

As ever, Tower was decisive. 'We can't tow that big heavy thing, you'd better come aboard with us.'

Sadly Brinton saw the logic. First he saw his two able-seamen off the craft . . . then, sprinkling petrol over the decking, he set fire to it . . . scrambling finally aboard Tower's own craft. The young officer explained they were en route to Ramsgate and Brinton's heart sank – just a week of bad luck from start to finish, out of it before he'd even begun. The one bright spot was meeting an officer like this, a born commander if he ever saw one – and it wasn't likely *their* paths would cross again.

For the men of Dunkirk the end was foreseeable in hours now, though few knew it: the mind almost anaesthetised by pain and shock, home had dwindled to a faraway dream. Trooper Dennis Cartwright, Birmingham-bred, lay back on the dunes, eyes closed, reshaping the cries and the chaos to a companionable Saturday afternoon roar: West Bromwich Albion football team playing on the home ground. Major Cyril Huddlestone of the East Yorks dreamed of eating cucumber sandwiches and watching the pretty girls in their swimsuits at the Mere Country Club, Knutsford, Cheshire. Twenty-four hours later he was doing just that; the Army had obliged by evacuating him there.

Private Walter Osborn, of the Suffolks, still holding out on the canal near Furnes, thought about his wife Louvain, back in Ipswich. Somehow Osborn felt they'd make a go of it if he got back though they had been married barely a month before he wrote that letter to Winston Churchill. Always a man to do things on impulse, Osborn had applied for compassionate leave from France on the grounds of his marriage – though he'd only broken the news to Louvain on arriving home.

When she rebuked him, 'You're daft, we haven't two halfpennies to rub together,' Osborn's formal proposal held a note of despair. 'All I know is this, gel – if I don't go back with a marriage certificate I'll be in the clink.'

In the end the special licence hadn't come through until days after Osborn was overdue; he'd only narrowly escaped the guardhouse then.

Strange delusions multiplied. Second-Lieutenant Alexander Lyell believed he *was* home: the Dunkirk landscape melted to a mirage of the road from Arbroath to Dundee. Sapper Robert Nevison saw a sight he'd never seen in his life – his father heading a Leeds choir in the chorus 'Glory to God in the Highest', from *The Messiah*. Lieutenant Laurence Harley lived a whole week of fantasy . . . piously attending religious services he later found never took place . . . convinced he was alone on the beach like a military Robinson Crusoe . . . following tank-tracks, Crusoe-like, for three miles on his commander's orders until they petered out. In fact, the tracks were those of his Humber staff-car – and the commander had issued no orders at all.

Some men hardly cared any more: adapting themselves as readily as water to a tumbler, they'd decided it was safer ashore. Corporal John Hudson, a sapper, keeping things going at the lorry jetties, christened them the 'dune dwellers': men who would make no move now the shelling was hotter, sitting it contentedly out like spectators in an amphitheatre.

Short on home comforts, they did the best they could . . . digging foxholes with steel helmets and empty corned-beef tins . . . topping them with mattresses, driftwood and corrugated iron . . . some setting their alarm clocks daily for 6 a.m . . . Bombardier 'Darky' Lowe and his mates bedding down between bales of sheep's wool on the Mole itself with a table, white linen cloth, milk, tea, sugar and a four-pint engraved silver teapot . . . Private Mervyn Doncom, having quested for fresh treasures, snuggling down in a deserted hotel basement with a cask of rum, swaddled in a silk eiderdown quilt.

One man who wasn't going home if he could help it was Lord Gort. As the Germans closed in on La Panne, he knew the last 100,000 men of his Army were in dire straits. It was more than flesh and blood could bear to leave them now.

Already, hazarding that the easternmost beaches would be in German hands next day, Gort had changed plans drastically. Now the 6,000 men of General Dudley Johnson's 4th Division holding the eastern perimeter at Nieuport must trek ten miles along the beaches to Braye Dunes – there to be taken off by Ramsay's 'special tows', a fifty-strong force of lifeboats and pulling boats drawn by tugs. Meantime the troops already at Braye must move westwards through Malo-les-Bains towards Dunkirk.

The trouble was, plans had changed so rapidly that Ramsay, as Gort knew, had had no time to inform the 'special tows' of the switch. If the minesweepers acting as watchdogs of the whole operation didn't latch on fast enough, the troops might arrive to find no boats at all.

Hence Gort's reluctance to leave, for none knew better than he that the perimeter was shrinking hour by hour.

Hour by hour the fears for Gort's own safety were increasing too. Well briefed by Lord Munster that 'Tiger' Gort would fight to the death, Winston Churchill was giving the Admiralty no peace – but the Navy could hardly keep track of him. Commander Colin Maud, of *Icarus*, unaware that the special dispatches he had sent ashore for Gort were a summons to return, made tracks for Dover with a load of troops. No sooner had he made fast than a Whitehall official approached him surreptitiously. 'Do you have a very important person on board?'

When Maud shook his head, mystified, the official fled in consternation – later to approach Lieutenant Courtney Anderson, whose Motor Torpedo Boat 67 had just tied up. In desperation the official urged: 'But you went to get him.'

Now Anderson remembered: days back he had sent an urgent summons ashore to Gort but the reply had been final. Gort was too busy evacuating an Army to consider coming.

'So far as I know,' Anderson answered unhelpfully, 'he's still sitting on the beach in France.'

In fact, though he would much prefer to have been, Gort wasn't. Already that afternoon he had phoned the Chief of the Imperial General Staff, Sir John Dill, at the War Office, explaining the change in plans . . . a last meeting with Major-General Alexander to lay down final instructions . . . Alexander to work under Admiral Abrial to the end, with leeway to surrender if it seemed the troops were in too great a jeopardy . . . a silent session, alone in his bedroom, cutting medal ribbons from a tunic he would have to leave behind.

Ascetic to the last, Gort was carrying his own two suitcases as he strode down the beach in the fading light with his Acting Chief of Staff, Brigadier Oliver Leese.

From then on all was routine . . . a long pull in an Army pontoon boat to Admiral Wake-Walker's flagship *Keith* . . . as shells fell astern of the pontoon, Gort didn't even bother to look round. Alongside, he found the destroyer's scrambling net harder going;

the Admiral's Flag-Lieutenant, Lord Kelburn, bounding on deck in the twilight in answer to a summons, glimpsed a mountain of a man floundering at the rail. Promptly, grasping him round the waist, Kelburn heaved. With a resounding thud two peers of the realm hit the deck as one.

In a moment Gort got up and walked away, almost too angry to speak. It was as if the cancer of humiliation was so deep within him now that even well-meant gestures were taken as an affront.

Yet his reluctance to quit the port that had seen the ruin of all his hopes was plain. Immediately aboard *Keith* he changed his mind; he wanted a transfer to the minesweeper *Hebe*, where he knew Commander John Temple. As the motor-launch sped off, Wake-Walker turned to Kelburn and heaved a sigh of relief: 'Well, thank heavens that's over.' Still Gort seemed unwilling to move. For close on six hours, while *Hebe*, her 4-inch guns blazing at German raiders, shook like an aspen leaf, Gort hugged the bridge, binoculars levelled, impassively surveying the scene. Watching him, Captain Eric Bush, R.N., couldn't understand why he was nursing a lantern he'd brought aboard.

Not until midnight, after a brief rest in the chart-house, did he step aboard Lieutenant Trevor de Hamel's Motor Anti-Submarine Boat 6 which was to ferry him to Dover. In the wheel-house, Leading Telegraphist William Coom, greatly daring, asked for his autograph.

Without demur the general signed 'Gort' in greenish-blue ink, with a bold backward-sloping hand – it seemed to Coom he was too tired even to protest. Rooted to the wheel-house with Oliver Leese as the little boat skimmed towards Dover, so weary that he nodded off to sleep even in mid-sentence, the commander of the beaten army went home.

As shell after shell came shattering into the little village of La Panne, Bill and Augusta Hersey knew that luck was still with them. Slumped dejectedly on the garage floor, Augusta had almost resigned herself to never seeing Bill again; but miraculously an ordnance corps captain had intervened.

As Hersey once again clambered into his truck to collect another load of troops from the perimeter, the captain – though the Herseys never knew why – stepped forward. He told Bill Hersey: 'Look, lad, you've done enough. From now on, you stop here with your wife.'

It was daylight when the order came through: 'Move down to the beach now. Go gradually, in ones and twos.' Slowly the Herseys set off . . . over cobbled streets, looped by trailing cables and choked with the swollen cadavers of horses . . . past the charred black ruins of seaside villas . . . Bill with his kit-bag hoisted, Augusta still lugging the suitcase that held her trousseau.

At the edge of the beach they ran into trouble. In the clammy heat Augusta had discarded her army greatcoat and her neat blue topcoat was plainly visible. At once an army beach-master stepped forward: 'No women allowed on the beach.'

Reasonably Hersey replied: 'She's my wife.' But the officer's voice was curt, final: 'I said, no women allowed on the beach.'

'I said, she's my wife!'

As the officer thrice rapped out his veto Hersey, eyes blazing, jerked his rifle to the ready, snicking back the bolt. After an ugly pause, the officer turned and walked away.

Still the Herseys' troubles weren't done. Another officer, overseeing the queues, was friendly but just as final. The Senior Beach-master must issue a written permit before Augusta could join a queue.

Desperately Hersey began a frantic search for someone who could allot the magic passport, but the crowds were too dense: numb with despair, he had to give up. Miraculously a friendly gunner now donated Augusta some battledress trousers, an army captain weighing in with a greatcoat.

As night curtained the water, Bill and Augusta slipped into the queue stretching out along the trucks – General Alexander's improvised jetties were working even now. Again Augusta looked every inch a soldier, though the men packed around were too tired to care. Drowsy with fatigue, their eyes bloodshot, they stared patiently into the darkness, while shells and Very lights, green, yellow and red, stitched the night sky to the east.

It seemed hours before they reached the jetty's end, but now an impasse arose. The ship's whaler bobbing level with the pier had room for just one more.

Hersey thought fast. Whatever happened he mustn't leave Augusta now. Lacking any word of English, they'd be wise to the ruse as soon as she reached the ship. They might even turn her back.

Quickly he turned to the soldier behind him. 'One more, lad – jump in here.'

The soldier gaped: 'What about your mate?'

Seeing Augusta sway with fatigue, Hersey, on an inspiration, steadied her with his arm. 'Oh, he's drunk – I'd best stay with him, see him through.'

Still their luck was holding. Almost at once another whaler loomed from the darkness; they scrambled in. They could read the legend on the sailor's cap: H.M.S. *Ivanhoe*.

The Herseys were just in time. At midnight on 31st May time was running out for Gort's Army. Of the last 5,000 souls to be lifted from La Panne beach before the Germans moved in, Bill and Augusta numbered two.

Though five destroyers, including *Ivanhoe*, were anchored offshore, they mustered only fifteen whalers between them. It was a full hour before the Herseys' whaler reached *Ivanhoe* and they began the spiderlike crawl up the scrambling nets.

But Augusta's crisis wasn't over: collapsing awkwardly on the destroyer's deck, she all but knocked herself cold with her rifle.

Curiously a sailor asked Hersey, 'What's up with your mate?' Never at a loss, Hersey replied: 'He's punchy – got a bit of shell-shock.'

Stumbling, half-unconscious now, Augusta was guided to the crew's mess-deck. Gently Bill Hersey helped his wife to sink to rest beneath a table – packed amongst soldiers, many of them naked, all in the last stages of exhaustion. But Augusta no longer cared. Next instant she had drifted into sleep, and as she slumped sideways her steel helmet rolled away to expose her sleek dark hair.

At Dunkirk, others realised the bitter truth: they were not going home at all. At Rosendael, the old château three miles east of the Bastion, housing many of the Dunkirk wounded, Major Philip Newman had ominous instructions from Major-General Harold Alexander. For every wounded man, one doctor and ten other ranks must stay behind.

Already Rosendael was bursting at the seams with wounded men; with the château long since jam-packed, scores lay beneath bushes in the grounds, nothing to quench their thirst save water from the goldfish pond. There were few dressings to treat them; the larder was down to fifty tins of baked beans. Unless hospital ships got through and fast, hundreds were destined for captivity.

In the Officers' Mess, by the flaring light of acetylene lamps, Newman and sixteen others drew lots. As the unit's priest, Father Joseph O'Shea, drew the names from a bowler hat unearthed in the cellar there was no sound in the room at all. Newman, drawing No. 17, felt a cold lump coil in his stomach: he would be one of the three to stay. Overcome by the pathos of it, though he was leaving for England, Theo Pathé, the French liaison officer, wept silently.

Thousands faced up to decisions affecting their entire lives. Captain Malcolm Blair, cut off from the Royal Fusiliers, was already aboard a destroyer when he heard his unit was still holding the Nieuport line; at once, hitching a ride in a whaler, he splashed ashore and trudged twenty miles to report. Half an hour later, the shell that wiped out Battalion Headquarters killed him outright. At Dover, aboard the destroyer *Mistral*, the Abbé Castel was just leaving for Cherbourg when word came that *Siroco*, of the same flotilla, must return to Dunkirk. As flotilla chaplain, the Abbé saw what he must do; deftly transferring to *Siroco*, he explained: '*Mes enfants, je ne puis vous laisser partir sans aumonier dans cet enfer.*' (My children, I cannot let you sail into this hell without a chaplain.) When German bombers and E-boats tore the heart from *Siroco* off the Kwinte Buoy, thirty-three of the crew were saved – but not the Abbé Castel.

To others it seemed time to contract out: accepting the stark shame of defeat, they found the truth unpalatably bitter. In the paddle-minesweeper *Glengower*, Lieutenant Gilbert Chapman, R.N.V.R., tried to coax a sea-soaked Tommy from the sponson that housed the paddles; below it was warm and dry. But the man was at lowest ebb: 'I'm so bloody fed up I want to catch pneumonia.' Some saw death as in a mirror: Lieutenant Cyril Murray, in the dunes at Malo, checked the chambers of his revolver, decided five for them, one for me. He thought there could be no mercy if the Germans took him prisoner; his identity discs were stamped 'Jew'.

A few found consolation in their blood. As Lieut.-Colonel Marvo Martin, an Irishman, commanding the 4th East Yorks, led his party to the Mole a naval officer halted them: there were no more ships that night, and when the next were coming heaven alone knew. When Martin, deeply stirred, cried, 'To think that I should lead the battalion to this,' Major 'Rosy' Lucas, his Irish second-in-command, had a word of cheer: 'Never mind, sorr – at the worse we can always claim our neutrality.'

Yet slowly the totals mounted – and no man knew greater joy than Winston Churchill. At the British Embassy in Paris, where

Churchill had flown to settle the last details of the French evacuation, Detective-Inspector Walter Thompson, his bodyguard, could find no peace. Even at midnight, Churchill had issued a post-haste summons to his suite.

When Thompson entered, Churchill, hugging himself like a small boy propounding a riddle, jabbed an ever-present cigar: 'Thompson, how many men do you think have been taken off at Dunkirk – from the beaches alone?'

Thompson, bewildered, gave up. He didn't even know how many were there. But Churchill, capering with glee, pressed him: 'Guess, Thompson – guess!'

In no mood for small-hours party-games, Thompson did his best. He hazarded, 'Perhaps fifty thousand?' Elated at scoring, Churchill first scoffed: 'Fifty thousand? Close to *double* that number, Thompson – and many more will come.' Then he added a solicitous rider: in his room, Thompson was cut off from all bulletins, but if he bedded down right here in the annexe, Churchill could give him a shake each time fresh totals came through.

Inwardly Thompson groaned. For the men of Dunkirk he felt as keenly as any Briton – yet the prospects of a good night's sleep now seemed very far away.

At La Panne they faced a bottle-neck. Hersey's own division – General Dudley Johnson's 4th – were in a desperate plight; there just wasn't a sign of the Navy. But now Johnson had an inspiration. Though the underwater cable from La Panne to Dover had been short-circuited by a bomb the day before, its frayed end was plainly visible down a cavity four feet deep.

In minutes a signalman had re-established the connection. Calling Ramsay at Dover, Johnson announced flatly: there were no boats. The troops were supposed to be embarking at the rate of 1,000 per hour – instead it was more like 100. Ramsay groaned: on this pitch-dark night of chaos, it was impossible to know whether the minesweepers had contacted his 'special tows' or not.

Brigadier Christopher Woolner, who'd looked in, never forgot the tension in the little villa: the eerie shadowed light from a blue hurricane lamp ... Johnson pacing silently up and down ... a staff officer linked by phone to the War Office, repeating stubbornly, 'But there *aren't* any boats' ... long ticking moments of silence.

Finally the War Office made a solemn vow. By daylight there would be boats to take off 6,000 men at Braye Dunes and Dunkirk.

Now the only way out for Johnson's men was westwards along the open sands, with enemy guns pounding the beaches, the staccato crack of musketry splintering the night, the grim prospect of enemy fighters when daylight came. Doggedly, moving in small compact groups, 6,000 men began the nine-mile trek.

Half the ships would never have known, if it hadn't been for the Naval Signals Officer, Lieut.-Commander James McLelland. Just before 1 a.m. he had called Ramsay's headquarters from La Panne: Gort had gone and he was closing down the telephone. Now, making his way along the beach towards Braye, McLelland chanced on some soldiers firing rifles in the air to signal to ships at anchor.

His signal lamp already smashed by a shell splinter, McLelland saw one last resort. Despite a wounded ankle he plunged into the sea, swimming desperately for the faint riding lights of the ship. Scrambling aboard the minesweeper *Gossamer*, he managed to gasp out the vital news to Lieut.-Commander Richard Ross before collapsing. The troops were moving west – and this, too, was where the ships must go.

Not every ship got the news. Towards midnight, east of Dunkirk, the tug *Kenia*, with *Tollesbury* and *Ethel Everard* in tow, steamed into a living tableau of hell; the shifting red outline of the burning port to the east, the darkness split by white veins of light, the menacing muffled roar of the perimeter guns.

To Skipper Lemon Webb it was a heart-stopping sight.

Without an auxiliary engine, without navigation lamps of any kind, a damaged rifle was the old barge's only weapon of defence. At midnight, as the tug slipped the one-and-a-half-inch wire, Webb and his crew were on their own.

Now, using the *Tollesbury*'s 'sweeps' — massive 24-foot oars — Webb and his crew began to row the barge ashore. Already Mate Edward Gunn had fashioned a life-line of rope, coiling it in loops over the fanciful yellow scrollwork adorning *Tollesbury*'s black-painted sides. If they chanced close to troops in the water, the soldiers would be able to cling on.

Abruptly the three ceased rowing. The motion of the 'sweeps' was lighting up the water with an uncanny phosphorescence — a phenomenon seen only on a dead calm sea. But Webb thought the shimmering wavelets might be enough to get the Luftwaffe curious.

Now, as the *Tollesbury* drifted closer, a strong sound arose on the night — to Webb, a Suffolk countryman, it was like the bleating of sheep on the salt-marshes. Next instant he knew the cries were human. 'Barge, barge, barge,' they were crying, then, on a rising note of hysteria, 'Skipper, Skipper, don't let her go aground.'

In the darkness none of them could see *Tollesbury* was flat-bottomed, drawing only three feet of water.

Deftly Webb brought the setting booms into play: long 15-foot poles topped with an iron spike, they operated much like a punt-pole to stop the barge from going too deeply into the mud. With a rattle the seven-ton anchor went out. Head on to sea, stern to the beach, *Tollesbury* had made her Dunkirk landfall.

Then as Webb lowered the hold-ladder to the waiting troops, the old barge shifted slightly. The ladder snapped like dry kindling.

At once Webb went into a frantic huddle with Mate Edward Gunn: the soldiers, shoulder-high in water, were in no shape to scramble aboard unaided. Within minutes they had the solution.

Swinging the barge's lifeboat in the davits over the side, they lowered only the stern tackle. Now, suspended almost vertically, the lifeboat could do service as a ladder.

One by one, uniforms black with water, the weight of their equipment almost tugging them backwards, the troops floundered like sodden sacks on to *Tollesbury*'s sky-blue decking. For a moment the old bargee felt his arms almost wrenched from their sockets. Then came an angry bull-roar from the shore: 'Who is in charge there?'

Webb, striving to make himself heard above the frantic cries of the troops, replied, 'Only the skipper.' At once the voice rebuked him: 'Well, you don't know much about handling men.'

The troops' shouting died to a soft murmur, like wind through grass. The Germans were very close now, close enough to hear the shouting.

But Webb was almost beside himself; he was a sailor-man, wasn't he, not a sergeant-major? Angrily he retorted: 'Well, at least *I'm* getting 'em aboard.' The interchange gave him fresh heart. Forgetting it wasn't his mission to get troops aboard at all, Webb told himself no brass hat should show him how to skipper his barge.

It was plain, too, that the biscuits and the 10-gallon tank of water he had been ordered to put ashore wouldn't be offloaded now. These men were starving. Just a few had strength to teeter along the deck to the bows; shortly Webb found the lifeboat from the Ipswich barge *Beatrice Maud* was ferrying them to a destroyer. But many more collapsed where they lay – in the foc's'le, in the sail cupboard, even in the coal-bunkers.

In fascination Webb watched as the famished men – among them a major-general and his aide – fell on the cheese and loaves of bread, tearing at it in handfuls, gulping gratefully at the cold clean water.

But as the sky grew paler, Webb knew keen anxiety: *Tollesbury* was anchored no more than eighty yards from the shore. If she wasn't clear of the beach by dawn the shells might shatter her to matchboard.

In the wheel-house, Webb wrestled with the decision. His orders were to beach his beloved barge and get away fast. But there were the men to get back now, at least 250, he estimated – in fact it was 273. It was high time to push off into deeper water. He yelled crisp instructions to Edward Gunn and Percy Scott.

Five minutes passed in the darkness . . . ten . . . fifteen. Then Gunn, sodden and dispirited, reported the worst news yet. The *Tollesbury*'s 17-cwt. rudder, a massive wooden affair like a tree-trunk, was wedged immovably in soft silting sand.

As the minutes raced and the tide receded, *Tollesbury* was going harder aground. Now Webb tried desperate expedients . . . exhorting the soldiers to try and rock her off . . . yelling to a passing motor-boat for a tow. Regretfully the answer floated back: the engine just hadn't the power.

Until two hours after dawn when the tide rose to refloat her, *Tollesbury* was a fixture. Webb had to accept that, like it or no, but he knew that whatever happened he'd be with her to the end. Softly he spoke aloud the words that were his credo: 'You don't leave a barge to die.'

CHAPTER NINE

MOST CHAPS HAVE GONE, YOU KNOW

Saturday, 1st June
1 a.m.–12 p.m.

Cresting the dunes at first light on Saturday, 1st June, Brigadier Evelyn Barker, a veteran soldier of the 4th Division, was at first struck dumb by the sight that greeted him. For ten clear miles the horizon was a dark unending smudge of men packed as densely as a hive in swarm.

Deeply stirred, Barker burst out: 'Good God, I never thought I'd see the British Army reduced to this.' Then turning to his aide, Second-Lieutenant Peter Young, he grumbled, 'You know, the men don't *care* that we're going back to England.'

Young thought the men cared all right – but that now, beaten, bewildered and misled, they would relish a fight only on equal terms. And by 5 a.m. it was plain that the odds were weighted against 65,000 men – the cream of Gort's Army – from reaching England at all.

Stepping ashore at Dover from Motor Anti-Submarine Boat 6 in the chill dawn of this Saturday, the same black truth had crossed the mind of Gort himself. At that hour, Leading Telegraphist William Coom recalls, there wasn't a soul on the quayside: only a lone sentry who almost dropped his rifle as it hit him he was presenting arms to the commander-in-chief.

But within seconds a Government Rolls had purred to a halt with a party headed by the general's military assistant, Lord Munster, and a Whitehall official, bustling forward, expressed relief the C.-in-C. was safely back.

At once Gort flashed angrily: 'That *I've* come back safe, huh? That isn't what matters – it's that my army gets back.'

In truth, all Gort's fears were justified. On the British sector of the canals girdling Dunkirk, an eight-mile loop from Bergues in the west to Les Moeres in the east only 39,000 British troops remained. Westwards, in the French sector, 50,000 *poilus* held fast.

But as the troops drew back from strong point after strong point, the chances of the rear-guard holding out dwindled perilously. To Major-General Harold Alexander, now headquartered in the Bastion, it seemed Admiral Abrial's plan to contract the perimeter further would draw the Germany artillery closer still and put paid to all embarkation.

On the other hand, Alexander was convinced, the British couldn't hold the line above another twenty-four hours. Brigadier Miles Dempsey, visiting the Bastion, always recalled Alexander on the phone to the War Office announcing curtly, 'I just don't propose to hold beyond Sunday night – after that we're all coming home.'

As the phone went down with a bang, Dempsey thought: 'Thank God – there's a man who's in control.'

The tragedy was there were hostile forces even Alexander couldn't control – among them the Stukas of Baron von Richtofen's 8th Flying Corps. All night the reconnaissance planes had been too active for comfort, the pure white lights of their magnesium flares dazzling eerily on the harbour waters. The R.A.F.'s dawn patrol – three crack Spitfire squadrons whose talents included such up-and-coming air-aces as Flight-Lieutenant Douglas Bader and Flight-Lieutenant Bryan Lane – could see there was trouble ahead.

And by 5 a.m., 4,000 feet above the target, their worst suspicions were confirmed: the grey wheeling shapes of a dozen Messerschmitt 109s, darting like sharks into cloud cover, orange flashes winking from their noses as they fired. What the pilots still lacked in technique they compensated in cold courage: within seconds the hazards were mounting . . . Flight-Sergeant George Unwin looping so close beneath a Messerschmitt it blew up above his head . . . Flying Officer Gordon Sinclair screaming after another ME in a dive that took him within fifty feet of ground level . . . Flight-Lieutenant Douglas Bader pouncing like a hawk on the first ME 109 he'd ever seen, watching the great spurt of orange flame whoosh back at him like a blow-torch, and thinking: 'It's true – they *do* have black crosses.'

Others were in direr straits. Pilot Officer Roy Morant, of Bader's squadron, his port engine gone, struggled to fight his way from a cockpit choking with glycol fumes, then belly-flopped into the sea. Briskly he showed Colonel Daniel Beak's South Lancs how to blow up the plane by firing at the petrol tank, then joined them in their trek along the sands. Sergeant Jack Potter, of No. 19 Squadron, stopped a cannon shell on the port side, then crash-dived his Spitfire 4,000 feet in the sea before clambering aboard a French fishing-smack.

By 6 a.m., claiming a total bag of fifteen German fighters, the dawn patrol was heading for base – and to the second wave closing the target soon after, it seemed all was quiet. In their whole forty-five minute patrol, Squadron Leader John Thompson's 111 Squadron never saw a Messerschmitt: by 7 a.m. they, too, had returned to base. The next sortie was timed for 9 a.m.

At 7.20 a.m., after first tentative probings along the beach, von Richtofen struck.

It was masterly timing. To Skipper Lemon Webb, still grounded aboard *Tollesbury*, it came without a scrap of warning: in his varnished pitch-pine cabin, aft, the old bargee was fixing breakfast on his Primus when a roar came from above. The major-general, whose name Webb never knew, had shouted to his aide, 'My God, Tony, look out!' Then, with the demon howl of hurtling metal, a bomb burst amidships within two feet of *Tollesbury*'s side.

As the barge bucked and shuddered like an animal in pain, Webb felt a twinge of guilt. If he'd been top-side, a judicious turn of the wheel when the bomb struck might have eased *Tollesbury*'s rudder from the sand bar.

Yet luck, it seemed, was on *Tollesbury*'s side. First Webb sent Mate Edward Gunn hastening to the barge's well to see if she was making water. In minutes Gunn reported no: the old lady was holding up. Now, oblivious to the sharp-edged snarl of bombs, the rocking explosions, the fountains of spray, Webb detected a faint motion. The tide had turned and *Tollesbury* was free.

At once he ordered the mate: 'Get all the sails set, Gunner – flying jib as well. We'll see if we can't make a board.'

Men on the beaches still recall that Dunkirk offered no stranger sight that day: von Richtofen's Stukas screaming from the sun like eagles cast in green metal, so close that Engineer Fred Reynard, in the *Bee*, felt he'd only to stretch his hands to catch the bombs, the little *Tollesbury*, rust-coloured sails streaming, pushing out into deeper water, as Webb tried vainly to 'make a board' – tacking to get wind and tide in his favour.

That morning, though, the south-west wind was light, the tide easterly – given her head *Tollesbury* would have drifted straight for the Nieuport guns. Phlegmatically, Webb decided he could do only one thing: weigh anchor and sit it calmly out.

The mood was universal. Though wave upon wave of bombers

darkened the morning sky, the keynote was suddenly patience – as if men through suffering had in these last hours gained a new resilience, a true self-sufficiency.

None set the tone more than General Alexander himself – sometimes surveying the battle from a deck-chair on the Mole, sometimes moving amongst the troops munching an apple. Forty-eight years old, the British Army's youngest general, the dark, imperturbable Guards officer who had led a cavalry charge against the Bolsheviks as a twenty-seven-year-old colonel lifted the hearts of all who saw him. The fate of the thousands still trapped at Dunkirk rested in his hands – yet his calm immaculate bearing showed nothing of this.

Alexander understood men very well. Without a steel helmet, despite whirling shell splinters, he told Captain Edward Bloom, a heavy smoker, to take a truck to an abandoned supply dump nearby so that everyone could have a smoke. He greeted Major Allan Adair, courtly commander of the 3rd Grenadiers, as blandly as if both were at Ascot Races, even offering tea from a well-stocked picnic basket. He told Lieutenant Frederick Turner, Adair's quartermaster, it was high time he got his men back to England.

When Turner didn't understand – for the full truth about the retreat still hadn't dawned – Alexander elaborated kindly: 'Most chaps have gone, you know.'

Only when Captain William Tennant opined that if things got much worse they would have to capitulate, did a glint of steel show through. As Tennant asked, how did one capitulate, Alexander answered grimly, 'I have never had to capitulate.'

On the beaches, men felt the same. As German fighters zoomed low, bullets triggering tiny fountains of sand, they met a new and startling phenomenon: the massed rifle-power of thousands ripping the thin air like fabric.

The incorrigibles acquitted themselves as well as any. Private

Walter Osborn of the Suffolks fired clip after clip, insensible of the kick of the butt against his shoulder. With exaltation he thought: I'm a fighting man again. Private Mervyn Doncom of the Hampshires had put aside his silk eiderdown quilt to annex a Bren-gun and was popping at a low-diving Dornier. He whooped with joy as it plunged towards a church steeple, pulling momentarily from the spin before nose-diving into the ground. Overjoyed, Doncom, like a Wild West sheriff, solemnly inscribed the butt: 'One Dornier.' The bren-gun would be the finest take-home gift of all.

It was a paralysing sight . . . the guns of eight destroyers crumping as one . . . ten rounds a minute at a seven-mile range . . . the screaming, wheeling planes . . . the blazing rifles of the men hitting back.

On the bridge of the destroyer *Codrington*, Major-General Bernard Montgomery seemed in his seventh heaven: with every wave of planes the captain, George Stevens-Guille, noted Montgomery's interest grew keener. Above the crescendo of battle he kept up a running commentary: 'Ah, another lot coming in now . . . what do you think their tactics are going to be? . . . I wouldn't come in all at once if I was them . . . if they came in one at a time I think they'd have a first-class chance of hitting us.'

Covertly Stevens-Guille mopped his brow. He had never heard of Montgomery until now, but it struck him this was the coolest customer he'd ever met.

It was no-holds-barred from the first: if the Stukas were out to finish the destroyers, they could expect no quarter on land or sea. Guardsman Thomas Heal saw a Stuka that had strafed the beaches crash-dive on the sand; at once, hands above head, the pilot leapt out shouting '*Kamerad*'. He fell colandered with bullets. There was little discrimination either. Sergeant Robert Copeman saw a pilot bale out from a burning plane; within rifle range scores of rounds of massed fire slammed into him. Whether he was German, French or British no one even knew.

Morale did more than hold up: it stirred thousands to an uncanny peak. Major Hubert Joslen's battalion of the Duke of Cornwall's Light Infantry not only decided Dunkirk was safer than the beaches: they marched there, dressing by the tide-mark, as if from Bodmin Barracks, Cornwall, a piper tootling in the lead, Regimental Sergeant-Major 'Sticky' Hill setting the swinging pace.

Some showed unconcern in doing things by the book. As Colonel 'Nipper' Armstrong of the East Surreys marched his men along the sands, a guardsman, grimed and whiskered, came to the salute. Mislaying his own unit, he had plans to join the Surreys. Armstrong accepted him – after a blistering lecture on regimental tradition had sent the man doubling for a wash and shave.

More showed it by superhuman nonchalance: caught between the Luftwaffe and the deep blue sea, there was still but one way to behave. Colonel Arnold Cazenove of the Coldstream stood bolt upright on the dunes, shaving at the height of an air attack; his batman, kneeling to hold the mirror, never turned a hair. Farther along, Captain John Hay Drummond Hay of the Royal West Kents was hailed by his servant whom he hadn't seen in days. The man apologised: he'd been chasing the captain for twenty-five miles with a pair of neatly-pressed trousers he now presented.

Captain Edward Scott-Clarke, another West Kents officer, made a lively book at a penny a bet: of the 100-plus Stukas crash-diving through space, which would drop a bomb nearest to them? Others didn't even watch the sky: some playing chess on a full-size board; a man near Private James Wilson dismantling a wireless set to see how it worked; a few reading peaceably. Staff-Sergeant Frederick Parks was determined to finish *Gone With the Wind* before joining a queue . . . Second-Lieutenant Alexander Lyell browsed through Chesterton's Father Brown stories . . . Lieutenant Edward Ford of the Grenadiers, ensconced in a fox-hole six feet deep, read Homer's *Iliad* in the original Greek.

And the ships were as bad – as if, in caricature of traditional British reserve, no one must make a fuss. In the *Medway Queen* a sailor sat peacefully fishing from the stern: he explained to yachtsman Richard Brett there was always the chance of landing a German helmet. Sub-Lieutenant Stanley Jones-Frank stood by his ship's gangway, hands on hips, steel helmet tilted on his head, bawling like a pierhead barker, 'Any more – any *more* for the *Brighton Queen*?' Lieutenant Barnard Bredin of the Royal Ulster Rifles, boarding the Isle of Man steamer *Ben-My-Chree*, had to step over a dead man at the head of the gangway; hastening to the saloon, he urged a white-jacketed steward to bring beer.

Gently the steward rebuked him: 'Not until we are three miles out, sir – but you can have some tea.'

Three-mile limit or no, more and more showed their unconcern in rousing saloon-bar tradition, marching with singsongs that echoed to the sky . . . Captain Joe Broadbent's company of a Yorkshire artillery regiment roaring 'I do like to be beside the seaside' . . . another group proclaiming 'There'll always be an England' . . . one battalion singing a song all its own:

> *Three hundred went to walk, walk along the sand-dunes*
> *Three hundred went to walk, walk along the sand-dunes*
> *Each mile that they walked they got a little fewer*
> *Where's our grub, they sang in tune,*
> *Where's the bloody brewer?*

And Capitaine de Corvette Pierre Fontaine, clinging to the wreckage of the destroyer *Foudroyant*, witnessed a spectacle that touched him to the quick: as the swift-running tide bore the survivors to the east, his whole crew passed before him as if in review chanting in superb defiance the words of 'La Marseillaise'.

Over beleaguered Dunkirk now, all hell was breaking loose, and the bombers were making their mark . . . the destroyer *Keith,* so badly holed that Admiral Wake-Walker had to transfer his flag for the tenth time, was down to thirty rounds of ammo before she listed to port and sank . . . the minesweeper *Sutton* hadn't one round left . . . the destroyer *Havant,* going full speed ahead in huge circles, couldn't stop – all her engine-room staff were dead or dying . . . *Basilisk* was a floating hulk . . . ship after ship was listing. Yet still among the men calm prevailed. Telegraphist Harold Marsh counted ninety-six bombs drop close to *Westward Ho!* then gave up; amidships, the 3rd Motorised Division's General Langlois watched the combat, his face a graven mask, then awarded both Lewis-gunners the *Croix de Guerre.* Aboard *Speedwell,* a superstitious sailor comforted Major Jack Lotinga of the Royal Fusiliers: 'We'll be all right – a speedwell's a very tenacious plant.'

Not every bomb was worth its weight in high explosive: from the Bastion's roof, Captain William Tennant counted no less than twenty-seven dive-bombing attacks on the *Clan MacAlister.* Partially gutted by Wednesday's raid, she had providentially settled, a perfect decoy duck, in shallow water on an even keel. Later Admiralty experts estimated her presence saved Britain £1,000,000 worth of shipping.

Aboard H.M.S. *Ivanhoe,* Augusta Hersey was too absorbed to know what was afoot; her cat-nap on the crew's mess-deck had been brief indeed. Within minutes of nodding off, the curious sailor who had watched her scramble aboard reappeared. One glance at the discarded steel helmet and Augusta's sleek dark hair was enough: 'I always thought that was a woman!'

When Bill Hersey, on the defensive, claimed her as his wife the sailor was understanding: 'That's O.K., mate – but this is no place for a woman. She'd be better off in sick-bay.'

Soon after the *Ivanhoe*'s baffled captain, Commander Philip Hadow, shot into the dispensary: 'I'd heard there was a woman aboard my ship. What are you doing here?' Forced to repeat the question in French, Hadow himself hastened to the crew's mess-deck to find Hersey: 'You'd better get up with your wife.'

When Bill Hersey scaled the companionway to the sickbay he couldn't help thinking of that first meeting at the Café L'Epi d'Or when Augusta had tried out her first-aid on him. For now his wife sat compassionately by a wounded soldier's side, feeding him sips of water. From another bunk a second Tommy, his eyes heavily bandaged, spoke up: 'Give us a fag, mate.'

Augusta told them to be quiet: the surgeon-lieutenant in charge had said the man mustn't be disturbed. Gently Bill Hersey offered a cigarette and the man drew on it painfully. 'Thanks, mate,' he murmured, 'I can stand anything now.'

There was still much to endure. Neither of the Herseys could know it but *Ivanhoe*, her guns pounding, was at that moment cutting in to the aid of Skipper Lemon Webb and his human cargo. Ever resourceful, Mate Edward Gunn, a First World War naval signaller, had used some yellow and red semaphore flags he'd put by to signal *Ivanhoe* they had troops aboard.

Then, as *Ivanhoe* moved in to the rescue, disaster struck: a bomb tearing like a juggernaut into her forward funnel sliced clean through the main steam pipes, spraying the boiler-room with a jetting cloud of steam at 300 lb. pressure. On deck at that moment, Lieutenant Andrew Mahony, engineer officer, recoiled in horror: it seemed as if the screaming from the boiler-room would never stop. In fact it went on for twenty unforgettable minutes.

At this instant blast struck the five-inch machine-gun mounting, canting it forward to train, still firing, at *Ivanhoe*'s bridge. Everywhere men fell dying.

In the dispensary it was a petrifying moment. With the thunderclap of breaking glass, every bottle on the shelves showered forward on Augusta Hersey's steel helmet. With one scream she leapt forward — clean on to the stomach of the man with the bandaged eyes.

He, too, yelled more in torment than in terror; for like Augusta he had missed the fearful sight Bill Hersey saw — the other patient's head whistling like a nightmare projectile into space, smashing the sick-bay door to smithereens. Now Hersey, too, leaped, grabbing at Augusta's steel helmet, endeavouring to wrest it from her head.

Resisting, Augusta cried, 'Leave it — leave it.' Then, her grappling hands encountering Bill's, she understood. The helmet's outer shell was a warm red paste of blood — yet still, reeling with nausea, she hung on. The thought possessed her: I have *my* life — I must wear it for protection. But Hersey, determined to spare his wife such horrors, prevailed and cast it aside.

In the gangway it was like a dam breaking. A flood of fear-stricken Tommies were clawing frantically to the upper deck; hastily anticipating panic, naval ratings had first clamped down the hatches on the forward hold. Hemmed in by darkness, Corporal James Trodden of the East Yorks was one of hundreds who first felt the ship 'rock like a biscuit tin', then, as the lights went out, a man's voice intoned: 'Let us pray.' Kneeling on a coil of rope, Trodden prayed for his wife and children, but even prayer wasn't proof against the hope of deliverance as the hatch again swung open. With scores of others he fought towards the sunlight — to an upper deck canting so heavily men scrambled on all fours over the butchered bodies of sailors.

Above the panic, instilling a measure of calm, Bill Hersey's voice rang out: 'Make way for the Navy, lads, they can do the job better than us.' As the minesweeper *Speedwell* closed to take off survivors, Commander Philip Hadow hailed her captain: 'For God's sake watch it — our magazine may go any moment.'

Yet still *Speedwell* drew alongside, both ships listing so heavily on the fearsome bomb-created swell that many men, jumping too soon, were crushed between the heaving sides. But one man found time for the courtesies. 'Hold on,' Augusta Hersey heard a sailor call, 'there's a lady coming aboard.' As Augusta and Bill jumped as one, kindly hands stretched forward to catch them.

Major Jack Lotinga of the Royal Fusiliers, one of the first to help Augusta to safety, never forgot Hersey repeating with dazed pride, 'She's a great kid, you know – she's a great kid.'

But Augusta, conducted to the captain's pantry by a friendly steward, was too far gone to take in tributes. All of them were crouching beneath the pantry's bar and the steward pressed a glass into Augusta's hand. Sick and numb, she swallowed it all, thinking vaguely it was lemonade. Only later did she realise she'd drunk her first – and last – half-tumbler of neat whisky.

It was no fault of *Ivanhoe*'s – but to Skipper Lemon Webb it seemed *Tollesbury* was still a long way from safety. For minutes the barge shook to the pounding blast of under-water explosions, the spume geysering eighty-six feet to the very tip of *Tollesbury*'s topmast. Yet Webb was more determined than ever that she should make the return journey. The other barges were beached and grounded now, as the Navy had ordered: Skipper Harold Miller's *Royalty*, Charlie Webb's *Barbara Jean*, Harry Potter's *Aidie*, the *Ena* under Captain Alfred Page. *Tollesbury* was the last of her line: she *must* survive the carnage.

Worse, Webb had seen with a prickle of horror the *Doris*, sinking rapidly and abandoned, drifting on the remorseless tide towards the Nieuport shore. His own brother-in-law, Captain Fred Finbow, was the skipper.

As in a mist, Webb saw one hope of salvation: the old Thames tug *Cervia*, under Captain William Simmons, was moving in to take them in tow. Now a fresh problem arose: no sooner was the tow-rope secured to the *Tollesbury* than Simmons, anxious to put Dunkirk behind him, went ahead fast.

It was too much for the barge. With an unearthly splintering the tug tore her bit-head — the stout wooden casing of the windlass — clean out by the roots. Again *Tollesbury* was adrift on a sea burnished red with the blood of men whose voyaging was over.

The day was marked by such courage. At Bergues, key strong-point of the western perimeter, the Loyal Regiment had stood fast for two days, but as the line contracted, artillery pressure on the old walled town stepped up. To man the stout seventeenth-century ramparts Lieut.-Colonel John Sandie had only 26 officers and 451 men; for the rest the garrison were stragglers doing their best ... a transport company of ex-London bus-drivers who'd indented for a musketry instructor ... the Rev. Alfred Naylor, Deputy Chaplain General, holding one gate of the town for three days with a mixed bag of chaplains. Barred from active combat by their cloth, Naylor and his cadre did sterling work questioning suspected fifth-columnists.

And the civilians weighed in too. At Steene, west of the town, General von Kleist's tanks were advancing steadily, but Mayor Jean Duriez, an industrial alcohol manufacturer, turned the faucets of his ten vast stills to send two million gallons of raw spirit gushing across the already flooded land. As Duriez watched a chance artillery shell, exploding like a thunderclap, transformed the waters to a raging sea of flame — 'like a gigantic Planter's Punch'. In fascinated dread Duriez saw two of von Kleist's tanks trapped by the torrent, glowing white-hot as the holocaust engulfed them. The advance from the west was stalled.

But by Saturday midday the Loyals could no longer hold Bergues itself. Already the troops dug in on the ancient ramparts sweltered from the heat of burning buildings — the smoke so dense even dispatch riders groped through the town on foot, mouths and noses bound with damp cloths. By noon the exposed canal bank beyond the northern ramparts had become the Loyals' last stockade – with men toppling like ten-pins under devastating artillery fire. Now in Captain Henry Joynson's company the troops were so tired the officers had to haul them across the road like sacks of coal.

Then by a miracle the wind changed – impelling a black choking banner of smoke from the burning town into the heart of the German lines. Even von Kleist's tanks could no longer advance: the few that did try, foxed by the smoke, tilted dangerously into the canal. The infantry advance held off – though not until 9 p.m. could the Loyals withdraw, doubling between waves of mortar fire towards Dunkirk. Many, by order of Major-General Harry Curtis, had left their rifles propped in position. Bound with a contraption of string, weights and slow-burning candles, they would keep firing at intervals, creating the illusion of a tough task force still on the alert.

Three miles to the east the East Lancashire Regiment had it as bad; with all ammunition spent, their 1st Battalion fell back towards Dunkirk, only a forty-strong force under Captain Harold Ervine-Andrews, to cover the thousand-yard front as they withdrew. A thick-set, heavily-built Irishman, Andrews was venerated by his men for his genially informal manner, though senior officers were less sure of him. On pre-war service in India and China his feats had become an eccentric legend – walking fifty-six miles for a £5 bet, shooting a black buck in the jungle, then carrying it home draped round his shoulders.

All that night Andrews and his men crouched under annihilating shellfire until it seemed the end was near. Already they had been blasted from their farmhouse quarters; now the Dutch barn to which they'd retreated was in flames, too. As they doubled behind a hedge, sparks and blazing straw eddying, they sighted the German infantry moving in a spaced dangerous line through growing dusk.

Andrews exhorted his men: 'Look, there are 500 of them,

maybe thirty-six of us – let them get a bit closer and then here goes.' His whistle shrilling, Andrews leapt forward, weaving towards the advancing hordes like a footballer moving in to tackle. As the howling mob of East Lancs followed at his heels the Germans fell back, seeking cover.

Scrambling to the roof of a barn with a rifle, Andrews picked off no less than seventeen Germans – then seizing a bren-gun, he lunged forward again. Private John Taylor, in the thick of it, recalls: 'It was a right do – when the ammo ran low we kicked, choked, even bit them.' After fifteen blood-stained minutes the Germans fell back in confusion. The line was held – but Andrews, after sending his wounded to the rear, was down to eight men now.

Resolutely, at the head of his little band, he struck across-country, splashing for a quarter of a mile through the flooded fields towards Dunkirk. He was to win the first Victoria Cross awarded to any officer in the Second World War.

On the beaches, the savage fury of the attack had one result. By 1 p.m. – six hours after the raid began – every man and woman still had one resolve: the only thing that mattered now was the lives of others.

Jog-trotting along the Eastern Mole, Colonel Sidney Harrison's 6th Lincolns had their own wounded slung like sacks over their shoulders – but they stumbled on, negotiating yawning four-foot gaps somehow, loading them on to ship after ship. In the shadow of the Mole, Gunner Albert Collins saw an officer bent on a task to tax Samson: a rope bound like a yoke round his forehead, he swam valiantly for a Dutch *schuit*, towing a Carley float with six men aboard.

Lance-Bombardier George Brockerton took risks as great as any he'd taken as a Wall of Death trick cyclist: finding eighty-one men trapped in a bombed cellar he worked for two hours to free them with hammer and chisel, using French hand-grenades in lieu of gelignite. Oblivious to the crash of bombs, he helped out every man then, to keep their peckers up, did some conjuring tricks.

Private Walter Allington of the Lincolns was in his element too. Already he'd spent one whole night trying to help a man crazed by a head wound . . . then, taking a vest and shirt, he'd plugged a terrible hole in another man's shoulder. Now, despite the writhing pains in his abdomen, he saw a bullet aimed at the diving Stukas had gone too low. A long way off, a man had fallen, the bullet lodging in the small of his back.

Somehow, though other men were nearer, Allington was again first to help – but the big gentle man had used his only field-dressing on that Belgian cripple. Working doggedly on his own, he found an abandoned ambulance, checked it was in running order, and loaded the man aboard. Then, despite the swooping Stukas, he drove until the Channel water was lapping over the bonnet. Standing on the roof of the truck, he flagged a destroyer's whaler to ferry the man away.

Everywhere men plumbed unsuspected depths in themselves. Brigadier Evelyn Barker was at the water's edge when a shell dropped close, shattering a soldier's arm so that it hung by a thread. Without more ado Barker borrowed a knife from his Brigade Major and honed it on a carborundum stone as coolly as a butcher. Lacking narcotics, he first gave the man a nip of cherry brandy before taking his arm off at the shoulder.

Then, improvising a tourniquet with handkerchief and pencil, Barker and his aide carried their patient along the beach on a mackintosh to place him in a doctor's charge.

Able Seaman Samuel Palmer, with twenty years' naval service, didn't know a crankshaft from a camshaft but he took the motor yacht *Naiad Errant* over with a crew of three – then after losing them took her back with nine thankful Tommies helping out the one engine still operative with paddles fashioned from shattered doors. Stoker David Banks from Sheerness did even better . . . making seven trips as skipper of the motor-boat *Pauleter* . . . doing his trick at the wheel . . . manning the bren-gun when the Stukas dived . . . rescuing 400 single-handed. Off the same beaches Commander Charles Lightoller, former second officer of the *Titanic*, was packing them in aboard his yacht *Sundowner*: his biggest kick was the stupefaction of Ramsgate's naval authorities when they found his 60-footer had brought back 130 men.

The tiros were well to the fore. Captain 'Paddy' Atley of the East Yorks found the barge *Ena* grounded where Lemon Webb's flotilla had lain, took her back with forty men, on the strength of five sailing holidays in Norfolk. It took fourteen hours, including a surprise return to Dunkirk, but they made it finally. Captain David Strangeways of the Duke of Wellington's Regiment hit on another barge, appropriately named the *Iron Duke*. Naked save for the skipper's doormat, which he wore like a sarong, Strangeways brought back twenty-six men, navigating with compass and school atlas.

To the doctors, life-saving was a dedication, but it was an uphill fight now. In Private William Horne's ambulance unit the only medication to deal with searing phosphorous burns was a bottle of acriflavine tablets diluted in water. At Rosendael, the dressings were all but exhausted; Major Philip Newman, the surgeon, did one last amputation by torchlight, then gave up. The ambulance unit at La Panne had packed up, too, after a record 2,000 operations in one week, but many doctors carried on as and how they could.

Where equipment was lacking, they improvised. Captain William MacDonald, in a dugout in the dunes, sterilised wounds with abandoned petrol. Captain Joseph Reynolds, lacking the Thomas splints used for compound fractures, secured fractured femurs with rifles. And scores cut off from their units or families lent a ready hand . . . slicing up battle-dress trousers to make bandages . . . ransacking abandoned homes for sheets . . . pretty Solange Bisiaux, a French doctor's wife, wringing out blood-stained bandages in salt water . . . other men working eight to a relay to carry stretchers on board the ships.

Round every ambulance and aid-post Sapper George Brooks noted the same hushed aura: the 'undercurrent of grief that moves like a wind when a coffin is carried from a house'.

Injuries or no, some men were determined to make the journey home. Lieutenant J. P. Walsh of the Loyals, knocked down by a lorry near Bergues, still plodded the five miles to Dunkirk: later the surgeons found his pelvis was fractured. Captain John Whitty of the Royal West Kents, wounded in the stomach, slogged some of the fifty miles from Flêtre, where his battalion was trapped, then, at last gasp, hailed a passing motor-cyclist and rode pillion to the beaches. Bundled into an ambulance and driven to the Mole, Whitty found the wait tedious; he climbed out, exhorting other wounded to follow him, and got them all passages on a home-bound boat.

There was the same spirit on the ships. Aboard the trawler *Brock*, a Surgeon-Lieutenant coped with grievous burn cases and a shortage of tannic acid by filling a zinc bath with tea and immersing his patients up to their necks. The destroyer *Whitehall*'s doctor, Surgeon-Lieutenant David Brown, went so swiftly to aid the wounded aboard the minesweeper *Jackeve* that he left his instruments behind. Nothing loth, he amputated with the engine-room's hacksaw, sterilised with blazing chloroform, the ex-trawler's fish hatch serving as operating table.

Whatever one's own problems, the needs of others took priority. In the hospital ship, *Dinard*, a wounded soldier pleaded with Stewardess Amy Goodrich not to fetch him soup if it meant running into danger, but Mrs Goodrich reassured him: she had her Mae West firmly strapped over her uniform. With shell splinters lancing like daggers across the deck, she walked aft to get it. And in the ward-room of *Leda*, Surgeon-Lieutenant Richard Pembrey saw a sight which moved him to tears: a dying man to whom he'd given morphine and a blanket, raised himself slowly on one elbow, watching another man shiver in the first stages of pneumonia. Silently the dying man stripped off his blanket, passing it to the man in greater need.

But at Dunkirk Captain William Tennant was forced to harden his heart: as the pace of evacuation quickened perceptibly, he recognised an inescapable truth. One wounded man on a stretcher was taking up the place of eight robust men – and Britain, hemmed in by enemies, could only hope to survive by giving fighting troops priority.

By 2 p.m. Tennant reluctantly sent orders to all his staff: from now on only walking wounded could be allowed to board any ship aside from hospital ships.

For the first time a painful truth dawned on many: in the last resort it was kindest to kill. Ambulance Orderly William Horne, looking sadly at a man with a shell-splinter through his breast-bone, knew he had but a few hours to live; meantime the man was in agony and there was no chance of moving him into Dunkirk itself. Lifting him gently, Horne gave him a last nightcap of whisky and water. Within two minutes he was dead.

At all levels it was the same: Tennant's decision, not lightly made, applied even more stringently to animals. Lance-Corporal Eric Stocks managed to smuggle 'Tippy', his little dachshund, into a sandbag and aboard a trawler – but Captain Edward Bloom, slated to board the destroyer *Vanquisher*, knew he would never get Hugo to England now. Yet the massive sledge dog, with his pathetic brown eyes, was too big and slow to fend for himself. All his life he had known kindness: he had not been made for a world like this.

Gently, his hand in Hugo's collar, Bloom walked away from the beaches, back into the dunes, where the marram grass grew in coarse tufts, but there were few men about. He thought afterwards he'd talked to Hugo for a while, but he could never remember what he said. The dog was sitting upright, pink tongue lolling, soothed by the words of his newfound master, as Bloom took out his .45.

The report was scarcely audible above the hubbub of Dunkirk. A blue chrysanthemum of smoke hung in the still air and Bloom walked fast away, not looking back.

On the Bastion roof Captain William Tennant was numb with horror. At 6 p.m. on this Saturday it seemed the Navy was paying a bloody price for daylight evacuation.

Out of forty-one destroyers that entered the fray only nine were left now – and the shipping losses were mounting out of all proportion to the men still to be saved.

Even as Tennant watched six Stukas came snarling from the sky at the old destroyer *Worcester* . . . pounding her every five minutes without mercy . . . sending her limping from the harbour at a crippled ten knots . . . burdened with a horrifying casualty list of 350 dead, 400 wounded.

Now, leaping to his feet, Tennant told Major-General Harold Alexander flatly: 'I'm sorry – but that finishes it. I'm sending a signal to Ramsay to stop any more stuff coming in by day.'

Within minutes his signal was drafted: 'Things are getting very hot for ships . . . over 100 bombs on here since 5.30 . . . many casualties . . . have directed that no ships set sail by daylight.'

And he wound up: 'If perimeter holds will complete evacuation to-morrow, Sunday night, including rest French. General Alexander concurs.'

The irony was, the Luftwaffe saw it all as the last fling of the dice. Pilot after pilot felt the same: what was any sortie but a token gesture now? The British had all but gone . . . within a week there'd be peace . . . the targets were too scattered to do the kind of damage that hurt.

And newcomers found it more of a puzzle still. Ten thousand feet above Dunkirk, in a fast-flying Heinkel III, Oberleutnant Alfons Vonier caught his breath; he called to radioman Paul Strobel, 'But this is fantastic – just *look* at all that shipping.' All along Vonier had believed that once the British were surrounded they'd make peace with Hitler. The magnitude of the exodus had never struck him.

Nor had the concept of danger – for the sky teemed with twisting grey Messerschmitts, fighter protection in plenty. But as Vonier watched the fighters had fled, vanishing west towards Gravelines. In the ominous silence Vonier appealed to his crew, 'Why in the world have they gone?'

Next moment they knew. From astern came a sudden rending burst of flame and in brief focus Vonier glimpsed the long mullet-head cowling he was to know well. A Spitfire – and hard on their tail.

Within seconds the Heinkel to port was in trouble – yawing violently, its starboard engine gone, it made tracks for Antwerp. The Heinkel to starboard was hit, too – smoke bannering from both engines, it spun downwards to crash-land west of Dunkirk.

With grim satisfaction Vonier watched radioman Strobel send a full 75-round magazine hosing into the Spitfire's fuselage. Shuddering, the plane spiralled sideways and flames blossomed from its wing roots as it rocketed in a droning crash-dive towards the sea.

It was a costly victory. The Spitfire's first burst had gone home; in silent dismay Vonier saw the Heinkel's instrument panel shattered beyond repair. From the rear turret Strobel called: 'I can't call up the others any more, Skipper – the radio link's out.' Vonier was philosophic, 'Time we got out of here.'

Gingerly he began to nurse the plane towards the emergency air base at Ghent – happily unaware that five bullets had lodged in the ignition fuse-box two inches above his head.

Others felt the same: the British, flying in two-squadron

strength, were a force to be reckoned with now. Reefing above the target in his Messerschmitt 109, Leutnant Hans Dudeck, a steel-nerved twenty-four-year-old of No. 2 Fighter Group, kept a wary eye open, boring hard for cloud-cover each time he saw a Spitfire. Why they flew always in formation like an air-pageant had him licked – but Dudeck had no taste for a dog-fight at close range.

The pilots seemed to manœuvre like stunt men, firing one burst, climbing like hawks, then swooping back to blast you from the rear.

And Major Oscar Dinort, in his slower-moving Stuka, never stood a chance: about this time, Oberstleutnant Hans Seidemann, von Richtofen's chief of staff, recalls he touched down at Beaulieu airfield cursing like a trooper. He spluttered impotently, 'Those Spitfires – when *they* come you just get into that damned smoke and stay there.'

It was different for the R.A.F. All week luck had been against them ... first that bitter stream of criticism ... the losses mounting on each under-strength patrol ... the mortifying knowledge that the copy-book tactics of peace-time just weren't paying off. Now, almost 100 sorties wiser, they were out for blood.

For Squadron-Leader George Lott, commander of No. 43 Squadron, the need was especially pressing. That very morning over breakfast the thirty-four-year-old Hurricane pilot had read in *The Times* that he'd been awarded the D.F.C. Over Dunkirk at 19,000 feet, Lott's resolution was both modest and urgent: he must do something to earn it.

The chance came fast. In minutes the eleven pilots of Lott's squadron heard their skipper's urgent tally-ho: '109s coming down behind.' Then the sky blurred to chaos: without warning, Lott was alone in a milling cloud of fifty German fighters. So strenuous was the tussle that he never thought of opening fire ... twice he had to scream to 3,000 feet ... twice he spiralled to 17,000 feet ... twice he flicked into a spin.

Only sheer aerobatics took him unscathed from the combat – but now, to his astonishment, he was lined up behind two unsuspecting Messerschmitt 110s.

Carefully, at a steady 300 m.p.h., Lott stalked them. His brain seemed ice-clear now – those flicks and rolls had been as good as an alcohol massage. He drew closer, but luck flew with him – at 400 yards they still hadn't seen. Nearer now and the sight rock-steady. At 100 yards he jabbed the firing button.

At once angry black smoke bellied from the Messerschmitt's engines. Beyond control, it zoomed steeply into a dive. But Lott was making sure: at 3,000 feet he was still on the ME's tail, jabbing the button in a murderous five-second burst, the plane bulking hugely in his sights as orange tracer chopped home. Next second the ME was gone, plunging like a stone into clouds.

Lott's first thought: he flew straight and steady for too long. His second: and so did I. His hands were shaking on the stick, his flying overalls drenched in sweat – but the sky was too empty for comfort. Swiftly he set course for home base – but that decoration seemed less embarrassing now.

The pilots were learning new skills. At 4,000 feet Flying Officer Hilton Haarhoff, blithe young South African rear-gunner of a Coastal Command Hudson bomber, had positive orders: stay low, ward off enemy attempts to interfere with shipping. To Haarhoff it was easier said than done: the Stukas, boiling in a two-mile circle, dived fast and climbed faster, balking his chance to take aim.

Then, three miles west of Dunkirk, the Hudson sighted trouble – a whirling vortex of twenty Stukas swooping like gannets at a fish. And Haarhoff, spotting their target, felt a stab of anger: what chance did one tug towing a barge stand against twenty Stukas?

Haarhoff of course couldn't know it, but the tug *Cervia* once again had *Tollesbury* in tow – though Skipper Lemon Webb, clinging grimly to the wheel, was almost inured to bombs now. What troubled him most as he steered dead for *Cervia*'s wake was the fear of mines: if the tug hit one of those he must be ready to cut adrift the tow in seconds.

To Haarhoff and his pilot, Flying Officer John Selley, a fellow South African, it seemed Webb was already doomed. As they watched a vast mushroom of water engulfed both tug and barge – but as the spray cleared, *Cervia* with Webb in her wake was still plodding gamely on. It was so moving Haarhoff wanted to cheer.

But both South Africans were decided now: somehow they'd find a way to spike the Stukas' guns. And, in an instant, it dawned. In the fifteen vital seconds before a Stuka dived it poised motionless, powerless to break away.

At once Selley rammed over stick and rudder, hot on the trail of the soaring Stukas. Boring to the centre of the vast circle, they jockeyed for position until the first Stuka was in their sights, as steady as a clay pigeon on a range. Then it was jerking violently under the Hudson's two-second burst, spiralling like a thunderbolt towards the shining sea.

Another Stuka zoomed past, and as it readied for the dive Haarhoff, at seventy yards range, opened fire again. Incredulously he watched the plane heel drunkenly on its back like a dying fish, then vanish in a streaming column of flame.

It was third time lucky too. Within thirty yards of the next plane, both men opened fire, so close they saw the fuselage vibrate like a tuning fork beneath tearing tracer. For a second splinters of olive-green metal flew like chips from an axe. Then the plane looped sickeningly into its death-roll; the pilot baled out with seconds to spare.

Thrice more the Hudson climbed, guns squirting, but the Stukas had had enough. They broke for base.

For Lemon Webb now there was a safe passage home – and for Haarhoff and Selley to end their day, the same surprise as Squadron-Leader Lott. Both were awarded the D.F.C.

It was a bitter blow for the Baron von Richtofen. At dusk he watched the last of his Stukas limp home, knowing the end was in sight. Again like a capricious child the Führer had lost interest. Orders had come that from Monday on all planes must be in readiness to bomb the airfields girdling Paris. The Stukas' Dunkirk sorties were all but over.

In his office, the baron, opening his leather-bound diary, penned his own bitter epitaph on the whole campaign: 'The Luftwaffe can't halt the Dunkirk embarkation at this last moment . . . the Army should have taken a firmer stand days ago. A victory over England has been thrown away.'

At Dover Admiral Ramsay was at his wits' end. Already the reports flooding in to his chief of staff, Captain Vaughan Morgan, showed both ships and crews near the limits of endurance. Only that morning, Morgan, hastening into his office, had beseeched he take time out to hear a destroyer commander's report. When Ramsay agreed, Morgan sped to fetch the officer – to find him as dead with lassitude as a man under morphia. The two men couldn't even shake him into wakefulness.

Yet within minutes Ramsay was reading the copy of a signal from Sir John Dill, Chief of the Imperial General Staff, to Major-General Harold Alexander: 'We do not order any fixed moment for evacuation. You are to hold as long as possible in order that the maximum number of French and British may be evacuated.'

It was plain calculations had gone sadly awry. There was no chance of winding up the evacuation this Saturday night. Somehow the ships' crews must gird themselves for fresh efforts.

But every port could tell the same story. As Commander Grenville Temple took the minesweeper *Sutton* into Harwich, not one of his crew had strength to throw a heaving line; the dockyard launch that made them fast found every man flat out where he'd fallen. Homeward bound on the bridge of *Leda*, Commander

Harold Unwin went fast asleep in mid-Channel. At Dover, Commander Harold Conway of Tennant's party, sent home for a brief rest, was intent on getting back to Dunkirk as fast as might be; on the quayside he hailed a destroyer's sub-lieutenant: 'When do you sail?'

Hysterically the sub screamed back: 'Sail? We shan't sail . . . the captain's dead beat . . . the crew's dead beat . . . you bloody brass hats just don't know the score.'

Other destroyers were holding out, but narrowly. In *Icarus*, six trips to her credit, not one of Commander Colin Maud's officers risked full glasses in the wardroom now; their hands were shaking too much. In *Harvester*, Commander Mark Thornton kept going somehow, but getting sense from the crew was a tougher proposition. Only Thornton's shock treatment — clanging on their steel helmets with a hammer, firing revolvers behind them — kept them awake.

And the personnel ships, with civilian crews ungeared to battle, were in worse plight. The Isle of Man packet *Tyn-wald*, after five trips, 7,500 troops lifted, ceded the ship to the Navy. The *Ben-My-Chree* did only two trips before the crew threw in their hands; it took naval stokers armed with bayonets to keep them aboard until a relief crew arrived. The *Malines* had done yeoman work rescuing *Grafton*'s survivors, but now the crew found the strain too great. Without orders *Malines* left Dover, returning to Southampton.

As the day's losses mounted, Ramsay was forced to Tennant's view: there could be no more embarkation by day. All three approach routes were under lethal gunfire. The only sane plan was to concentrate the ships still in the battle off Malo beach and in Dunkirk harbour after dark.

Sending for his flag officer, Commander James Stopford, Ramsay made this signal to all ships in his command: 'The situation makes it imperative that you should make one last effort. I am sure you all realise what is at stake.'

And at Dunkirk Major-General Harold Alexander took final steps to implement his conference with Tennant: the signs suggested Admiral Abrial was right. The perimeter must be shrunk to the walls of the Bastion itself, with the British withdrawing from the front line through the last rearguard of all – over 30,000 Frenchmen under Général Barthélémy, few of whom would escape.

The sole defence for both Bastion and beaches would be the seven 20-mm. guns of the 14th Anti-Tank Regiment under their last commander, Major William Mitchell. Summoning Mitchell to the Bastion, Alexander, reclining on a string bed, told him: 'I want those guns up here.'

Mitchell demurred. The guns had been set up on the hard sand at Malo-les-Bains at low tide – a last-ditch precaution in case German tanks gained the beaches. But Malo was almost two miles away; there wouldn't be another low tide between now and dawn on the Sunday.

But Alexander, shrugging, was implacable: somehow the guns must be got to Dunkirk. As Mitchell set off on a hair's-breadth ride to Malo one factor caused him mounting unease: he had left orders for the guns to be blown at 9 p.m. Could he reach his battery in time to countermand the order?

After a hellish bone-shattering ride through burning streets, Mitchell made it with just fifteen minutes to spare. Cursing, sweating, heaving, the sixty men left to him began to manhandle the guns through soft powdery sand towards Dunkirk: seven guns to defend the last perimeter of all.

CHAPTER TEN

HAVE YOU SEEN MY JOHNNY?

After 1st June

Around 4 p.m. on Saturday, 1st June, as the minesweeper *Speedwell* inched slowly in towards Dover's Admiralty Pier, an embarkation staff officer on the quayside hailed her captain, Commander 'Lucky' Marnisell: 'How many aboard?' At once Maunsell's reply boomed back through the loud-hailer: 'Five hundred and ninety-nine men – and one woman!'

As the roar of laughter travelled like a shock-wave through the ship, Augusta Hersey, lining the rails at Bill's side, almost flinched. In these last moments she was so tired that rescue seemed an anti-climax – and even humour at a premium. Irrationally she had hoped that Dover's white cliffs, in contrast to the inferno of Dunkirk, would be cloaked in tranquil silence.

Yet in these last hours the harbour was still as clamorous as a railway terminal in a rush-hour ... the ships packed stem to stern in tight unending ranks ... a thousand voices bawling through loud-hailers ... the frenzied barking as quarantine inspectors rounded up truck-loads of shivering, ownerless dogs.

As far as Augusta could see there was nothing but a surging irresistible mass of men in soiled khaki piling down gangplank after gangplank . . . French *poilus* with loaves of bread skewered on their bayonets . . . British Tommies ducking their heads like thirsty horses into zinc buckets of water . . . the wounded of all nations lying blood-stained and exhausted on green canvas stretchers. Tirelessly the Red Cross and Women's Voluntary Service workers moved among them with apples, chocolate and cups of tea.

And for Augusta worse was still to come. For hours, in a tiny over-heated waiting-room, Bill had to argue bitterly with a major in security, who was convinced both Herseys were spies; only Augusta's marriage certificate and Hersey's Army paybook talked them out of that. Within minutes came a tearful parting, and despite all Hersey's protests the military police were adamant. His wife would be taken to a civilian transit camp, but he himself must board a troop train with the rest.

In the nick of time Hersey contrived to scribble his mother's address in Addlestone, Surrey, on a scrap of paper. Somehow, some time, he would see Augusta there.

After that, time passed with agonising slowness. Seeking refuge from the babel of tongues, Augusta sank to sleep on a stretcher; she woke in disgust to find herself surrounded by wounded German prisoners. It was twilight by the time that they packed her, along with other French civilians, into a London-bound train – and as it halted at every station while welfare workers thrust bread-and-cheese through the windows, her spirits sank still lower.

Her trousseau and everything she had ever owned were gone now – abandoned a lifetime ago in that split-second escape from *Ivanhoe*. From the other civilians in the compartment she could glean no facts, only an excited buzz of rumour. And when and how, speaking no word of English, would she contact Bill again?

Above all the tidal wave of cheering from the close-packed

ranks lining every street and railway embankment bewildered her. Had they after all a special reason to cheer?

In all logic it seemed a time to mourn. True, the vainglorious British Expeditionary Force, 390,000 strong, 'as well if not better equipped than any similar army', was home, but with its tail between its legs. Only a handful of men – above all Major-General Bernard Montgomery's 3rd Division – remained mobile to repulse Hitler's onslaught.

Yet all along the coast and forty miles inland to London the ovation was the same – a surging Niagara of cheers all England seemed to echo. The slogans 'Well done, B.E.F.' daubed in chalk and whitewash on sooty back-garden walls . . . the gay bunting of Coronation year brought forth to do new service . . . the nurses and Women's Voluntary Service Workers thronging every port and railway terminal . . . these were the tokens of the way the British felt.

It was a time of tributes. That day the *New York Times* had declared: 'The rags and blemishes that have hidden the soul of democracy fell away. There, beaten but unconquered, in shining splendour, she faced the enemy.' The *Daily Express*, too, had bannered: 'Tired, dirty, hungry, they came back – unbeatable.' In Germany the *Hamburger Fremdenblatt* was moved to praise: 'They defended themselves . . . with the proven tenacity of the Anglo-Saxon race which Germany has never underestimated.' The *Daily Mirror*'s headline was inimitable: 'BLOODY MARVELLOUS!'

Yet the ordinary Tommy could hardly credit it. As his destroyer slid in towards Dover's quayside, Private Ronald Le Dube of the Loyals paled beneath his Dunkirk tan: 'My God, they'll give us hell for this.' Passing through Peckham Rye Station, South London, Lieutenant Patrick Needham of the Grenadiers felt sick with shame; from the platform a Salvation Army Band had struck up, 'See the Conquering Heroes Come.' It was left to Sergeant Leslie Teare, scanning the *News of the World* en route to London, to elucidate the riddle: 'Do you know why they're waving as we come along? We're all bloody heroes.'

Aboard a Sun tug fussing into Ramsgate, Captain John Gibbon of the Border Regiment heard a French liaison officer voice an outsider's bewilderment: 'If this is how the British celebrate a defeat, how do they celebrate a victory?'

The query was apposite. If thousands like Bill Hersey had brought their rifles and equipment all the way, thousands more had nothing but the clothes they stood up in. Corporal Holt of the Duke of Wellington's Regiment came ashore enveloped in a sugar sack in which he'd punched holes for his arms and legs. Corporal Ivan Miles, a sapper, wore only the black shorts and vest of an Ipswich youth club. Some were rigged as for a fancy dress carnival . . . Capitaine de Corvette de Toulouse-Lautrec wrapped in a blanket like a Sioux . . . Private Roland Cotton wearing a battle-dress top over a woman's scarlet jumper with French army breeches and French golf stockings.

Few scored as well as Signalman Douglas Peckham; wearing the greatcoat of the *Scimitar*'s captain with white tennis flannels and sneakers, he was saluted by his own sergeant, later to be ushered to balcony seats in the local cinema.

Though their costumes were rag-bag, they were in no mood to be patronised. Aboard the *Javelin* Captain George Anderson and his fellow-officers heard one military policeman yell to another: 'Here they come – like a flock of ruddy sheep.' As the gangplank went down, scores of men hurtled forward; pounded almost insensible, the Redcaps were tossed bodily into the harbour.

Already the final easing of tensions saw the first crack-ups. As Brigadier Christopher Woolner, one of General Montgomery's stalwarts, composed a message to his wife in Dover Post Office, the postmaster cautioned: 'I'd make it a greetings telegram, sir – no day for ordinary telegrams.' Suddenly the iron brigadier's face crumpled and he cried. In the corridor of a London-bound train,

Driver Percy Case wept too; on a sudden he had remembered Laurence Binyon's *Ode to the Fallen*:

> *They shall not grow old, as we that are left grow old:*
> *Age shall not weary them, nor the years condemn.*
> *At the going down of the sun and in the morning*
> *We will remember them.*

These were conditioned crack-ups: the minds of many men would be scarred for life. Sergeant Sidney Tindle, the perky little Irishman, was now, within seven days, a true Dunkirk veteran: white-haired, his teeth smashed, gaunt with the horrors he had seen. In a Devon transit camp he and two-score others went berserk without warning, smashing the barrack furniture to matchwood, howling like wolves. On the London-Dover railway line Police Inspector Richard Butcher noted a disturbing sign: the whirling flurry of sparks as broken men pitched their rifles from railway carriage windows. And Lance-Corporal Guy Cobbett, on the same journey, knew a hair-raising moment: the sudden cry of an approaching express train matched by the shriller screaming of a bombardier blundering from his compartment, the screams echoing in awful unison as the man lurched away up the corridor.

The civilians felt it too: despite the flags, the carnival atmosphere, the air held an ugly tension. In Kensington, West London, Mrs Kathleen Heal knew something was wrong: still sodden with the waters of Dunkirk, her husband, Tom, had sprawled fully dressed on the best bed – something a guardsman would never do in normal times. At Dorchester, Dorset, Mrs Edith Williams recoiled at her husband Fred's condition – bearded, hollow-cheeked, reeking like a polecat. For her and other wives the Army had an ominous advice: 'Don't worry if your man screams at night or throws himself down when a plane flies over the back garden.'

Some men were overdue; for their wives and sweethearts the

days became a lifetime of railway platform vigils, praying for one face to materialise. As his train rattled towards Devizes, Lance-Sergeant Billy Mullins saw it time and again: one pale strained face ducking through a forest of waving hands, the despairing cry.

'Have you seen my Johnny?'

'Don't know, love – what unit?'

'Dorsets – 2nd Dorsets.'

'Some Dorsets in the next coach up – you never know, perhaps he's there.'

Second Officer Daphne Lumsden, of Ramsay's W.R.N.S. staff, couldn't help knowing her husband was in peril; she herself had decoded the message: 'H.M.S. *Keith* bombed. No news of survivors.' Though Lieutenant Graham Lumsden was the *Keith*'s navigating officer, she bit her lip, forcing herself to work on.

When the lieutenant turned up a day later, garbed in a French sailor's jersey and pom-pom hat, Daphne Lumsden mistook him for the office cleaner. On recognition her first reaction was wifely: 'My God, how wonderful to see you – but you smell of French scent.'

Some were less lucky. At Ramsgate Station, Mrs Rosa Bishop moved like an automaton now. For seven nights she had not left her bivouac in the railway carriage. For seven days she had not stopped serving chocolate or tea or posting soldiers' letters. Tired, sleepless and numb with anguish, she was conscious of only one truth. Of the 44,000 men who entrained at Ramsgate Sergeant Tom Bishop had not numbered one.

In fact Bishop had landed at Plymouth, not Ramsgate – but the first reunion made it plain that the romance was finished. The irony seemed too bitter: their love had ended weeks before yet they had not known.

To Petty Officer Arthur Brinton in the Petty Officers' Mess at Ramsgate, it seemed as Saturday slipped into Sunday that life hadn't even begun. With cold over-riding anger he told himself that to the last he was being excluded from the Navy's greatest triumph since Nelson's time. First he'd had to wait while all the others got a boat, then his own boat proved useless, now he was out of it for good.

Gloomily sipping tea from an enamel mug at 5 p.m. on Sunday, 2nd June, Brinton thought of Tower, the young sub-lieutenant who'd taken him aboard. Twenty-three years in the Navy, Brinton normally jumped only to the orders of commanders and above – yet from the first there'd been something electrically different about Tower. He saw him going a long way up the ladder – maybe one day he could say it took a First Sea Lord to rescue him from Dunkirk beach.

At that moment, looking up, Brinton saw Tower in person. Stunned he heard him say: 'We're having a final evacuation tonight, Coxswain. Only fast boats of a certain speed are allowed to go.' And Tower went on: he himself was taking the motor yacht *Rosaura*. Would Brinton come?

Only later did the petty officer realise he'd answered yes – since Tower now urged: 'Ask your two able-seamen if they'll come too.' Oh, Brinton assured him, they would come. A grin creased Tower's young face: 'You'd better ask them,' he insisted. But Brinton had already guessed the answer he received ten minutes later. If Tower was the skipper, they would go.

Tower issued final instructions. Brinton and his crew must be aboard *Rosaura* not later than 10 p.m.; it was the last chance to take off the thousands still waiting patiently. Then he was gone, his slight compact figure shouldering briskly through the swing-doors.

Once, thirteen years back, Tower and his sister Penelope had been taking their enforced after-lunch rest on their beds at Hurstpierpoint College, Sussex – their father, the Rev. Bernard Tower, had been headmaster there. As youngsters will, they had one day talked romantically of dying – given the chance how would the other really choose to die?

Afterwards Penelope could never remember her answer: she

thought it had been comfortably, in bed. For a time, as often when pondering something, 'Bill' had said nothing – but finally the iron-willed eight-year-old broke silence. 'I'd like to die rescuing people,' he decided, then, as an afterthought, 'In a small boat, I think – because I like small boats.'

Even then Penelope, just ten years old, felt 'a small cold frog jump in my heart'.

Brinton did not know this.

In the Church at Crombeke, twenty miles from Dunkirk, John 'Warrior' Linton saw his last chance running out like sand in an hour-glass.

Though his legs were yellow and hard now, swollen like tight bladders beneath their constricting splints, Linton was fully alert for the small signs that spelt disaster. As the hours wore on, he had all too many yardsticks as to how bad things were.

Already, the nursing sisters had gone on ahead – without the wounded. But as they came round with army field-service cards to be filled up and posted in England, the tears were running down their cheeks.

A regimental soldier to the last, Linton had still wanted it straight from his commander. He and Colonel Whitfeld had held their small despairing council-of-war for three days now. As if on the appointed hour, Whitfeld came over and sat on his stretcher.

'What's the position today, sir?'

Whitfeld couldn't beat about the bush. 'I'm sorry, Linton – it's hopeless.'

Outside the church door there was a sudden urgent commotion. Soon Linton saw the orderlies wheeling in a wounded civilian on a small hand-cart. As it passed on the way to the altar, Linton noticed the village priest's black three-cornered hat poking grotesquely from the cart. It seemed only moments since he had been bustling importantly in and out of the church.

A small sick fear gnawed in Linton's mind: if they'll shoot a priest, what'll they do to us?

Lying there, the pain sweeping through his legs in waves, the young West Countryman tried thinking of anything rather than capture ... about writing letters ... he'd have to let 'Raygo's' mother know what had happened somehow ... about food, because the pain had driven out hunger now and he could remember nostalgically, but without longing, the steak and onions and French fried potatoes his mother had cooked him after his first pay-packet ... about the good times when he and his brother Bob had gone crazy over films, taking tram-rides from cinema to cinema to see Al Jolson in *The Singing Fool,* then on to the revival of *Ben Hur.*

More commotion now. His footfalls hollow on the flagstones, an orderly had come running with a message for the unit's commander, Lieut.-Colonel Tristram Samuel. As in a dream Linton watched Samuel roll down his sleeves, don coat and service cap, carefully adjust the Red Cross band on his sleeve. Then, straightening his tie, he marched from the church.

The thought went through Linton like an electric current: 'He's doing that to get ready to surrender.' He had no means of knowing that Samuel had been ready three days back — when orders came from Dunkirk: 'Can take no more wounded. Stand fast until you fall into the hands of the Germans.'

The same instinct must have touched others too; not even the badly wounded were groaning now. Through the whole length of the Church of St Blaise, there was not a curse, not a mutter, not even a cough. With agonising clarity Linton recalls the tension: 'Root your eyes on the ceiling, grip the side of the stretcher, make your mind a blank and wait, wait, wait ...'

He did not have to wait long. Abruptly the aching silence was broken by the grinding of a tank's gears somewhere in the village of Crombeke. At the same moment Linton heard voices shouting— German voices.

The voices came nearer. The church door shattered open and fifty yards away with nightmare clarity Linton saw the enemy he had feared almost more than death itself: two armed German soldiers in field-grey.

They snapped to attention and an officer strode in — jack-boots, long grey leather coat, cane tucked beneath his arm. He took in the whole shadowed length of the church and his lip curled. He said quite matter-of-factly, '*Englischer Schwein*,' and still there was the unearthly silence, not a cough, not a mutter, not even a curse.

In London Winston Churchill had business to do. Two days from now he must render his report to the nation. In the long lit Cabinet Room at 10 Downing Street, pacing slowly, he marshalled thought. On the far side of the room, poised at the noiseless Remington typewriter, only Mary Shearburn, his secretary, stood vigil. To sit closer — within complete earshot — would never do. The Old Man liked freedom to pace.

Almost thoughtfully, Churchill began: '*We must be very careful not to assign to this deliverance the attributes of a victory. Wars are not won by evacuation.*' Swiftly Mary Shearburn's fingers flew over the keyboard, each paragraph in the triple spacing that was the Premier's whim.

By the unlit fireplace, Churchill marched: from fireplace to velvet-draped french windows and back. Often he rumbled, 'How many?' and the answer must come pat: the total of words dictated already. Sometimes he growled, 'Gimme!' ratcheting paper from machine to scan a phrase.

Still he marched. Once he took thought on history: '*When Napoleon lay at Boulogne for a year with his flat-bottomed boats . . . he was told by someone "There are bitter weeds in England."*' He mused on a parallel: there were certainly a great many more since the B.E.F. returned.

Past midnight now. The room was colder. As yet Miss Shearburn had no sense of a disciple's role. She was tired and now, as often, Churchill was gripped by the pain of gestation. His voice had grown faint. She could barely hear.

Moving myopically, head bowed, he struggled with tears.

Loving him because his feelings were naked to the bone, Miss Shearburn yet invoked a silent curse on his mumbling. Now sobs shook the firm foundation of his voice.

'. . . *we shall not flag or fail. We shall go on to the end. We shall fight in France, we shall fight in the seas and oceans . . . we shall defend our Island whatever the cost may be. We shall fight on the beaches, we shall fight on the landing-grounds, we shall fight in the fields and in the streets, we shall fight in the hills . . .*'

It came home to Mary Shearburn then as the most painful of all dictations. Racked by grief for his stricken land, he could not go on.

A full minute passed. Almost trumpeted, the next sentence hit her like a fist: '*We shall* NEVER *surrender.*'

It was the turning-point. 'All the tears,' Mary Shearburn recalls in wonder, 'had gone from his voice.' Her fingers had flown to the keyboard. Churchill was marching again.

'. . . *and even if, which I do not for a moment believe, this Island or a large part of it were subjugated or starving, then our Empire beyond the seas . . . would carry on the struggle . . .*'

On and on Churchill marched, faster and faster, his voice a drumbeat, charged with faith, thundering to a finale.

'. . . *until, in God's good time, the New World, with all its power and might, steps forth to the rescue and liberation of the Old.*'

Sub-Lieutenant 'Bill' Tower had spoken no less than the truth. Already at Dover Castle, Admiral Ramsay had dictated a last-ditch signal to Flag-Lieutenant James Stopford: 'The final evacuation is staged for tonight and the Nation looks to the Navy to see it through.' And he went on: 'Every ship must report now on her fitness to meet this final call.'

None knew the stark facts better than Ramsay. While only 3,000 British troops remained the shrunken Dunkirk perimeter now held fast only through the valour of 30,000 French troops – and tonight seemed the last chance to bring them off.

Tired beyond belief – he had insisted on personally scanning every signal that came in – the admiral was in no mood for post-mortems. When his chief of Staff, Captain Vaughan Morgan, sighed: 'It's a pity we hadn't more time to plan this,' Ramsay's retort was acid: 'If we'd had months to plan it, we'd have done no good – nobody could have foreseen the size of the problem.'

As the admiral's message passed from ship to ship, the tension grew. Aboard *Sabre* Commander Brian Dean laid it on the line: 'It'll be risky . . . the Germans may be in the town by now . . . but I think we should go.' In the Isle of Man steam packet, *Lady of Mann*, Captain Thomas Woods sent for his firemen and engineers; earlier they had decided flatly, no more Dunkirk trips. Now Woods tossed across Ramsay's signal: 'Read that then tell me whether you'll go.' Not a man held back.

Danger or no, scores were anxious to get in on the act. In the Clacton lifeboat, Wilfred Pym Trotter hunted out a pocket dictionary; if French troops were involved it would come in handy. Author David Divine, briefed to take across Rear-Admiral Alfred Taylor, 'Dynamo's' maintenance officer, stole a twin-screw motor cruiser named *White Wing* to make sure of the ride. In London a willing volunteer rang the Admiralty: he was booked for this week-end but could he go on a roster for the next?

And each ship had its own way of doing things on this Sunday night. Aboard *Ben-My-Chree* ack-ack gunner Richard Charters thought the boilers must surely burst; the ship was heading so fast for Dunkirk the throbbing engines drowned all speech. To Commander Harold Conway, it seemed the French Railways' ship *Côte d'Argent* would never move at all; no sooner had she left Dover than Capitaine Georges Grailhon, weighing anchor, sat down with his officers to a sumptuous five-course dinner, topped off by coffee and kummel. Then, as Conway fumed, Grailhon, draining his last cup of coffee, leapt to his feet, crying '*Aux armes!*'

At a foaming twenty knots, the *Côte d'Argent* thrashed towards Dunkirk – destined to bring back 1,100 men that night.

Aboard *Rosaura*, a sleek 35-footer, once the shining toy of the Deputy Leader of the House of Lords, Lord Moyne, Petty Officer Alfred Brinton chafed too. From the first hair's-breadth moment that they skimmed across the darkened Channel, Sub-Lieutenant 'Bill' Tower had seemed transfigured . . . practising with a bren-gun that a soldier had left behind, determined to pot a German plane if one showed up . . . shrugging off the yacht's broken compass.

'It's all right, Coxswain,' he assured Brinton. 'I can steer by the stars.'

Hunched in the little cockpit beside Tower, Brinton felt a glow of pride: here, he'd known all along, was a born seaman. But as the Eastern Mole loomed ahead and Tower swerved in at speed-trial pace towards the inner harbour the Petty Officer felt the glow fade abruptly. He cautioned Tower: 'I'd go slower than that if I were you, sir . . . dangerous if we hit some of that wreckage.'

Tower, though, setting his lips, had merely steered dead ahead. 'I can't help that – there are men here who want rescuing and I'm going to rescue them.'

For a second anger welled inside Brinton. The young pup – why, he'd learned his seamanship when this one was in diapers. Then strangely the anger was metamorphosed to anger against himself: he was showing the yellow streak, a thing he'd never done before. In a way the whole purpose of this night was symbolised by Tower, who saw that the one thing paramount was the saving of souls. What was needed tonight was the courage to go straight ahead, as Tower was doing. Tonight seamanship and everything else must come second.

It took courage indeed. At La Panne, Major Hans Sandar and his gunners had the range of the harbour to perfection now; at precise ten-minute intervals the command of the lean, disciplined S.S. officer cut the darkness of the foreshore: '. . . on target at 17,000 metres . . . up one degree . . . eighty-two degrees . . . Fire!' Already, as Admiral Wake-Walker's fast motor-launch weaved skilfully through the wreckage of the inner harbour, directing the first ships to their berths, shells were soaring and screaming among the close-packed craft.

To Captain William Tennant, sweating out his last hours in Bastion 32, it seemed that the thousands still remaining would need the luck of the gods to make good their escape. Worse, scores of French troops, cut off from their officers, were still hiding up in the cellars of the town or in the sand-dunes by Malo-les-Bains, unwilling to run the gauntlet of fire without a firm directive.

As always, the Navy did their best: if the troops weren't at first sight apparent they must go and find them. Burly Commander Edward Conder, of the destroyer *Whitshed*, annexing a bicycle, rode perilously through the blazing town, trumpeting '*Reveillez, mes braves*' to every group of *poilus* he saw. From the bowels of the Clacton lifeboat, Wilfred Pym Trotter kept exhorting '*Courez, courez, bateau ici.*' (Run, run, here's a boat.) Organising small-boat work off Malo-les-Bains, Rear-Admiral Alfred Taylor sent Lieutenant Seymour (now Mr Justice) Karminski into the town to drum up survivors; a gifted linguist, Karminski could make himself understood in most languages. To the admiral's dismay he returned empty-handed: 'The only chap speaking any known language said I'm a stranger here too.'

Many, put to strange shifts, surprised themselves. Cadet Rating Keith Horlock, working from the Western Mole, had to inch down a narrow iron ladder carrying a tiny baby in his arms; to his amazement the tot, enchanted by the firework display of tracer, crowed delightedly. Lieutenant R. C. Watkin, anxious to speed up the flow of French troops, yelled 'Comme ça,' then to show how easy it was, leapt fifteen clear feet from the Mole to the destroyer *Winchelsea*. Faced with the transportation of a crippled French grandfather, Sub-Lieutenant Bernard de Mathos of *Southern Queen* solved it by lowering him with a bowline.

Aboard the Channel ferry *Autocarrier* Assistant Steward Jimmy Knott had positive instructions; foreseeing a long parting from their homeland, the *poilus* were swarming aboard with eiderdowns, parrot cages, even silver-framed family photographs, but the ship was there to save souls, not property. Consigning their treasures to the water, Knott next seized a hamper like a wicker cat-basket which a *poilu* had thrust at him – only to recoil as the owner, with a screech of horror, leaped to wrench it away.

Inside, fast asleep, lay a six-months-old baby. The 'soldier', its mother, had hit on precisely the same disguise as Augusta Hersey.

It was, Knott thought whimsically, the strangest thing: this morning he was a crack steward who had waited on Winston Churchill, tonight he was in blazing Dunkirk warming a bottle of milk for an unknown French baby on top of the galley's tea-urn.

Inexorably the minutes ticked away. On the roof of Bastion 32, Major William Mitchell glanced nervously at a sky lit as by summer lightning, then at his watch; his seven anti-tank guns had been positioned round the Bastion's approaches for twenty-four hours now, the sole artillery support left to Major-General Harold Alexander's 1st Guards Brigade. To Mitchell they seemed inadequate armament to halt a German advance.

In the hospital at Rosendael Major Philip Newman scanned a new order from General Alexander: all those wounded who were semi-ambulant should have a chance to get away on the last trucks. Minutes later, Newman saw a sight to recall the coming of Jesus to Bethesda: as medical orderlies passed the news through the corridors and gardens of the château, more than a hundred men, sliding from stretchers, scrabbling from beneath bushes, began a racking convulsive crawl towards the four trucks remaining – struggling on their knees, propelled by their elbows, hobbling on crutches made from coal hammers and garden rakes.

Quietly Newman and his orderlies settled down to perfect the German sentence which was the key to life: '*Nicht schiessen – Rotes Kreuz*' (Don't shoot – Red Cross). Only long after did they discover the tragic truth neither they nor Tennant realised – enough ships had arrived to take away all the wounded, and to the very end the roads from Rosendael to Dunkirk remained navigable.

In the harbour, despite the seeming scarcity of troops, the boats kept loading – cloaked now by the thick velvet pall of smoke that crawled seventy miles up the coast. To Chief Engine-Room Artificer Claude Feben, aboard the corvette *Kingfisher*, it seemed the Thirty-Fourth Psalm he'd read that morning had come true: 'The angel of the Lord encompasseth about them that fear him.'

Not all were destined to be saved. Discipline was rigid, impeccable now; as the last British troops filed through, 100 men of the 5th Green Howards, a self-appointed cordon under Captain Dennis Whitehead, stood guard with fixed bayonets, rounding up stragglers from the beaches, siphoning the Tommies in orderly lines to the narrow corridors of the Moles. Already, though, the shells of Sandar's gunners struck anvil sparks from the slippery stone; to Private 'Yorky' Giles, teetering perilously across a twelve-foot plank, a temporary bridge the Navy had thrown across breached stonework, it was a journey he'd never forget. The only handhold was a length of rope lashed by the sailors, and as the shells struck and men plunged seventy feet to the dark water the plank heaved and bucked like a trampoline.

Hundreds, like Sergeant Alexander Reid of the Cheshires, one of a compact party spaced fifty yards apart, were guided at the last only by a naval officer with a megaphone hailing, 'At the double — towards me.' Then, with a high whining sound the shells came falling, but as the troops dropped flat Reid looked up to see the officer, megaphone in hand — still standing. On they clambered, over the bodies of men writhing in agony, and still the officer shouted, 'Keep moving. The evacuation must go on.'

At 11.30 p.m. in the stifling heat of the Bastion, Captain Tennant scanned a last report from his piermasters. Between now and 4th June another 52,000 men would be brought off, the bulk of them French, but Tennant's main task was done. As his craggy face cracked in a rare smile, he announced: 'This is going to be rather fun.' Then, to his signals officer Michael Ellwood, the shortest signal of the whole bloodstained campaign: 'Make to Vice-Admiral Dover — B.E.F. evacuated.'

But still the Navy had three hours to go, and to many it seemed that these encompassed the most heartrending sights of all. Aboard *White Wing* author David Divine saw the silhouettes of a thousand Frenchmen outlined against the lightning flash of bursting shells: without warning the ship they sought to board was blown sky-high. Still under shellfire, without hope of rescue, they retreated back towards the broken town — 'quite the most tragic thing I have ever seen in my life . . . we could do nothing with our little dinghy'. Lieutenant George Davies, R.N.R., felt the same: as the last of the French soldiers he could carry made to board the motor-launch *Thetis*, the man stepped back, yielding place to another. In explanation he pointed to a third man, already aboard: '*Son copin*' (His friend).

It was a weird and unforgettable picture . . . the sea as still as a mountain lake . . . the choking inky smoke . . . the angry yells each time a soldier's equipment tangled with a launch's searchlight mechanism, bathing the harbour in a white, uncanny light . . . the blurting of the destroyers' sirens . . . the pale flicker of Aldis lamps.

Above it all came a steady flow of signals and exhortations:

'Come on now, double up, let's keep this column moving!' . . . '*Sutton* to *Niger, Sutton* to *Niger,* I am leaving now . . .' . . . '*Passez vite, passez vite*' . . . 'Are there any more British troops here, this is your last chance.' . . . 'Senior Naval Officer to *Thetis,* remember Cinderella, repeat remember Cinderella, don't be around here after 2.30 . . .' Lastly the message telegraphists would always remember: 'On receipt of signal "Blue Peter" no further evacuation can be carried out. Ships return to base.'

Lacking wireless link-ups, the small craft never got this message direct – it was the job of the parent ships to see them safely away. Petty Officer Arthur Brinton's first intimation that the evacuation was over came only as *Rosaura* once again cut away from the Chinese river gunboat *Locust,* at anchor outside the breakwater.

For three hours *Rosaura* had shuttled steadily back and forth from the inner harbour ferrying French troops to *Locust* – yet now, once they were well clear of the gunboat, Tower, to Brinton's puzzlement, lifted the loud-hailer. 'I can't go back with her empty,' he shouted to *Locust.* 'I'm going back for one last lot.'

Brinton had no means of knowing that minutes earlier *Locust*'s captain, Lieutenant Anthony de Costobadie, had told Tower: 'Orders are quite definite – no more troops to come off after 2.30 a.m. Back to England now – you've done enough.'

But to Tower, whose father's precept had always been 'The deadliest sin is self', it was unthinkable *Rosaura* should return to Ramsgate without troops. As so often happened, 'Bill' Tower had made his own final decision – knowing he was too far away for de Costobadie to do more than fume impotently.

The resolve made sense to Brinton too. Within the shadow of the Western Mole thirty-three *poilus* and two officers – a doctor and an engineer – were still huddled, and Tower had given his solemn promise he'd bring them off. And it took only minutes to load them aboard and set course for England – Tower easing skilfully through the harbour's wreckage then, a quarter of a mile off shore, increasing speed with a rush.

It was then Brinton noticed that though the engine still revolved furiously, *Rosaura* was no longer travelling through the water. Above the engine-roar he warned Tower: 'Hear that, sir? She's racing.'

Nodding briefly, Tower eased the clutch, in an effort to slacken *Rosaura*'s speed. Abruptly he speeded up, seeking extra power. Still *Rosaura* wasn't moving: as Tower cut the engine altogether there was a moment of almost total silence. Together Brinton and Tower went down and took the cover off the engine.

A swift glance and both men knew how bad things were. Though the eight-cylinder engine was still sound enough, its impetus could no longer reach the propeller at all. The propeller shaft was torn clean away from the engine coupling.

There was no time to lose. For emergency electrical break-downs, *Rosaura* carried a supply of cable; now, aided by the French engineer, Tower and Brinton lashed it, using a wire-rolling hitch, round the coupling and shaft.

That way, Tower, the dedicated mechanic, knew, even the full power of the drive from engine to propeller shaft wouldn't make the knot give way. On the contrary it would tighten the knot – but could the same be said about the wire?

As yet Tower couldn't know, though to Brinton he still seemed his calm quietly confident self – hadn't he, time and again, coped with problems like this on his old rattletrap cars? Then, too, it was a question of 'needs must'; there was no one in sight to give them a tow.

The destroyers *Shikari* and *Whitshed*, the minesweepers *Kellett* and *Ross* – all the Sunday night mercy fleet had gone now, and in the outer harbour the blockships were moving in. It seemed likely *Rosaura* held the unenviable distinction of being the last boat out of Dunkirk.

Tower doubled back to the wheelhouse. Gently, with infinite patience, he tried to turn the engine over on the self-starter. Below Brinton and the French engineer kept tense watch on the shaft, meshed tightly round with the clumsy electric cable. If it just lasted long enough for them to overtake the rest of the convoy, they'd catch a tow in no time.

Above their heads the self-starter whirred. The engine sprang violently into life – and Brinton's heart sank. One twirl of the shaft and the cable had snapped like twine. Though the engine went beating remorselessly on, the shaft lay still and useless.

Tower tried one last gamble. Unwinding the useless cable, he now disconnected the engine coupling altogether. Next, sweating, cursing, smeared with oil and grease, the three men gingerly eased the propeller shaft along until it made direct contact with the engine. It might just work – though *Rosaura,* if she could be steered at all, could manœuvre only stern first.

Within minutes Tower gave up. From the *poilus* in the stern-sheets had come a despairing wail of protest; the mighty wash of water as the yacht went astern had all but drowned them. Reluctantly Tower ordered: 'Drop anchor – we'll try some other way.'

Already dawn approached. The sky grew paler. A light sea mist curled gently across the surface of the water, but not so thickly that Tower failed to see, motionless across the bay, three or four abandoned motor-boats. The nearest was perhaps a mile away.

Tower made up his mind. 'I'm going to swim for one of those, Coxswain – I'll bring it back and tow us home.' But the decision, so swiftly reached, appalled Brinton. He urged: 'Don't do it, sir. Those boats are farther away than you think.'

Already, though, Tower, folding his uniform in neat methodical piles in the wheelhouse, had stripped to his underwear. 'I'll put on my Mae West,' was all he said, struggling into it. Then, handing Brinton his watch, his wallet and his binoculars, he dived cleanly over *Rosaura*'s side, striking steadily for the nearest of the boats.

For a moment Brinton didn't know what to think. Should he have argued with Tower more — yet how could you argue with a man who had a core of steel inside him? Swiftly he handed the young officer's binoculars to Able-Seaman Corry in the stern-sheets, ordering: 'You keep a watch out for Mr Tower.' To the other seaman in the bows he called: 'You watch for the officer too.'

Soon it was hard to distinguish Tower's head from the jetsam bobbing gently in the early mist. To ease his mind Brinton had one last attempt to get *Rosaura* under way, but by now the batteries were flat; he couldn't even make the engine turn over. Looking over the side, he saw a soldier, an old man with a Mae West, struggling feebly in the water.

There was no hope of reaching him; he had drowned within minutes. But, Brinton recalls thinking, that won't happen to Mr Tower. He's got a bright future ahead of *him*. As if to vindicate him, he heard Corry cry from the stern-sheets: 'He's got the boat anyway.' When finally he trusted himself to speak, Brinton could only say gruffly: 'About blooming time too.'

Anxiety fading, Brinton watched the small boat get under way, savouring the blessed peace. No howling Stukas, no cursing, singing soldiers, no cries from the wounded — he would hardly have known Dunkirk as the same place. Suddenly, eyes probing the faint mist, he lunged forward, snatching the binoculars from Corry's hands.

Aloud he cried: 'Where the devil does he think he's going?' The little boat with Tower at the helm was heading back towards Dunkirk.

His mind racing, Brinton watched. Was Tower seeking some bigger craft that would ensure them a better tow? Or was he hoping to pick up yet more soldiers from the inner harbour? But the boat was hidden by the mist now; there was no chance of hailing the young officer.

Nor would there ever be. A moment later, cruelly and

unbearably loud through the haze, Brinton heard one hammering staccato burst of machine-gun fire.

Still Brinton waited. Slowly, like the first dawn chill, he felt black ungovernable grief invade his body. What he wanted most now was to give up. He wanted the German Navy to come out in all their strength and take him prisoner. If Tower had gone, then life made no sense, no sense at all. At this moment Brinton hated himself, the other men in the boat, the whole futile bloody war.

The bitterness was all too human – yet, as Dunkirk drew to a close, more even than the life of Sub-Lieutenant 'Bill' Tower, remained irreplaceable. Not until five years later was Tower's death officially presumed – but Petty Officer Arthur Brinton and his cargo, picked up by an R.A.F. speedboat after two and a half days adrift, came back to a nation whose life hung in the balance.

Already for 68,000 fighting men, the war had ended. Of those, 40,000 faced only the cruel monotony of five years behind bars. On 1st June Lord Gort had announced: 'We shall meet them again. Next time victory will be with us' – but as the losses tallied up, Winston Churchill and his War Cabinet were appalled at the tight-rope line between survival and extinction.

Against the Germans' two hundred divisions, the British could now muster but a score – without equipment for a tenth of that number. To hold off Hitler's 'Operation Sea-Lion', as Winston Churchill later revealed, Britain had just 500 18-pounder guns and howitzers, many stripped from museums. The equipment of ten complete divisions was gutted or strewn across the fields of Flanders – and within fifteen days France, too, had been beaten to a standstill.

Worse, out of 200 destroyers only seventy-four were now out of dockyard hands – and the R.A.F. had fared no better. Of their first-line bomber strength, forty per cent had been lost in the Battle of France.

To many Germans it seemed but a question of time. At first

light on the Tuesday, Major Hans Sandar and his gunners, coming down to the shores of Dunkirk, stopped short in amazement; fully 50,000 vehicles were littering the beaches and promenades, choking the inshore waters. To his driver Sandar cried: 'Exactly what we were looking for – scrap my car, fish that Buick out of the water and get it working.' When his regimental commander, Oberst Priesz, noted, 'So the British are out,' Sandar jerked a thumb at the devastation. 'The British are finished.'

The top brass felt the same. Already on 1st June Hitler, paying a fleeting visit to General von Bock's Brussels headquarters, had found Army Group B's commander moody, withdrawn. Perhaps sensing constraint, the Führer was at pains to explain: 'You were probably surprised I halted the tank divisions – but I was worried about the French attacking from the south. I mustn't suffer the least check there.'

When General von Kleist, of the Panzers, raised the same grievance later, Hitler was airy: 'Possibly! But I did not want to send the Panzers into the marshes of Flanders and we will not hear much more of the British in this war!'

Had the Führer at the last been anxious to spare the British as von Rundstedt thought? Or had faulty intelligence on French fighting-power and a dread of the Flanders mud caused him to apply the brakes at the vital moment? The weight of evidence suggests that his motives, like most men's, were inextricably mixed, but one thing is certain: the bulk of the Army hierarchy expected a negotiated peace within weeks.

Only the prescient had doubts. On the Saturday, in Brussels, once the Führer had left, Oberst Hans von Salmuth, von Bock's chief of staff, retired to confide in his diary: 'so . . . in the discussions between the Führer and von Rundstedt on the 24th were borne these decisions that cost us an assured victory in Flanders.' A pause, then von Salmuth wrote on: '. . . and which perhaps have lost us the whole war.'

But nobody knew that then, or even later. On 4th June Winston Churchill was to rally the nation with his immortal vow to fight on, yet behind the defiance lay a hard core of anxiety. Brigadier Charles Hudson was one of many top brass summoned to the Royal Station Hotel, York, for a top-secret meeting with Secretary of State for War Anthony Eden and Major-General Harold Alexander – and as Eden finished speaking, a shocked gasp ran the length of the conference table.

For the Secretary, on a fact-finding mission for Churchill, had one cogent question. In the event of German invasion and southern England being abandoned altogether, how would British troops react to shipping out of Liverpool and continuing the fight from Canada? How loyal was the Army, in short, after the débâcle of Dunkirk?

As commander after commander had his say, one thing was plain: while regular officers and non-coms might obey to the letter, the bulk of wartime conscripts would fight on English soil or not at all – or take a chance with their families.

Hudson and the others left the conference room strangely chastened: the real gravity of the situation had gone home to them now.

These were the questions to vex the leaders in the months that lay ahead. To most mortals, the significance of Dunkirk would grow only with the years. The hardest business now was to take up the threads of a life they had counted as lost.

Engineer Fred Reynard left the *Bee* tied up at Newport, Isle of Wight, and hastened home. The Sunday roast was in the oven and in the sunlight people were filing from church; it was all as if he'd never been away. In the parlour the budgerigar whistled and cooed his party-piece, 'Where have you been, Fred, eh?' But Reynard didn't think you could explain – not to a budgerigar.

Captain Edward Bloom went to a party with friends. Clean and shaved and freshly pressed, he felt almost himself again – it just wouldn't do to think of Hugo yet. Lance-Corporal Eric Stocks was luckier – Tippy had gone into quarantine but the little dachshund was to survive as a pet until 1953. Private Sidney Morris, clutching his small boy's aeroplane, got back to his native Coventry easier than he got into his house. The sun of Dunkirk had tanned him walnut-brown, and in the twilight his wife wasn't keen on admitting a strange Moroccan.

Private Walter Allington got as far as Paddington Station, then the pain in his abdomen seemed to lance upwards through his brain and he fell in a dead faint. Hours later a surgeon found that Allington, the Dunkirk samaritan, had retreated all the way with an appendix inflamed to bursting. Private Mervyn Doncom was at first beside himself – at Dover the military police had annexed his cherished bren-gun just as if it had never bagged a Dornier at all. Philosophically Doncom broke camp and went to the movies, consoling himself that if he hadn't looted some safety-pins at the last his tattered uniform would have fallen apart in the stalls.

Private Walter Osborn had it out with his commanding officer: 'Look, sir, you let me out to fight, then back into the clink – I did my share same as anyone.' To his joy, Lieut.-Colonel 'Tony' Milnes saw his point: with his last fourteen days remitted, Osborn was just a fighting man again.

All the fight had gone from some. On London River, at Gravesend, the *Tollesbury* was once again tied up after her journey into hell; the crew had gone home, but Skipper Lemon Webb had stayed behind. He didn't know brother-in-law Fred Finbow had left the *Doris* before she even sank – it would take time before Webb could face his wife Mabel and reveal her brother's fate. His cabin door locked, the old skipper fell face downward on his bunk, sobbing like a child. He had brought his beloved barge back but the strain had been too great. Two voyages later he retired.

In the church at Crombeke, the odds had seemed too great to fight. In tense unearthly silence John 'Warrior' Linton had first watched the German soldiers move all the stretchers closer together, one by one. Then, as two men entered carrying a machine-gun, Linton closed his eyes: all along he had known the Germans were making ready to mow them down. It seemed hours before he could look again – then absurdly peace flooded his whole body.

By now the soldiers were almost out of sight, toting the machine-gun to make a defence point in the belfry. He was trembling all over with relief, but he couldn't stop. Within weeks German surgeons would amputate his left leg at the knee – but he'd been left behind to live, not to die.

Augusta Hersey reached West Byfleet Station, in Surrey, somehow; at the transit camp in West London they had bathed and fed her and checked her credentials before sending her on her way, but life in England seemed so strange she needed time to adjust. Twice she lost her way in the green Surrey lanes, and it was early afternoon when she first rapped at the door of 23 Addison Road.

Though the smile on the face of Bill's mother told her she was home she could say nothing save '*Bonjour*' – but somehow they made her understand Bill would come soon. She looked so lost at first, sitting with her hands folded on her lap in the back parlour, that Bill's mother handed her a work-basket and some mending.

Beyond the cottage the river glittered in the June sunlight and there were green fields as far as Augusta could see. Sometimes she smiled timidly at Bill's mother, but only the ticking of the parlour clock broke the silence. It was as quiet as the shadowed rooms of the Café L'Epi d'Or, seven days back, but suddenly she knew the difference without need of words: the silence of freedom had supplanted the silence of fear.

FACTS ABOUT DUNKIRK

This is not the whole story of Dunkirk — merely the story of a group of people whose lives were bound up in that fateful week. It does not embrace all of the facts or anywhere near all of them; no one man could present truthfully the mammoth nine-day exodus involving countless million men and women. And since the people themselves were often too shocked, too busy or too bewildered to note their actions from hour to hour, even basic statistics must be accepted with reserve.

With these cautions in mind, here is an attempt to answer some major queries:

How many men came home? All sources agree on the final count: 338,226. On the other hand, these figures ignore the 27,936 men already landed in England by midnight of 26th May, swelling the grand total to 366,162 — 139,911 of them Allied troops. Of the bulk total 98,671 were taken from the open beaches, the remainder from the Moles and harbour.

How many ships took part? Probably the most vexed of all Dunkirk questions — while some official lists include ships on patrol work, others take cognisance only of those ferrying troops. Captain

S. W. Roskill (*The War At Sea*, 1939-45, Vol. I) quotes 848 British and Allied ships taking part; the Ministry of War Transport's summary, though, lists 1,040 vessels, but even this does less than justice to French efforts. Personal research to date reveals a total of 1,210 but even this seems likely to be incomplete.

Who came off when? Biggest lifts were accomplished on the 30th and 31st of May and 1st of June – 53,823; 68,014; 64,429 respectively. Peak day for the beaches was the fogbound 30th May – 29,512 lifted. For the harbour: the 47,081 who embarked at the height of von Richtofen's 1st June air-raid.

Who did the bulk of the lifting? Again, figures are incomplete – since the 'useless mouths' lifting of 26th May doesn't figure in Admiralty computations. During the main evacuation, though, destroyers took off the largest number (102,843), followed by personnel ships (87,810), minesweepers (48,472), trawlers (28,709), and *schuits* (22,698). According to Dr Hervé Cras (*Dunkerque*) French naval and merchant vessels lifted 48,474 men – of whom 3,936 were taken direct to other French ports.

What were the Navy's casualties? In terms of ships, heavy – out of 848 ships, Roskill shows 235 lost through enemy action or other causes, almost double the 121 estimated by the Ministry of War Transport. But even Roskill's total is probably incomplete for small craft. Again destroyers took the biggest beating (9 sunk, including 3 French destroyers, 19 damaged) with personnel ships close behind (8 sunk, 9 damaged). Personnel casualties never were estimated – though 125 civilians and merchant seamen were killed, 81 wounded.

What did the Army leave behind? In terms of hard cash, no figures are available – but the following totals give a pointer . . . 2,472 guns . . . 63,879 vehicles . . . 20,548 motorcycles . . . 76,097 tons of ammo . . . 416,940 tons of stores . . . 164,929 tons of petrol. On the credit side, Gort's Army *did* bring back 322 guns, 4,739 vehicles, 533 motorcycles, 32,303 tons of ammo, 33,060 tons of stores, 1,071 tons of petrol. At least £2,090,000 – vide the Comptroller and Auditor General's Report for the year – never was accounted for.

What were Allied casualties? In fact, Gort lost 68,111 men – killed, wounded or taken prisoners-of-war. Roughly 40,000 men, some of them French, were taken prisoner when Dunkirk fell. Of those wounded in the campaign, 8,061 Britons, 1,230 Allies were evacuated to Britain – though thanks to streamlined hospital care, only 1.7 per cent died of their wounds.

Where were the R.A.F.? They *were* over the target – though of the 32 squadrons taking part, only 16, through home defence commitments, were ever operative at one time. Between them they put in 101 patrols, 4,822 flying hours, in nine days, claimed 265 enemy aircraft destroyed. (The Navy's claim: 35 destroyed, 21 heavily damaged.) Final stages saw them down to bare bones: by 30th May, airfields in southern England had only 283 aircraft immediately serviceable, 362 pilots to fly them. Total losses: 177 planes in nine days, 106 of them fighters.

What were German losses? Major L. F. Ellis (*The War in France and Flanders*, 1939-40) quotes 240 aircraft destroyed and damaged in nine days – though David Divine (*The Nine Days of Dunkirk*) cites 156 only. The Luftwaffe's own Flying Personnel Casualty List, though, prepared for private circulation, not propaganda release, suggests a steeper total – 727 aviators killed or missing between 21st and 31st May, including 129 officers. Army casualties were never totalled up.

What did people say? There are no imaginary conversations in this book. Such dialogue as is quoted represents a genuine attempt by one or more individuals to remember what he or she said at the time.

When did various events occur? Official papers *do* confirm that 'Operation Dynamo' began at 6.57 p.m. on 26th May – and that Captain Tennant's 'B.E.F. evacuated' signal was timed 11.30 p.m. a week later. In between, though, there are wide discrepancies; every time given in the text follows an existing log or report, but in the flaring intensity of Dunkirk, days often elapsed before reports were made up. For instance, the account of Lieut. Robert Bill, R.N., timed the beginning of the shocking 29th May air-raid as 3.30 p.m . . . the *Lochgarry*'s Captain MacKinnon reported 2 p.m . . . the *Clan MacAlister*'s Captain Mackie made it 3.45 p.m.

Every care was taken to check that the incidents described pertain to the right day, but the time phases at the head of each chapter are a rough guide only. Inevitably some incidents began earlier and finished later than the compass of that chapter.

ABOUT THE AUTHOR

Richard Collier was a British historian, born in London in 1924. He was eighteen when he joined the Royal Air Force in 1942, and later travelled throughout the Far East as a war correspondent. He worked on numerous British and American magazines and wrote fifteen major works of military history. He died in 1996.

CHINDIT

BY RICHARD RHODES JAMES

With a new introduction by Al Murray

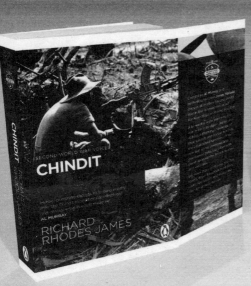

SECOND WORLD WAR VOICES

As selected by James Holland and Al Murray on their hugely popular history podcast, *We Have Ways of Making You Talk.*

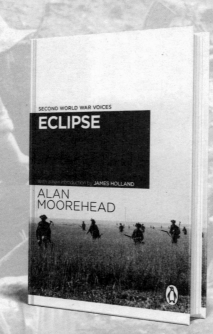